The Quantum Stock Market

The Quantum Stock Market

And the Road Not Taken in Finance

David Orrell

The MIT Press
Cambridge, Massachusetts
London, England

The MIT Press
Massachusetts Institute of Technology
77 Massachusetts Avenue
Cambridge, MA 02139
mitpress.mit.edu

The MIT Press would like to thank the anonymous peer reviewers who provided comments on drafts of this book. The generous work of academic experts is essential for establishing the authority and quality of our publications. We acknowledge with gratitude the contributions of these otherwise uncredited readers.

This book was set in Times New Roman by Westchester Publishing Services. Printed and bound in the United States of America.

Library of Congress Cataloging-in-Publication Data

Names: Orrell, David author
Title: The quantum stock market : and the road not taken in finance / David Orrell.
Description: Cambridge, Massachusetts : The MIT Press, [2026] | Includes bibliographical references and index.
Identifiers: LCCN 2026004030 (print) | LCCN 2026004031 (ebook) | ISBN 9780262055987 paperback | ISBN 9780262055994 pdf | ISBN 9780262056007 epub
Subjects: LCSH: Investments—Mathematical models | Stocks—Mathematical models
Classification: LCC HG4515.2 .O77 2026 (print) | LCC HG4515.2 (ebook) | DDC 332.6—dc23/eng/20260415
LC record available at https://lccn.loc.gov/2026004030
LC ebook record available at https://lccn.loc.gov/2026004031

EU Authorised Representative: Easy Access System Europe, Mustamäe tee 50, 10621 Tallinn, Estonia | Email: gpsr.requests@easproject.com

Contents

Introduction

> If, in respect of several questions treated in this study, I have compared the results of observation to those of the theory, this was not to verify the formulae established by mathematical methods, but to demonstrate only that the market, unwittingly, obeys a law which governs it: the Law of Probability.
>
> —Louis Bachelier, last sentence of his *Théorie de la Spéculation*, 1900

If classical quantitative finance has a patient zero, it would be the French mathematician Louis Bachelier. His 1900 doctoral thesis for the Sorbonne, *Théorie de la Spéculation*, was the first to model the stochastic process, later known as Brownian motion (or in discrete form, a random walk), which underlies theories such as the Black-Scholes (aka Black-Scholes-Merton) option pricing formula. Bachelier applied the method to price financial options on the French Bourse. In 1905, Einstein used the same idea to estimate the mass of an atom, though he was apparently unaware of Bachelier's work.

From 1909 until the outbreak of war in 1914, Bachelier gave lectures as a "free professor" at the Sorbonne (he started being paid only in 1913).[1] One of the courses he taught was "Probability Calculus with Applications to Financial Operations and Analogies with Certain Questions from Physics." Topics may have included relating the diffusion of probability, as in his option pricing model, to the diffusion of heat, as in the heat equation from nineteenth-century physics.

One student at the Sorbonne who probably didn't take that class was Louis de Broglie. He graduated in 1910 with an arts degree but then decided to switch into theoretical physics. After serving during the war in the wireless telegraphy section—he was stationed at a post in the Eiffel Tower—he resumed his academic studies. As he later noted in his Nobel lecture, what attracted him to theoretical physics was "the mystery enshrouding the structure of matter and the structure of radiations, a mystery which deepened as the strange quantum concept introduced by Planck in 1900 in his research on black-body radiation continued to encroach on the whole domain of physics."[2] When de Broglie published his own thesis in 1924, *Recherches sur la théorie des quanta*, on the wave properties of matter, Einstein remarked that he had "lifted a corner of the great veil."[3] His prediction of electron waves was confirmed experimentally in 1927.

At the same time that quantum mechanics was in the ascendant, Bachelier's work in finance sank more or less out of sight and remained there for several decades. His thesis was only discovered in the early 1950s by the economist Paul Samuelson, who later told a BBC interviewer, "I was able to locate by chance this unknown book, rotting in the library of the University of Paris, and when I opened it up it was if a whole new world was laid out before me. . . . After the discovery of Bachelier's work there suddenly came to the mind of all the eager workers the notion of what the Holy Grail was. There was the next step needed. It was to get the perfect formula to evaluate and to price options."[4]

Given that the field of quantitative finance originally had its roots in physics, it seems strange that the two fields could have grown so far apart, to the point where an economist could see a version of a nineteenth-century heat equation as a "whole new world" as if it had been concealed by a great veil. Even stranger, perhaps, is that modern quantitative finance is still using essentially the same methods.

In this book, we will present a model of the stock market that is based instead on probabilistic wave equations. The aim, therefore, is to "update" quantitative finance to the kind of mathematics that was being used in the early twentieth century, before quantum mechanics developed its own specialized notation. After all, if particles can be associated with a wave, as de Broglie had shown, then it doesn't seem such a challenge to say that prices can too.

To give a brief overview of the structure, chapter 1 sets the stage with some background and describes how the quantum model helped to both explain and predict a number of empirical results from finance. Chapter 2 presents a model of transactions based on classical probability, which helps pave the way for quantization. Chapters 3 and 4 present, and relate to finance, two paradigmatic models from quantum mechanics: the infinite well and the quantum harmonic oscillator. Chapter 5 shows how the same quantum methods can be applied to convert the probabilistic model of transactions from chapter 2 to a dynamical model. Chapter 6 introduces a quantum model of asset price, which is similar to an older model from the 1970s, but with a twist. Chapters 7 and 8 look at how the quantum model can be used to price options, model implied volatility, and reveal problems with standard techniques, with chapter 9 giving the example of the widely used VIX index. Chapter 10 presents a design for an investment strategy that exploits the insights brought by the quantum model, while chapter 11 discusses the relationship between explosive dynamics of the physical and financial sort. Finally, chapter 12 summarizes the main findings and argues that classical finance has reached the end of the road—and the way ahead is quantum.

The book's predecessor and companion volume, *Quantum Economics and Finance: An Applied Mathematics Introduction*, first published in 2020, took a broad look at quantum methods in areas such as decision theory, game theory, and finance. Although there is some overlap in content in the chapters on the quantum oscillator, the presentation here focuses only on the problem of asset price behavior and does not get into topics such as entanglement, which require more detailed knowledge of quantum probability. The advantage is that the methods are simpler and rely only on wave mechanics of the sort studied in a second-year undergraduate physics class (which at least was where the author was first exposed to them). For physicists, this may seem like a step back, but it provides a natural bridge to the probability distributions used in finance.

As a note on style, although the book is mostly equations, figures, and explanatory text, I have made the occassional diversion for things like context, humor, or related ideas. This might be unusual for a book of this nature, but it is consistent with the theme that economics has been stuck on the same track for too long and needs to loosen up its thinking.

Much of the content was developed in a series of around twenty technical articles and columns for *Wilmott* magazine and talks for the Certificate for Quantitative Finance Institute. The author would like to thank Paul Wilmott for many useful discussions over the years that have helped shape this research. In an important sense, he was a codiscoverer of q-variance (chapter 1) because, while I was lucky enough to have a model that told me to look for it, he was the one to see it was an interesting and relevant phenomenon, out of all the crazy ideas floating around, and draw attention to it. Thanks also to Dan Tudball and the editorial team at *Wilmott*, and to Larry Richards and Asghar Qadir for useful comments on research papers. I am grateful to Catherine Woods, Executive Editor at MIT Press, for her confidence in this project and for her guidance throughout its development. I also thank Caroline Helms and Roger Wood for their careful management of the editorial and production process, Alka Ranjan for meticulous editorial assistance, Margarita Encomienda for the perfect cover design, and two anonymous reviewers for helpful and insightful reviews. Finally, thanks as always to my family, who have been my companions on this quantum road trip.

My hope is that the reader will discover something of interest here too. We begin with an overview of three anomalies that spurred the development of the quantum model.

1

Anomalies

> Suppose the paradigm not only describes the subject matter of the field; suppose it also describes the field's appropriate methodology. In this case, observations that contradict the existing paradigm will be dismissed if they violate the prescribed methodology.
>
> —George A. Akerlof, 2020

> If you change the way you look at things, and the language you use, you come out with completely new ideas.
>
> —Bob Coecke, chief scientist at Quantinuum, speaking about quantum music (Ball, 2023)

Quantum physics was invented because classical physics could not make sense of a number of anomalous results. Perhaps the most basic, or alarming, of these was known as the ultraviolet catastrophe. According to classical theory, an object when heated would radiate an infinite amount of energy in the high-frequency ultraviolet spectrum. An iron poker left in a fire would glow red, then white, and then vaporize anyone in the room. In general, atoms would just radiate away all of their energy, leading to the collapse of all matter and the death of the universe. Since this apparently hadn't happened, a new theory was called for.

Finance too has its anomalies, even if they aren't quite as dramatic. Few people outside a very specialized area would even notice them. In fact, they are so unimportant that, unlike in physics, some of them weren't discovered until a model predicted them—and even then, they didn't become more widely known. They only concern the nature of financial markets, not the structure of the universe. They can't be used to build a bomb either, unless, as we'll see, you include the financial kind.

But otherwise, the same principle holds: The existence of these anomalies means that a new theory is called for.

1.1 Price Impact

The first anomaly concerns the effect of large transactions on markets. A good way to learn about a system—in engineering, biology, or even finance—is to study its response to perturbations. A well-known empirical result in quantitatve finance is the so-called square root law of price impact. Suppose that the normal daily transaction volume, measured in units per day, for a particular asset is V. Then an excess transaction of size Q will boost the price by an amount about equal to $\sqrt{Q/V}\sigma$, where σ is the daily volatility.

This result poses something of a challenge to classical theory. One paper on the topic writes, for example, that "understanding market impact is one of the most puzzling and difficult issues in finance ... theory suggests a market impact function has a linear functional form, with price impact proportional to the number of shares traded, while empirical evidence suggests a square root model, with marginal price impact diminishing as the number of shares traded increases."[1] A number of attempts have therefore been made to develop models that match this observed behavior.

A related question, though, is what effect the large transaction has on variance. After all, when you perturb the physical system known as a bell, it doesn't just move to the side—it also vibrates. So when the market's bell is hit by a large order, how loudly does it ring?

To get some definitions out of the way, if the N daily closing prices for an asset are given by S_i, then the daily log returns are $y_i = \log(S_i/S_{i-1})$. The daily volatility σ is defined as the standard deviation of log returns

$$\sigma = \sqrt{\frac{1}{N\frac{1}{N}}\sum_{i=1}^{N} y_i^2} \tag{1.1}$$

while the variance equals the square of the volatility.

In classical finance, following Bachelier, price change is usually modeled as some version of a random walk. Time is divided like this into discrete intervals, such as a day, and at each interval, the log price is assumed to take a random step up or down by an amount related to the volatility. A property of a random walk is that the expected price change over a period T scales with the square root of time, so volatility is assumed to have dimensions of inverse square root of time. In this picture, the variance due to impact should therefore scale with the length of the period T over which the excess order occurs. Or as one 2023 paper put it, "The variance of impact depends linearly on T, as expected by the diffusivity of price."[2]

Although this appeared to be the general consensus, the only paper I could find to have tested it (which was also the cited source for the idea) was one from a team of researchers who had used a large database to measure the effect of large transactions on asset price.[3] The results were presented in a plot of variance versus Q/V. According to the authors, who were leading researchers in the area, the variance was a linear function of Q/V with a slope that was roughly constant. We will go into the calculations later, but this was consistent with the rest of their model. However, I had been experimenting with a quantum model that made a rather different prediction.

According to the quantum model, a large transaction that takes place over a short interval, such as a few minutes, should have a bigger effect than one that takes place over a long interval, such as a day. Variance didn't diffuse—it jumped. But here was an empirical study by a leading group that said the opposite.

Normally, if a relationship is linear, it is best illustrated in a figure where the axes are also linear, but in their paper, the authors had opted to use a log-log plot where both the horizontal and vertical axes had been transformed to a logarithmic scale. It was therefore impossible to confirm visually whether the relationship was actually linear. However, an obvious feature of the graph was that some of the curves crossed each other—and as Euclid knew, parallel lines don't intersect. The only way to find out what was going on was to replot the data using linear axes.

Although I was told the data was proprietary and therefore not available to share, it was still possible to digitize the plot, extract the coordinates for each point, and replot using regular axes. The results are shown in figure 1.1. The nine lines represent large transactions that unfolded over a particular period, ranging from about 3.5 minutes to 345 minutes, or about a full trading day. Each point represents an excess transaction of size Q, defined relative to the normal daily transaction rate V. For example, a point with $Q/V = 0.05$ represented an order that was 5 percent above the usual number.

The results clearly showed that the slopes of the lines were not parallel as claimed, but were high when the imbalance persisted over a short time (the dark lines) and almost flat when the imbalance extended over a longer time (lighter lines). This seemed to make intuitive sense and also agreed with the prediction from my quantum model. In fact, according to the quantum model, the variance slope should be roughly an inverse function of the period T. We return to this later.

When I presented this result in a 2022 article[4] along with a talk at a conference organized by the Certificate for Quantitative Finance (CQF) Institute,[5]

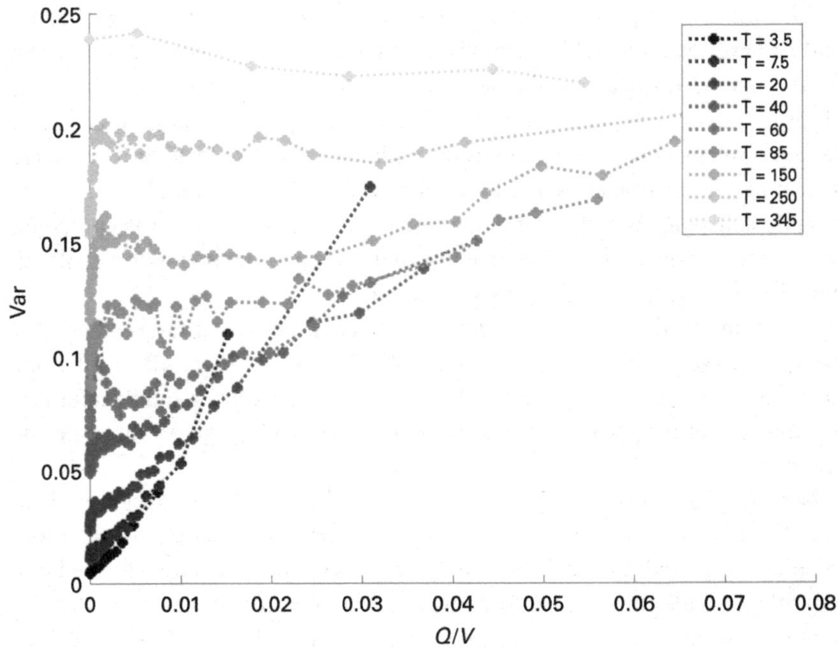

Figure 1.1
Plots of variance as a function of relative excess order size Q/V for large orders of durations binned into ranges with midpoints varying from 3.5 minutes (dark gray) to 345 minutes (light gray), which is about one trading day. According to the classical theory, these lines are supposed to be parallel.

there wasn't much interest, which was perhaps unsurprising given that it may have seemed like a dry and specialized topic. The model, meanwhile, was met with what might be called tired confusion. In fact, I might as well have been trying to pitch an idea for a perpetual motion machine.[6]

I would learn that using the word "quantum" tends to create what might be called a cognitive barrier in the world of finance, which wasn't overcome by the fact that the model produced the correct results. The finding might not have been that interesting in itself, but the reaction struck me as anomalous.

1.2 Q-Variance

The quantum model that I was using was not very sophisticated. It modeled the price of an asset using a quantum harmonic oscillator, which is the quantum version of a spring system. Here, the spring was a restoring force that resisted price change over the period. A large order perturbed the oscillator, shifting it to a different price point according to the square root law, while also boosting the variance. The model was very simple but did a reasonable job of fitting the data; indeed, it had predicted the effect shown in the figure, so it seemed to be on the right track.

But if the relationship between price change and volatility held for periods of a few minutes to a day, as in the impact studies, then if the model was going to work, it should apply to longer periods as well, such as a week, a month, or a year. To be more precise, if x is the log returns over a period T, the model prediction was that the expected variance over the same period was related to the normalized log price change over the period $z = x/\sqrt{T}$ by the simple formula

$$\mathrm{Var} = \sigma^2 + \frac{z^2}{2}, \tag{1.2}$$

where σ is a minimum volatility that occurs at $z = 0$. I later called this property q-variance, where the letter q can stand either for quantum or quadratic, depending on preference.

To be clear, q-variance wasn't something I had read about or come across in some other area of modeling or statistics. Instead, it was a prediction, or really a consequence, of the quantum model. Put simply, if you displace a quantum oscillator by an amount x, then the variance increases by this amount. If the formula didn't hold, at least approximately, then neither would the model. An unusual feature, at least for the world of finance, was that there was no adjustable parameter for the quadratic term. Also, it was supposed to hold for any period T. This meant that the model could easily be falsified. The only way to find out was to look at the data.

I started with long-running price indexes like the Standard & Poor's 500 and the Dow Jones Industrial Average. The results were better than I could have expected. Figure 1.2 was obtained from the S&P index since 1927 (it officially became the S&P 500 in 1957), and so covers almost a century (for historical context, that was the year of the famous Solvay conference whose group photo included Schrödinger, Heisenberg, de Broglie, Born, Bohr, Planck, and Einstein).[7] Each point represents the normalized log price change z and volatility (square root of variance) for a particular period of length T. The darkest points are for periods of a week, and the lightest are for periods of thirty-two weeks. The gray line is the expected volatility as a function of z. For example, its value at $z = 0$ is computed by looking at all the periods where the price change is nearly zero, and averaging the variance. The dashed line is the model prediction.

As we will see later, the same pattern is seen with a range of financial data including other stock market indices, individual stocks, and everything from bond yields to Bitcoin. Unlike the price impact case, this anomaly was easily checked using publicly available data. But if researchers couldn't understand

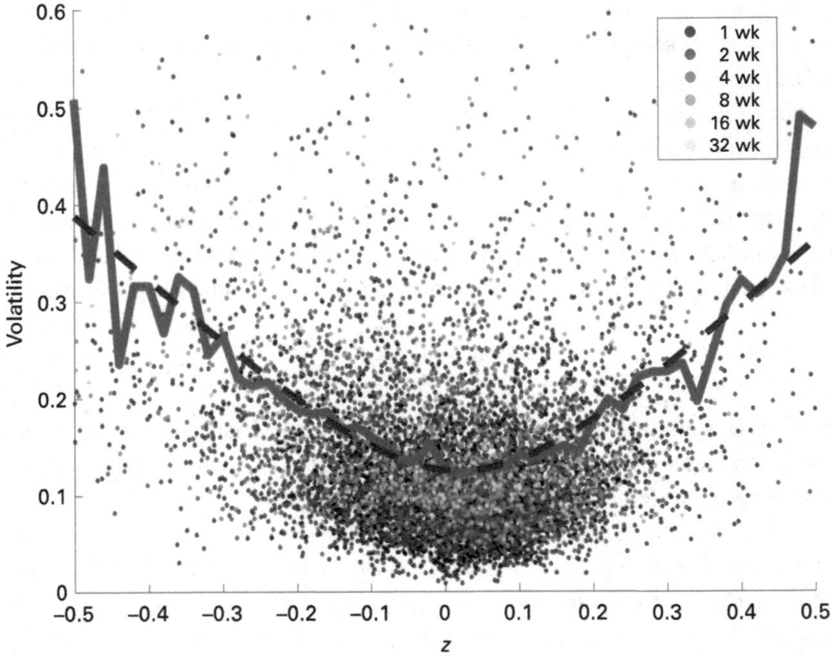

Figure 1.2
Points show volatility (square root of variance) as a function of z computed over periods T ranging from one week (dark gray) to thirty-two weeks (light gray) for the SPX index 1927–2024. Gray line shows the square root of average variance; the dashed line shows the quantum model. According to classical theory, the gray line is supposed to be flat.

my model of price impact, they simply couldn't see q-variance, even after it was pointed out using different kinds of graphs.

I presented the property at a number of conferences in 2022 and 2023[8] and followed up with some papers and columns that tried to draw attention to it,[9] but most people remained skeptical or just annoyed. One reviewer[10] wrote that "many models . . . have considered non-constant volatility," and so they were "very confused" by the claim that this was a new result. Another wrote that "this stylized fact is well known. . . . So there is nothing new here. . . . No, nothing leads to this equation which is a purely arbitrary choice of the author, and nothing guarantees that in practice volatility follows [it] (and it is of course not the case)." So it was either well known, or wrong, or both at the same time.

However, the reviewers didn't cite any works that mentioned the property, and I couldn't find any either. No one noticed or appeared to care that the equation could be falsified empirically. And unlike the first anomaly, which was rather specialized and technical, this one really mattered. As seen later, it is inconsistent with a classical random walk, and therefore much of quantitative finance.

I could understand a degree of skepticism—stock market data has been around for a while (the Dow Jones index dates to 1896), so it might seem that there is nothing new to discover about index prices. And claiming that your new discovery is quantum is going to raise eyebrows. However, q-variance was easy to verify using freely available online data.

By this point, I was starting to feel gaslit. I was doing the scientific thing of making a falsifiable hypothesis, testing it using data, and presenting the results in a clear and transparent manner, but the critics just looked confused and said there was nothing there.

1.3 Mona Lisa's Smile

While these two anomalies seemed, as far as I could tell, to be new findings, the third anomaly was more familiar, at least to experts in the field, and concerned the implied volatility smile seen in options trading. Say that a trader wishes to purchase a call option on an asset, with a strike price K equal to the current price S_0 and a time to expiration of T. The payout is then equal to $\max(S_T - K, 0)$, where S_T is the final price at time T. The value of the option, which is supposed to equal the expected payout, can be calculated by the Black-Scholes model, whose only free parameter is the volatility σ.

This number σ was in theory supposed to be a constant, but in practice, it seemed that traders were doing something different. Using the same formula, it was possible to compute the so-called implied volatility that traders were using by backing it out from the price that they paid. When this was done, a consistent pattern emerged: Traders were assigning higher volatility to options with extreme strike prices K than they did to at-the-money options where the strike price was close to the current price. This phenomenon became known as the volatility smile.

An example of the volatility smile, or actually a volatility surface since it shows different expirations T, is shown in figure 1.3. The data is derived from SPX options during the period 2004–2020. The option prices are averaged over each strike K and expiration T, and the implied volatility is plotted as a function of x and T where we now define $x = \log(K/S_0)$.

According to Derman and Miller (2016), "The modeling of the volatility smile is likely one of the largest sources of model risk within finance." The usual approach was to treat it as an irrational anachronism, probably caused by behavioral biases on the parts of traders. One theory is that it first occurred following the Black Monday crash of 1987 and reflects a degree of risk aversion.[11]

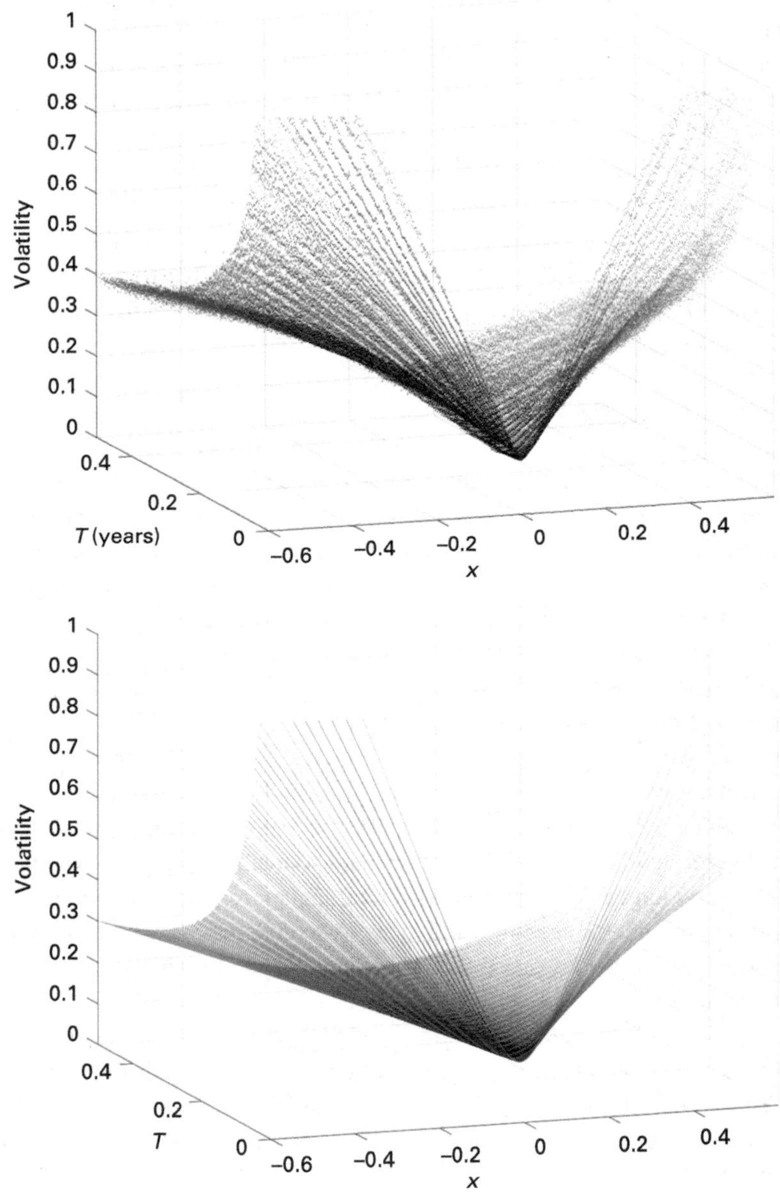

Figure 1.3
Top panel shows an implied volatility surface averaged from SPX options 2004–2020, plotted as a function of $x = \log(K/S_0)$ and time to expiration T. The smile is steeper for small T. The bottom panel shows the surface predicted by the quantum model equation 1.3 for the same values of x and T. The model's sole parameter is a base volatility σ. According to classical theory, the surface should be flat.

After all, in the classical model, you could only have one volatility at a time, so any model that "permits different volatilities for the same underlier ... is illogical."[12] Scores of papers and books had been written on the subject, and experts lined up with theories that claimed to model or explain the enigmatic smile, as if it were the financial version of the Mona Lisa.

To be clear, implied volatility is a complex phenomenon, and some of these models certainly had merit. But if the quantum model was right, then the implied volatility smile could be viewed at least in part as a reflection or weakened version of q-variance—or put another way, since implied volatility is calculated using the classical model, as a marker for model error.

There is clearly a connection between betting on a large price change (extreme strike) and expecting high volatility. Furthermore, the quantum model predicted that the implied volatility should approximately follow a modified version of the above equation given by

$$\sigma_q = \sqrt{2q^2\sigma^2 + (1-q^2)z^2}, \tag{1.3}$$

where $z = x/\sqrt{T}$, σ is a parameter, and

$$q = \frac{1}{\sqrt{2e}} \sum_{n=0}^{\infty} (2^n n!)^{-1} \sqrt{2n+1} \approxeq 0.95 \tag{1.4}$$

(long story, which we come to in chapter 7). In particular, if the quantum model was right, one would expect to see the same scaling in z, so the volatility smile becomes increasingly steep for small T.

Although the model was new, the idea at least that implied volatility should scale with log price change divided by the square root of the expiration time had been floated before. The reference that tended to come up was a Salomon Brothers report from 1995.[13] After contacting one of the authors, I learned that the last copies were apparently destroyed in 9/11. The effect was put down to risk aversion on the part of investors. In the quantum model, the reason was much simpler: The volatility smile was not a "logical inconsistency"[14] or primarily a psychological effect; instead, it was an attempt—influenced of course by many other factors—to capture an inherent property of markets that was neglected by the classical model. In other words, traders know about q-variance (they just don't know they know it).

Needless to say, though, the scaling of implied volatility with z had never made much of an impact on models of implied volatility. After all, it didn't seem to match with theory. Instead, as seen later, modelers would build elaborate models that used multiple parameters but held only for a particular time T. The quantum model, shown in the lower panel of figure 1.3, was hardly a perfect fit, but it captured the structure of the surface. In fact, as seen later, it can in a well-defined manner explain or account for over 80 percent of the implied volatility surface for the S&P 500 index using only a single parameter that applies for all periods T. For a mathematical model in the social sciences, that is a good result. But a more significant corollary, in my view, was that conventional methods were leading to a systematic mispricing of options, and risk in general.

I presented the research at another CQF conference, this one marking fifty years (1973–2023) of the Black-Scholes model.[15] The keynote speaker, who gave the last talk, was none other than the original paper's coauthor Myron Scholes. There was no indication that he had endured my own presentation. However, during a panel conference on the good old days of quantitative finance, a question from the audience was read out: "What would your response be to people who believe quantum economics/finance is too much of a stretch and is unrealistic?"

After everyone had a good laugh, the answer from one of the panelists, a leading quant who had trained in quantum mechanics, was, "I kind of agree—that it's too much of a stretch."

My own response (unrecorded since I was listening at home) was, "Really?" I give a talk laying out basic flaws in the models used in classical quantitative finance, which together lead to a significant error in the pricing of risk, and people are worried that the quantum version is unrealistic? That's the reaction?[16]

Later, I was able to share a polite and productive correspondence with the same quant, who it turned out hadn't heard about q-variance either. In 2025, Paul Wilmott (who had confirmed the result himself) and I made a direct request to readers of *Wilmott* magazine and the associated online forum for references to it, as well as some individual appeals to leading quants and other experts, but still nothing came up. As Paul said, "Tumbleweed."[17] Or as he summarized later in the opening session of a CQF conference that brought together leading authorities on the topic of volatility and risk in finance, "I've sent it to experts to look at. And nobody has seen this before. Nobody can explain it."[18]

Nor could they reproduce it: in late-2025 *Wilmott* magazine launched a competition to find a classical continuous-time model which could simulate q-variance using no more than three parameters.[19] The fact that no winning candidates emerged suggests a deeper disconnect with classical theory which we return to in chapter 6; the fact that modeling this basic empirical property was generally viewed as an intriguing brain-teaser showed just how novel it was to most people in the field.

It seemed that q-variance had been hiding in plain sight. The most interesting and anomalous thing about it was that no one could see it was an anomaly. Akerlof had warned that "observations that contradict the existing paradigm will be dismissed if they violate the prescribed methodology."[20] But here the phenomenon wasn't even seen or acknowledged, at least until Paul shone a spotlight on it.

But I had to wonder, was the problem the natural resistance to new ideas, or was I really bad at writing articles and doing presentations? Was it because I am not a member of the quant community? Or is it just that quantum is a no-go area for anyone who wants to appear serious?

1.4 A Different Path

Whatever the reasons may be—and this is a developing story, which we return to in the final chapter—the main point for now is that, even if quantum methods are over a hundred years old, their application outside of physics is still a niche pursuit. But the quantum approach seems particularly suited to finance and economics, where the use of money acts like a kind of measurement procedure that puts a hard price on the fuzzy concept of value. So before dismissing it because of its association with physics, researchers need to keep an open mind.

After all, mathematicians have developed many ideas that have found use in physics, such as the use of imaginary numbers to name one. It would seem churlish for physicists to deny mathematicians such as myself the opportunity to explore quantum techniques just because they came up with the idea first. And as the quantum computing expert Scott Aaronson observed, "The theory could have been invented by mathematicians in the 19th century without any input from experiment. It wasn't, but it could have been."[21]

Physicists also often (not always[22]) see quantum methods not as mere mathematical tools but as representing a deep ontological truth about physical reality, so any application (or in this view, misappropriation) outside of physics is either a flaky analogy ripe for debunking[23] or a kind of advertising gimmick to make the model look cool (if so, it is the least successful pitch in the history of advertising).[24] Classical models based on equilibrium mechanics get a pass. However, many quants and economists are dismissive of econophysics in general because it smacks of physics envy, which is ironic given that their fields were originally based on concepts from physics (e.g., Brownian motion). A self-respecting quant will probably be uncomfortable (fall about laughing) if you use the word "energy" to describe asset behavior; however, the models they use are often based on things like the diffusion equation that have energy terms in them, even if the finance versions don't use that word.

Non-physicists will be especially leery of quantum ideas, in part because physicists themselves have always drummed up the idea that they are incredibly complex (see, for example, the Feynman quote at the start of chapter 3). That may be true in the context of subatomic particles, but as we will see, building a wave function model of price is not so hard.

In the end, all the worries about what counts as quantum and so on seem rather unserious. The field of quantitative finance has never had anything along the lines of an ultraviolet crisis, but it could certainly use a wake-up call. Quants and "financial engineers" should use the best tools for the job and be careful about writing off a theory just because they are uncomfortable it has its roots in physics.

But anyone who is convinced that quantum ideas are too flaky/weird/fanciful for a real scientist to use outside the confines of physics should probably just look away now, and keep doing what they are doing, because such preconceptions are not themselves scientific and tend to be quite rigid. Although, they will need to come up with a model for empirical facts like q-variance that have eluded the classical approach for the last century.

For the rest of us, this book will now step back to the heady days when quantum ideas were first being applied to physics but before they became mainstream, and ask how Bachelier or one of his students might have applied wave mechanics to the stock market in the same way that contemporaries like de Broglie were applying them to the atom—and before anyone told them it was wrong. Consider it the path not taken by quantitative finance—the one where one of the luminaries at the 1927 Solvay conference (so before the 1929 crash) turned to another and said, "My shoeshine boy told me this is a great time to invest, but I'm uncertain."

In terms of mathematics, the treatment relies only on wave equations of the sort being used in the early twentieth century before quantum mechanics developed its own specialized and sometimes inscrutable notation. We will not go deeply into complex properties such as superposition and entanglement but simply use wave functions as a way to describe the evolution of probability as a dynamic system. Quants are used to working with static probability distributions, so the main difference is that now the distributions are dynamic and can move around.

In fact, as seen later, classical quantitative finance is in a way consistent with quantum finance. It can be described as a kind of Platonic special case in which inefficiencies or opportunities for arbitrage do not occur—but only because no transactions ever take place either.

As always, of course, the only justification for using quantum techniques is if they are demonstrably better than existing methods at explaining or predicting a system. In the next chapter, we therefore start with a model of transactions based on classical probability before showing how a switch to the quantum framework spins it into life.

2

The Propensity to Transact

> A long time ago, when economics consisted rather of glib phrases than of real analyses, a critic of the science said, "If you want to make a first-class economist, catch a parrot and teach him to say 'supply and demand' in response to every question you ask him. What determines wages? Supply and demand. What determines interest? Supply and demand. What determines the distribution of wealth? Supply and demand." In every instance the answer is right, but it explains nothing.
>
> —Irving Fisher, *Introduction to Economic Science*, 1910

> If you think that's the way atoms are, then you're back in 1910.
>
> —Richard Feynman, *QED: The Strange Theory of Light and Matter*, 1985

Adam Smith wrote in his 1776 *The Wealth of Nations* that the "propensity to truck, barter, and exchange" was inherent to human nature. Some 160 years later, the economist John Maynard Keynes formalized the concept into a "propensity to consume," which was counterbalanced by a "propensity to hoard."[1] Today, economists continue to use the term; Oxford Reference, for example, defines the propensity to consume as "the proportion of disposable income which individuals desire to spend on consumption," which they note "may be affected by factors such as the consumer's total assets, liquidity, and expectations of inflation."[2]

When applied more narrowly, the propensity to consume or to hoard a particular commodity (say oil, or housing, or ownership of a stock) will of course depend on its price. In mainstream economics, this relationship is captured by the so-called law of supply and demand. This imagines markets as consisting of suppliers on one side and consumers on the other. The propensity of the former to supply the good is represented as a function of price by an upward-sloping curve, so the dearer the good, the more is produced. The propensity of the consumer to buy the good is conversely represented by a downward-sloping curve of demand versus price.

The point where these two curves intersect represents the optimal price that gives a stable equilibrium and optimizes the utility of both buyer and seller. According to the neoclassical economist William Stanley Jevons (1871), following a transaction, both parties then "rest in satisfaction and equilibrium, and the degrees of utility have come to their level, as it were."[3] Or as Walras (1889) put it more drily (his italics), "*Production and exchange in a market ruled by free competition is an operation through which services can be combined into products of the kinds and quantities that give greatest possible satisfaction of wants within the limits imposed by the double condition that each service as well as each product has only a single price in the market, the one for which supply and demand are equal, and that the selling price of products is equal to their cost in services.*"[4]

The neoclassical picture is therefore of an economy at equilibrium. Economists speak frequently of the forces of supply and demand, which are visualized using these two lines. However, because the system is at equilibrium, the forces are assumed to perfectly cancel out, which means that they never need to be calculated or even expressed using equations. Bachelier's option pricing theory can be seen as extending Walras's model of the economy to include the market for options whose payout occurs in the future. This view was later completed by Eugene Fama's efficient market hypothesis[5]—variously described as "the best established fact in all social sciences"[6] and "probably the best-tested proposition in all the social sciences"[7]—which claimed that prices effectively adjust instantaneously to new information.

As a sidenote, it is often said that neoclassical economics is Newtonian because of its reductionist, mechanistic approach, but really, it would be better described as Aristotelian. According to Aristotle, whose word was considered sacrosanct well into the Middle Ages, the universe was made up of the four elements Earth, Water, Air, and Fire, plus the fifth element Ether, which was reserved for the heavens. Each element had its place, so Earth would tend to sink and Air would rise. In a vacuum, each element would find its level instantaneously, which was why "nature abhors a vacuum" (Medieval philosopher: "probably the best established fact in natural philosophy"). In neoclassical economics, the perfect vacuum exists, and it is the market. Prices always find their level, and dynamics don't really matter, although they are sometimes included as a kind of friction to slow adjustment, just as in Aristotelian physics.

Although many mathematical techniques from physics, including, of course, the heat diffusion equation, are forced into service in economics, there is no real sense of dynamics, let alone probabilistic dynamics of the sort encountered in quantum physics. So-called Dynamic Stochastic General Equilibrium models, for example, are really equilibrium models with some noise and frictions thrown in. The main qualities of the neoclassical model are therefore that it is static and deterministic; however, the economy is obviously a dynamic probabilistic system. In this chapter, we will show how propensity can be modeled in a probabilistic fashion before getting onto the question of dynamics in the following chapters.

2.1 The Propensity Function

The word "atom" is from the Greek *atomos* for indivisible. Its use in physics is derived from the Greek philosopher Democritus, who wrote that "Sweet exists by convention, bitter by convention, color by convention; but in reality atoms and the void alone exist."[8]

If there is a financial equivalent of an indivisible atom, it would be a transaction between two parties involving the trade of money for ownership of an asset. There can't be half a transaction any more than there can be half a contract. We are not used to thinking of a transaction as a kind of particle, but as we'll see, it can be a useful concept.

Suppose that a buyer wishes to purchase a unit of stock from a seller. Finance has its own version of the uncertainty principle, which is that the price of the asset is not perfectly known and can be discovered only through transactions, which in turn can affect the price. The buyer and seller therefore only have access to the opinions of others, their own beliefs, and an approximate going rate. The buyer will on average tend to offer a price that is a little lower than this going rate in order to avoid overpaying, whereas the seller will on average ask a little more in order to avoid a bad deal. The spread between the buyer and seller prices is a measure of the uncertainty in price.

At the same time, each party will have not a single price, but a range of prices at which they are willing to transact. This can be viewed as a kind of schedule, which we will depict as a normal curve centered at a preferred price. The probability of a transaction actually occurring will depend on the overlap of these schedules, which in turn will depend on the flexibility of the buyer and seller. For example, if both parties are stuck on their respective prices with little room for negotiation, then a deal is unlikely to be reached.

To make this more precise, we define the propensity function of the buyer to be a density function describing the probability of making a purchase as a function of price. Because it is a probability density function, the total probability should integrate to 1. Such a propensity function is illustrated in figure 2.1 for the buyer (curve on the left) and the seller (right). Both functions are assumed

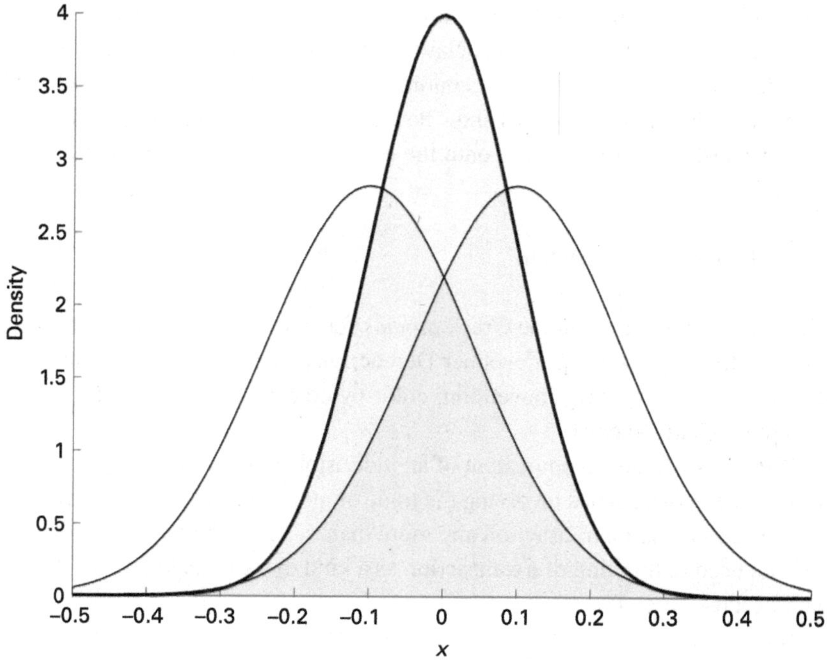

Figure 2.1
Propensity functions for the buyer (left), seller (right), and joint (middle). Here, the joint propensity is scaled to give a total probability of unity. Price x is treated as a logarithmic variable.

to be normal curves, with the mean ask price of the seller x_a higher than that of the buyer x_b. Price is treated as a logarithmic variable. For simplicity, we will also assume that the standard deviations of the two curves are the same, so $\sigma_a = \sigma_b = \sigma$, and the midpoint price is normalized to zero. We therefore have $x_a = -x_b = \epsilon$, where ϵ is the half-spread. (For the general case, see Orrell, 2020a.)

The probability of a transaction actually occurring is the joint propensity function, shown by the heavy black line in the figure, which is the product of the buyer and seller functions. It is a scaled normal curve, with mean and standard deviation

$$x_t = \frac{\sigma_b^2 x_a + \sigma_a^2 x_b}{\sigma_a^2 + \sigma_b^2} = 0 \tag{2.1}$$

$$\sigma_t = \frac{\sigma_a \sigma_b}{\sqrt{\sigma_a^2 + \sigma_b^2}} = \frac{\sigma}{\sqrt{2}}. \tag{2.2}$$

The scaling factor α, which describes the total probability of a transaction occurring over the trading period, is itself in the form of a normal equation

$$\alpha = \frac{1}{\sqrt{2\pi \sigma_c{}^2}} \exp\left(-\frac{x_c^2}{2\sigma_c{}^2}\right), \tag{2.3}$$

where $x_c = x_a - x_b = 2\epsilon$ and $\sigma_c = \sqrt{\sigma_a^2 + \sigma_b^2} = 2\sigma_t$. It has a maximum value at $x_c = 0$ of $1/\sqrt{2\pi \sigma_c{}^2} = 1/\sqrt{8\pi \sigma_t^2}$.

It might seem that we should model the propensity using something like a logistic function that is monotonically decreasing in price for the buyer and increasing for the seller. However, this would violate the condition that probabilities should sum to 1, and it would also have little effect on the joint distribution since it is easily checked that the product of two such logistic functions gives a bell-shaped curve.

2.2 The Transacton (Not a Typo)

We therefore need to calibrate the model so that the total joint probability accurately reflects the probability of a transaction occurring at some price during the period T. A question then arises about the role of the period T. If an individual is thinking about buying a house, for example, and they are likely to purchase one in the next month, then doubling the period to two months does not make them twice as likely to buy or mean that they will buy two homes. However, it does make it more likely that other potential buyers will arrive; and if we consider a stock market where there is a certain rate of turnover, then we want the total number of transactions in a period T to scale with T. We will return to this later when we discuss the quantum model.

A related question is how the price will evolve over time. Suppose we divide time into discrete steps so each period represents a separate short step of length T. If the probability of a transaction at some price is one, then the log price change would be a random draw from the normal distribution, and the price would evolve according to a standard random walk in a manner consistent with the Bachelier view of markets.

A variation on this would be to assume that the number of transactions n in a single time step follows a Poisson distribution. The transactions will perturb the price as in a shortened version of a random walk. This case is depicted in the left column of figure 2.2. The top three panels show the probability distribution after $n = 0, 1,$ and 2 transactions. The bottom panel shows the distribution where the number of transactions follows a Poisson process with a rate parameter (so

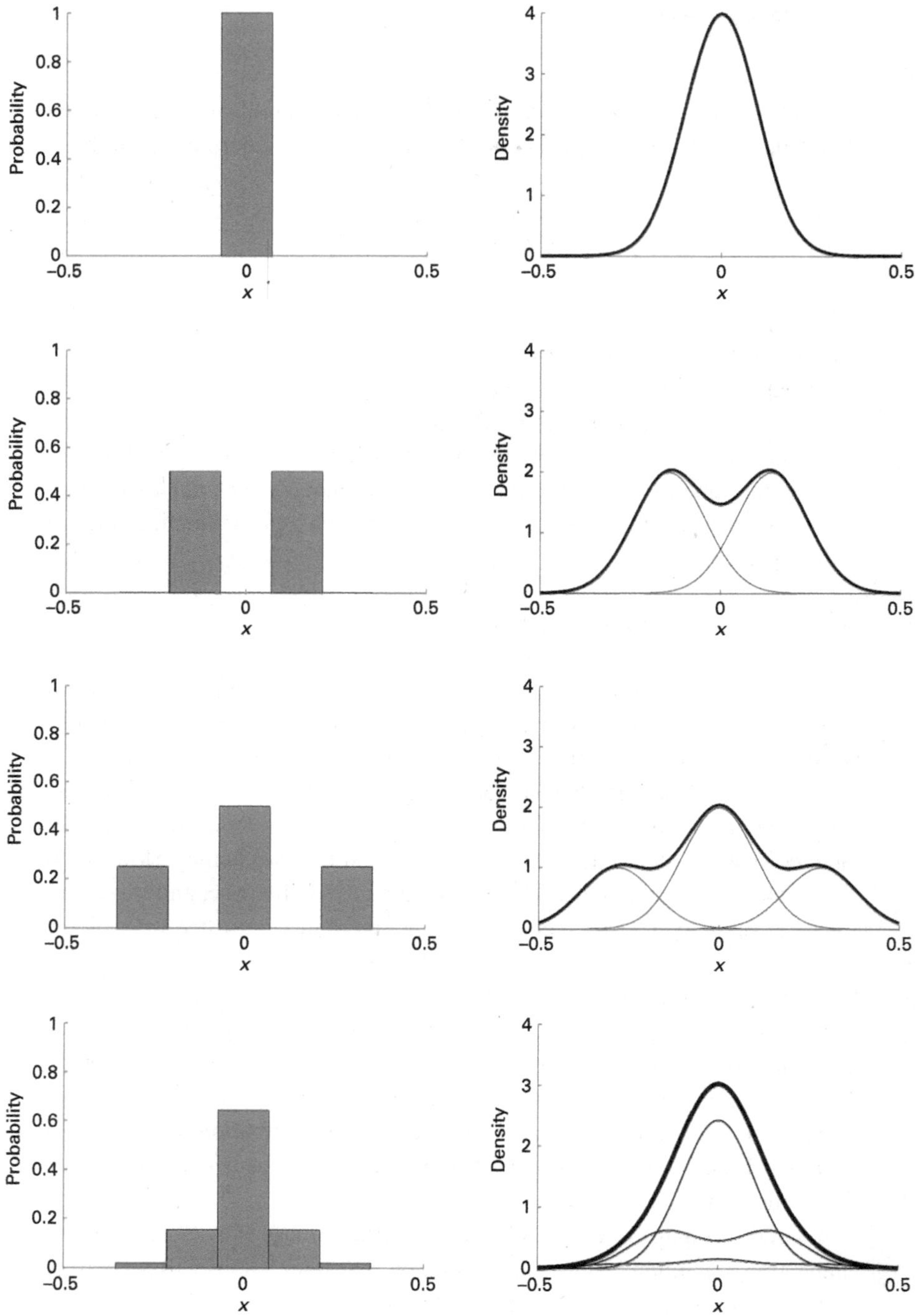

Figure 2.2
Left column shows the probability distribution for a sequence of transactions within a single time step T. Top three plots are for $n = 0$, 1, and 2 transactions. Bottom plot is the distribution after the time step if we assume that the number of transactions n follows a Poisson distribution with rate parameter $\lambda = 0.5$. Right column shows the same with an additional noise term. The bottom plot here compares with the probability density function of a jump-diffusion process as discussed later in chapter 6.

average number of transactions) equal to $\lambda = 0.5$. It can be viewed approximately as the weighted sum of the first three terms, with respective weights of 0.61, 0.30, and 0.08 (higher terms decay rapidly). The right column shows the case where an additional noise term is added, so the price is perturbed by an amount $\delta = \sqrt{2}\sigma$, where $\sigma = 0.1$ is the standard deviation of the noise term. (The choice of parameters is consistent with the jump-diffusion model discussed later, where a price is perturbed by normal noise together with a number of larger jumps, though there, the size of the jump also varies randomly, while here, it is fixed.)

Finally, we need a word to describe a potential transaction like the one depicted in figure 2.1. We will therefore coin the word *transacton* to denote a unit of stock that is up for negotiation between a seller and a buyer. A transacton is therefore like a kind of ghostly elementary particle that may or may not appear in the tangible form of one or more actual transactions, with a rate of success defined by λ. Setting $\lambda = 0.5$, for example, means that the odds are balanced, so the average number of transactions produced is one-half.

In the classical supply/demand model, the analysis takes place at an aggregate level over all buyers and all sellers. In an agent-based model, the analysis takes place at the level of individual buyers and sellers. In classical finance, it takes place at the level of price changes. By setting the unit of analysis to be the transacton, the probabilistic model described here puts the focus on the actual transfer that takes place between seller and buyer. Of course, the model is a simplification; for example, it deals in a single unit of stock, where trading may allow fractional units, and so on. However, as we'll see, it suffices to capture the key dynamics of the system.

2.3 Out of Balance

Suppose that we wish to model the effect of a large transaction on price. Since a transacton represents a potential transaction between two parties, we can view the market as being made up of a number of such models running in series. If the usual number of units being put up for sale is N_a and the demand is N_b, then when the market is balanced, we would have $N_a = N_b = N$. Assume, though, that the demand per available unit over the time step increases by an amount $\Delta N = \iota N$. In this case, the demand on a seller will exceed their regular rate of turnover. We can then ask how much the price should change in order to restore the original rate.

If we assume that the balanced price is $x = 0$, then since the propensity curves are normal, it can be checked that the price change needed to balance the effect is $x = \sigma\sqrt{2\log(1 + |\iota|)}$. A similar argument for the case where the number of sellers changes shows that, in general,[9]

$$x = \pm\sigma\sqrt{2\log(1+|\iota|)}, \tag{2.4}$$

where the sign depends on the sign of

$$\iota = \frac{N_b - N_a}{\min(N_b, N_a)}. \tag{2.5}$$

For small imbalances $|\iota|$, we can use the approximation $\log(1+|\iota|) \approxeq |\iota|$, so

$$x \approxeq \pm\sigma\sqrt{2|\iota|}. \tag{2.6}$$

However, the approximation only applies for small imbalances, while as discussed later, empirical evidence shows that this square root relation applies over a much larger range.

Another problem is that, as mentioned in chapter 1, large transactions don't just affect price; they also affect the variance, and it isn't clear how to address this. One approach would be to say that the imbalance increases the expected number of transactions n per transacton. The variance would therefore similarly increase in a linear fashion with the number of transactions.

Of course, the choice of structure and parameters for this model seems quite arbitrary. There is no apparent rationale for selecting the jump size δ or the rate parameter λ, or even why we need to consider transactons in the first place instead of just modeling price directly and assuming that jumps occur sequentially in time in the usual way (or perhaps by modeling individuals as in an agent-based model). It also isn't clear how changes to price and to variance are related. This might be why, to the author's knowledge, no classical model along these exact lines has been proposed previously in the literature, and why we have to invent a new word, *transacton*, to describe a unit of analysis that describes a fundamental interaction. As seen later, though, similar ideas and properties emerge naturally from the quantum model, which focuses on the role of transactions and takes dynamics into account.

2.4 Entropic Force

Before proceeeding to the physics-adjacent quantum model, an obvious objection will be that there is no equivalent in the social sciences of the forces found in physics. As mentioned earlier, economists speak, for example, of the forces of supply and demand, but these are just metaphors, and it is impossible to write them out as equations.

As seen in the first chapter, quantitative finance has its roots in nineteenth-century physics. Neoclassical economists of the time used analogies from physics to develop concepts such as utility, which was seen as a form of energy. As time went on, though, the fields of finance and economics increasingly distanced themselves from physics.[10]

However, although financial transactions may seem to lack tangible forces, they are the result of intangible processes involving the flow of information. And in physics, there is a direct link between information and force through the concept of entropy.[11]

In statistical mechanics, a force $f(x)$ with potential $U(x)$ acting on a single particle yields a probability distribution $P(x)$ for the position of the particle of

$$P(x) = C\exp\left(-\frac{U(x)}{k_B T}\right), \tag{2.7}$$

where T is temperature, k_B is the Boltzmann constant, and C is a normalization constant. Taking the derivative of each side, it follows that

$$f(x) = -\gamma \frac{P'(x)}{P(x)}, \tag{2.8}$$

where the term $\gamma = k_B T$ has units of energy. In physics, this term is the amount of heat required to increase the thermodynamic entropy of a system measured in natural units.

In other words, the force can be recovered from a knowledge of the probability distribution, which is a form of information. In physics, this so-called entropic force represents the system's tendency to maximize entropy by evolving to states that are statistically more probable. It follows that, given a probability distribution $P(x)$, we can derive a corresponding entropic force.[12] In particular, the bid and ask propensity functions in figure 2.1 can be viewed as the product of such forces.

Figure 2.3 shows the entropic force for a uniform probability distribution and a normal distribution. The first corresponds to the case where particles are confined to a box with position $|x| \leq 0.2$. If the walls are infinitely stiff, then the forces have infinite magnitude. The second corresponds to the case with a linear entropic force that pushes the particles toward the center. The next two chapters will derive quantum models for each of these situations.

It follows from this that if we can describe propensity using probability, then we can translate that information into an entropic force. The idealized, unmeasurable forces of supply and demand from neoclassical economics are therefore turned into something concrete. Suppose, for example, that the current price x is higher than the buyer's central price x_b. The propensity to purchase is then given by the function $P_b(x)$, and the resistance to changing to some nearby price $x + \Delta x$ will depend on the change in propensity conditional on (or relative

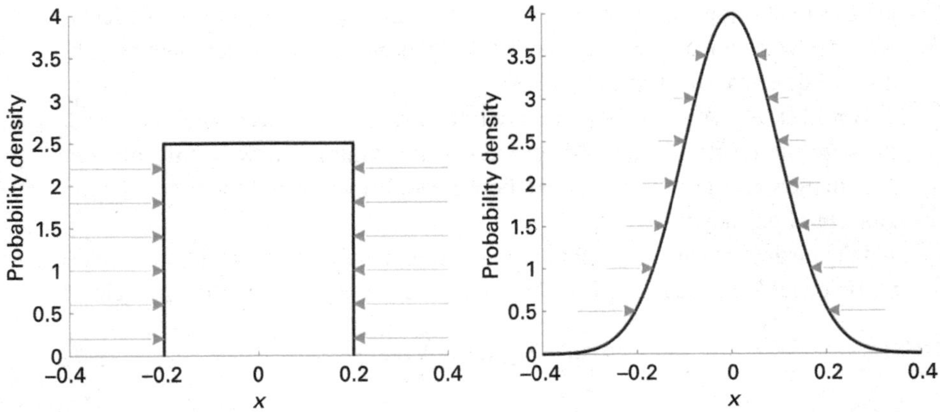

Figure 2.3
Left panel shows entropic force for a uniform probability distribution, as for particles confined to a box $|x| \leq 0.2$. Right panel shows entropic force for a normal distribution.

to) the current propensity. This is equal to the slope of the propensity divided by the current propensity or $P'_b(x)/P_b(x)$. We therefore define the supply and demand forces as

$$F_a(x) = \gamma \frac{P'_a(x)}{P_a(x)} = -k(x - \epsilon) \tag{2.9}$$

$$F_b(x) = \gamma \frac{P'_b(x)}{P_b(x)} = -k(x + \epsilon), \tag{2.10}$$

where

$$k = \frac{\gamma}{\sigma^2} \tag{2.11}$$

is a force constant, γ is a scaling parameter with units of energy, and we have set $\sigma_a = \sigma_b = \sigma$ and $x_a = -x_b = \epsilon$ as before.[13]

The forces therefore represent the mental desire for the buyer or seller to adjust the price to their own preferred level. The fact that the propensity functions are normal means that the corresponding forces are linear in price. They can therefore be viewed as a first-order approximation to the dynamics in the region of the central equilibrium point.

We can similarly define the transaction force as the entropic force generated by the joint probability, which is just the sum of the buyer and seller forces:

$$F_t(x) = \gamma \frac{P'_t(x)}{P_t(x)} = \gamma \frac{P_a(x) P'_b(x) + P'_a(x) P_b(x)}{P_a(x) P_b(x)} \tag{2.12}$$

$$= F_a(x) + F_b(x) \tag{2.13}$$

$$= -2kx. \tag{2.14}$$

The force is therefore directed toward the center with a magnitude that scales with displacement, as depicted in the right-hand panel of figure 2.3. The point at which the probability of a transaction is highest can be found by setting the derivative of the joint propensity function to zero, so

$$P_t'(x) = P_a'(x)\,P_b(x) + P_a(x)\,P_b'(x) = 0, \tag{2.15}$$

which occurs at the price

$$x_t = \frac{k_a x_a + k_b x_b}{k_a + k_b} = 0. \tag{2.16}$$

The equilibrium price is therefore the point where the supply and demand forces are in balance and $F_t(x) = 0$, as expected. The dynamics associated with a linear force are a simple oscillator, so the picture is of price bouncing back and forth around a central point.

So far we have modelled only a single transacton, but price change over a period is of course due to multiple transactions whose effects add together. If there are M potential transactions over a period T, and we model each as a separate transacton with spring constant k, then the total price change can be modeled by assuming that the springs act as if joined end-to-end in series, with an effective spring constant of

$$k_T = \frac{k}{M} = \frac{\gamma}{M\sigma^2}. \tag{2.17}$$

Comparing with equation 2.11, the variance of the series is therefore $M\sigma^2$. If we assume that M scales with time, it follows that we can model the system using a single representative oscillator whose variance also scales with time as in classical finance.

This entropic force argument may seem like an elaborate explanation for a restoring force on price, which is a concept that has already been tried in economics with little success. In fact, one of the first mentions of a mathematical model in economics was an oscillatory model of the stock market.[14] The fact that prices do not in fact oscillate was probably one reason why economists moved toward a model in which prices were always at equilibrium. However, just because prices do not behave like a classical oscillator does not mean that we should abandon the idea of dynamics altogether. The problem may just be that we are using the wrong kind of probability and the wrong kind of oscillations.

2.5 Summary

A model based on classical probability can be used to simulate transactions; however, it doesn't tell us anything new or surprising about the system, it is essentially static and so says nothing about dynamics, and some of its properties such as price impact are inconsistent with observed behavior. The main problem, though, is that it does nothing to help explain the anomalies described in the first chapter. These all involve the volatility, and in the classical model, this is treated as being a constant parameter. We can address this to an extent by considering individual transactons and selecting particular parameters, but the justification is unclear.

Note that in the description so far, we are already modeling price using a probability wave. However, the wave is not moving, so there are no dynamics, which seems to be a limitation if we want to talk about things like "impact." We can derive an associated entropic force, but it doesn't connect to anything. We need a way to make the wave move.

As we'll see, this can be addressed by making the wave function complex, so, for example, it can rotate around the real axis. But to do this, we need to look at how similar problems were modeled in physics a century ago.

3
Wave Mechanics

> The ideas which are here expressed so laboriously are extremely simple and should be obvious. The difficulty lies, not in the new ideas, but in escaping from the old ones, which ramify, for those brought up as most of us have been, into every corner of our minds.
>
> —John Maynard Keynes, *The General Theory of Employment, Interest and Money*, 1936

> I think I can safely say that nobody understands quantum mechanics.
>
> —Richard Feynman, *The Feynman Lectures on Physics*, 1964

The quantum revolution in physics came about when physicists realized that to explain the properties of matter, they needed to think in terms of probability waves. The key ingredients were Planck's idea of quanta and Einstein's formula for the energy of a photon. It might seem that neither of these have much to do with the stock market, but in fact, there are a number of common elements, including ones related to the discrete nature of the underlying system.

This doesn't mean that our aim is to use subatomic particles as a metaphor for the markets. Metaphors and analogies are, of course, central to how we think about and understand the world; however, mathematical models are a little different. Calculus was first developed to study planetary motion, but we can use it in an area like economics without saying people are like planets, and the same is true of quantum probability. Also, the whole point of a metaphor is to explain something that is abstract or unfamiliar by comparing it with something that is concrete and tangible, and for most readers—and certainly the author, who doesn't know his muons from his gluons—talking about markets in terms of subatomic particles is unlikely to help. However, we will unapologetically make use of concepts such as energy, mass, and momentum because these are useful to describe dynamic systems and also have meanings in areas including finance.

In this chapter, we introduce the quantum wave mechanics used in this book by applying it to a simple problem, familiar to any physics student, known as the infinite well—and argue that, although quantum physics may be impenetrable (picture someone staring into an infinite well), the quantum view of finance is actually quite intuitive. As Keynes knew (he met Einstein in 1926 and may have borrowed the title for his *General Theory of Employment, Interest and Money* from Einstein's general theory of relativity[1]), the problem sometimes lies not in new ideas but in escaping from the old ones.

3.1 Waves and Particles

To briefly recap the physics,[2] Planck's formula for the energy of light was $E = hf$, where f is the frequency and h is called Planck's constant. Einstein's theory of relativity, however, proposed that the energy of a photon is $E = mc^2 = pc$, where p is momentum and c is the speed of light. Solving for the momentum gives $p = E/c = hf/c = h/\lambda$, where $\lambda = c/f$ is the wavelength, and we have used the relation $\lambda = v/f$, where here, the speed of the wave is $v = c$.

In other words, a light wave of wavelength λ is associated with a particle with energy E and momentum p. But there is nothing in these equations to suggest that they apply only to light (hold that thought). In his doctoral thesis, de Broglie therefore argued that in the same way, a particle was associated with a wave. If the particle had energy E and momentum p, then the corresponding wave has frequency $f = E/h$ and wavelength $\lambda = h/p$.

It was later found that it was more convenient to work in terms of angular frequency $\omega = 2\pi f$ and $\hbar = h/(2\pi)$, which scales between this and energy. The de Broglie relations then become

$$E = \hbar\omega \tag{3.1}$$

$$p = \hbar k, \tag{3.2}$$

where $k = 2\pi/\lambda$ is called the wave number.

This wave idea was useful because it imposed a new kind of structure on the behavior of matter. For example, if an electron at some radius from the atom was to be represented as a standing wave, the circumference at that radius would have to be an integer multiple of the wave length.

At this point, physicists didn't known what the wave functions, as they became known, actually represented. However, in 1926, Max Born proposed that the waves expressed the probability of finding a particle in a particular state. If a particle had a wave function $\Psi(x, t)$, then the probability of finding the particle in the region $(x, x + \delta x)$ was $|\Psi(x, t)|^2 \delta x$. Since the particle had to be located somewhere, it followed that the wave function must obey the normalization condition

$$\int_{-\infty}^{+\infty} |\Psi(x,t)|^2 \, dx = 1. \tag{3.3}$$

To find the wave for a particular situation, an obvious starting point was to look for solutions in the form of basic waves such as $A \sin(kx - \omega t)$, which has wave number k and angular frequency ω. A problem was that such waves do not satisfy the normalization condition, but there were ways around this, such as using linear combinations that partially cancel out. More generally, since sine or cosine waves can be written as the sum of complex waves

$$\cos\theta = \frac{e^{i\theta} + e^{-i\theta}}{2} \tag{3.4}$$

$$\sin\theta = \frac{e^{i\theta} - e^{-i\theta}}{2}, \tag{3.5}$$

it made sense to look at linear superpositions

$$\Psi(x,t) = Ae^{i(kx-\omega t)} + Be^{-i(kx-\omega t)} + Ce^{i(kx+\omega t)} + De^{-i(kx+\omega t)}, \tag{3.6}$$

where the coefficients A, B, C, and D were to be determined.

The top left panel of figure 3.1 shows the real part of a complex wave function of the form $\Psi(x,t) = Ae^{i(kx-\omega t)}$ for a fixed time point. The complex component, not shown, is similar but out of phase. Here, the momentum $p = \hbar k$ is known precisely, but the amplitude including both real and imaginary components is constant (top right), which means that the particle can be located anywhere.

The lower panels show the same for a wave packet, constructed via Fourier's method from a particular linear superposition of waves. The probability amplitude is constrained to a particular region and so can be normalized. However, because the wave packet is constructed from multiple waves, the momentum is no longer well defined. In the other extreme case where the wave packet is localized to a single point (not shown) so the probability density is described by the Dirac delta function, the range of momenta in the waves is infinite.

If we define the uncertainties in position and momentum to be Δx and Δp, respectively, then applying Fourier's theorem to the wave packet of a particle, it was found that

$$\Delta x \Delta p \geq \frac{\hbar}{2}, \tag{3.7}$$

which is the Heisenberg uncertainty relation. It followed that one could never perfectly know both the position and momentum of a particle.

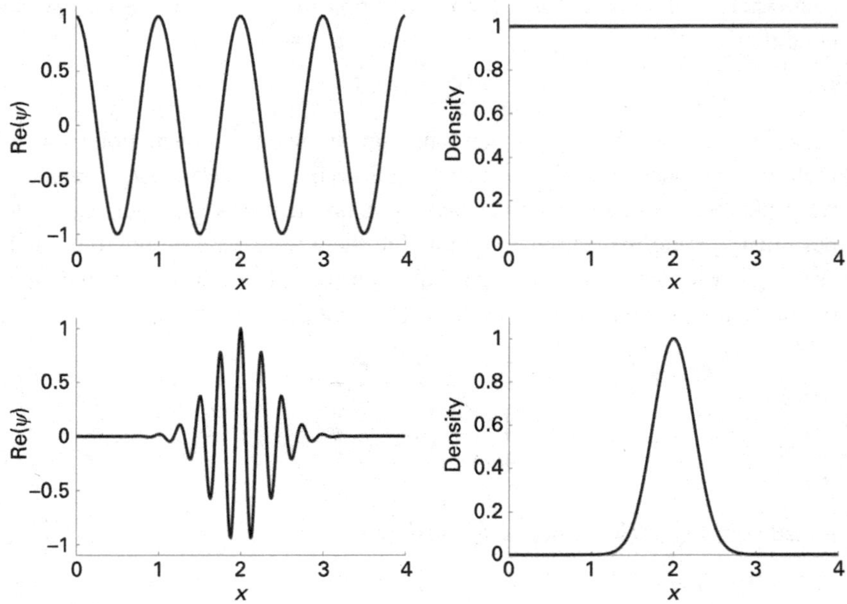

Figure 3.1
Top left panel shows the real part of a complex wave function $\Psi(x,t)$ at a fixed time. Top right panel is the corresponding probability amplitude, which is constant and so does not meet the normalization constraint. Bottom row shows the same for a wave packet, constructed from a linear superposition of waves. Here, the probability is confined within a certain region.

This observation immediately offered a solution to a long-standing conundrum. According to classical physics, an electron circulating the positively charged nucleus of an atom should radiate away its energy and spiral into the nucleus in about 10^{-12} seconds. According to the uncertainty principle, this couldn't happen because if the electron collided with the nucleus, then its position would be precisely known. The kinetic energy satisfies

$$\langle K\rangle = \frac{1}{2}m\langle v^2\rangle = \frac{1}{2m}\langle p^2\rangle = \frac{\sigma_p^2}{2m} \geq \frac{\hbar^2}{8m\sigma_x^2}, \tag{3.8}$$

where σ_p^2 and σ_x^2 are the variances, and we have used $\sigma_p^2 = \langle p^2\rangle - \langle p\rangle^2 = \langle p^2\rangle$ since $\langle p\rangle = 0$ by symmetry. As the position uncertainty σ_x approaches zero, the kinetic energy goes to infinity. The electron cannot therefore collide with the nucleus but instead will be located in a particular minimum band. However, as seen next, a particle that is confined to a particular region cannot have zero kinetic energy.

3.2 A Particle in a Box

Of course, quantum theory also led to a number of other conundrums of the philosophical sort. For example, was the wave function real or just an imaginary construct (for one thing, it involved imaginary numbers)? Physicists on the whole reacted to such ontological questions by ignoring them and focusing on applying the method to solving problems. Also, $\hbar$ was a small number, so the uncertainty was only considered to be relevant at the atomic scale. (In finance, we will use the wave function to describe price, which isn't very real either, but here, the effects do scale up.)

An early example of a simple application, which dates at least to a 1930 textbook *An Outline of Wave Mechanics* by N.F. Mott, is that of the infinite well, which is about a particle in a box.[3] It might seem to have little to do with finance, but going through the exercise of solving it will supply us with the basics for understanding how to combine probability and dynamics, which will become useful later for modeling the stock market.

Suppose that a particle of mass m and energy E is trapped in a one-dimensional box $0 < x < L$ (the situation was sketched earlier in the left panel of figure 2.3). The potential energy inside the box is $V = 0$ and outside the box is $V = \infty$. This means that the particle cannot leave the box, and its energy inside the box is purely kinetic.

Since the particle cannot leave the box, the wave function must be zero outside it, so if we assume the wave function is continuous, then we obtain the boundary conditions

$$\Psi(0,t) = \Psi(L,t) = 0. \tag{3.9}$$

At $L = 0$, we can write the general solution in the form

$$\Psi(0,t) = Ae^{-i\omega t} + Be^{i\omega t} + Ce^{i\omega t} + De^{-i\omega t} \tag{3.10}$$

$$= (A + D)e^{-i\omega t} + (B + C)e^{i\omega t} \tag{3.11}$$

$$= 0. \tag{3.12}$$

Since this equation must hold for all times t, it follows that all terms are zero, so $D = -A$ and $C = -B$. We can therefore write

$$\Psi(x,t) = Ae^{i(kx-\omega t)} + Be^{-i(kx-\omega t)} - Be^{i(kx+\omega t)} - Ae^{-i(kx+\omega t)} \tag{3.13}$$

$$= A(e^{ikx} - e^{-ikx})e^{-i\omega t} - B(e^{ikx} - e^{-ikx})e^{i\omega t} \tag{3.14}$$

$$= 2i\sin(kx)(Ae^{-i\omega t} - Be^{i\omega t}). \tag{3.15}$$

Applying the normalization condition gives

$$\int_{-\infty}^{+\infty} |\Psi(x,t)|^2\,dx = 4|Ae^{-i\omega t} - Be^{i\omega t}|^2 \int_0^L \sin^2(kx)\,dx. \tag{3.16}$$

It is easily checked that the term multiplying the integral is time dependent unless $A=0$ or $B=0$. If we choose the latter, then this term becomes $4|Ae^{-i\omega t}|^2 = 4|A|^2$, and

$$\Psi(x,t) = 2iA\sin(kx)e^{-i\omega t}. \tag{3.17}$$

The other boundary condition $\Psi(L,t)=0$ further tells us that

$$\Psi(L,t) = 2iA\sin(kL) = 0, \tag{3.18}$$

from which it follows that k can only take on the discrete set of values

$$k_n = \frac{1}{L}(n+1)\pi \tag{3.19}$$

for an integer n, where we use $n+1$ instead of n for later convenience.

The normalization condition then becomes

$$\int_{-\infty}^{+\infty} |\Psi(x,t)|^2\,dx = 4|A|^2 \int_0^L \sin^2(k_n x)\,dx = 2|A|^2 L = 1, \tag{3.20}$$

so

$$A = \frac{1}{\sqrt{2L}}e^{i\theta}, \tag{3.21}$$

where θ is an arbitrary phase factor. Choosing $\theta = -\pi/2$ gives

$$A = \frac{-i}{\sqrt{2L}}. \tag{3.22}$$

3.3 Energy Levels

So far, we have dealt only with normalization of the wave function and have not involved much in the way of real physics; however, this only concerns how we interpret the wave function. Because the particle's energy is purely kinetic, we have

$$E = \frac{p^2}{2m}. \tag{3.23}$$

Using the de Broglie relation $p = \hbar k$ gives

$$E = \frac{p^2}{2m} = \frac{\hbar^2 k^2}{2m}. \tag{3.24}$$

It therefore follows that energy is quantized and can only take on the values

$$E_n = \frac{\hbar^2 k_n^2}{2m} = \frac{(n+1)^2 \pi^2 \hbar^2}{2mL^2}. \tag{3.25}$$

Also, $E = \hbar\omega$, so the frequencies associated with each number n are

$$\omega_n = \omega(n+1)^2 \tag{3.26}$$

for

$$\omega = \frac{\pi^2 \hbar}{2mL^2}. \tag{3.27}$$

Putting this all together, equation 3.17 along with the formulas for A and k_n tell us that the solution in the region $0 < x < L$ is given by wave functions of the form

$$\Psi_n(x,t) = \psi_n(x) e^{-i\omega_n t}, \tag{3.28}$$

where

$$\psi_n(x) = \sqrt{\frac{2}{L}} \sin \frac{(n+1)\pi x}{L} \tag{3.29}$$

is independent of time. We can also write this in terms of the energy levels as

$$\Psi_n(x,t) = \psi_n(x) e^{-iE_n t/\hbar}. \tag{3.30}$$

The wave function $\psi_n(x)$ is known as an energy eigenfunction, and E_n is its associated energy eigenvalue. The number $n = 0, 1, 2, \ldots$ is known as the quantum number.

The corresponding probability distributions are

$$P_n(x) = |\Psi_n(x,t)|^2 = \frac{2}{L} \sin^2 \frac{(n+1)\pi x}{L} \tag{3.31}$$

for $0 < x < L$ and $P_n(x) = 0$ elsewhere. These are again independent of time and so correspond to stationary states. The wave functions and amplitudes for the first four energy levels are shown in figure 3.2, where the location of the box is $-0.5 < x < 0.5$ (this is equivalent to shifting the x coordinate to $x - L/2$ with $L = 1$). The wave function rotates around the real axis, so the thin lines show snapshots of the real component over a single period, ending with the heavy line.

The different energy levels resemble the modes of a vibrating string. If we tied the end of the string together, then the circumference would be an integer multiple of the wavelength. As mentioned above, de Broglie's particle wave hypothesis therefore justified the idea, first proposed by Niels Bohr, that an atom's electrons were limited to bands with discrete levels of energy.

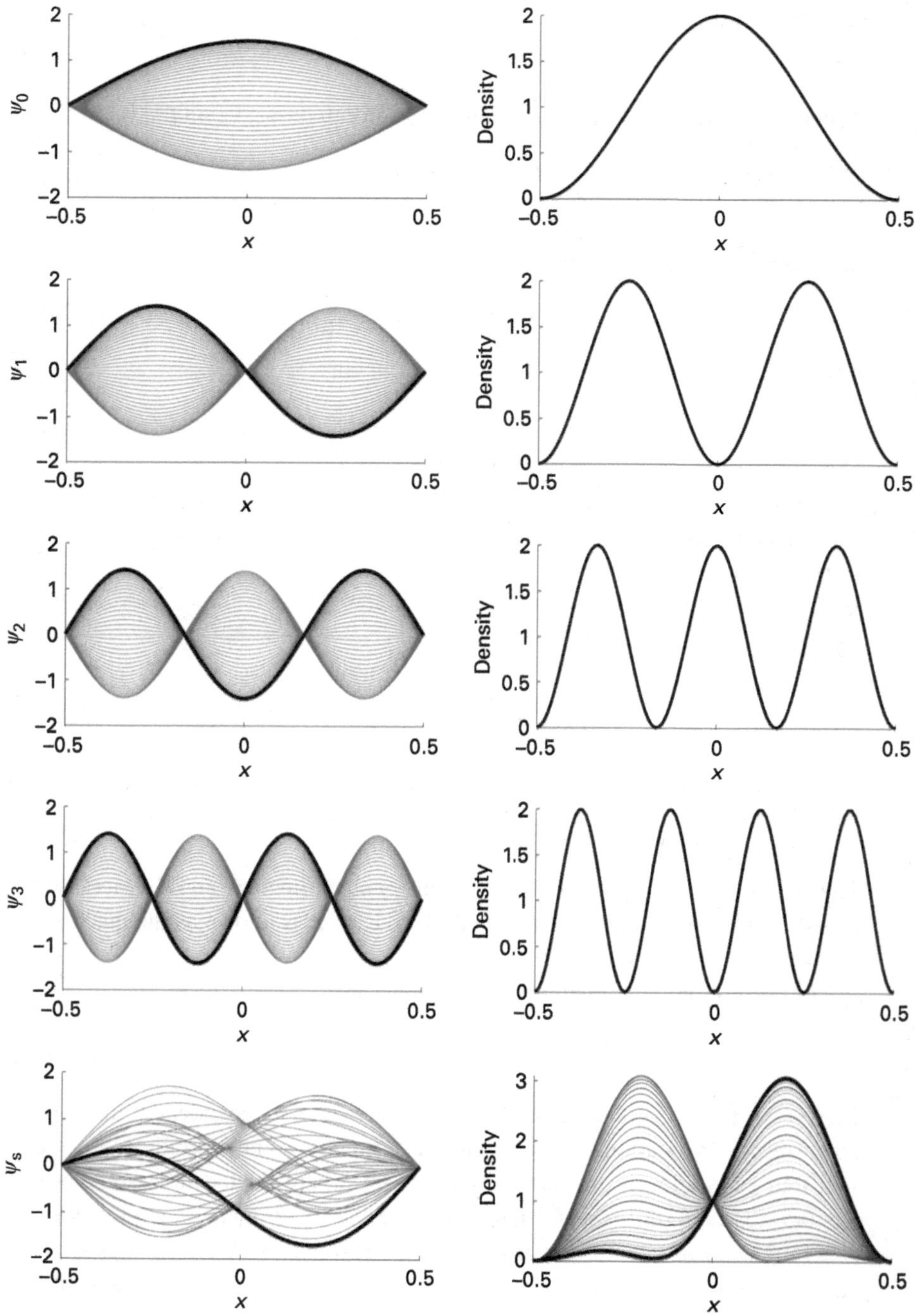

Figure 3.2
Figure shows real part of wave functions (left) and amplitudes (right) for the infinite well. First four rows are energy eigenstates $n = 0$ to 3. The wave function rotates around the real axis with time, ending at the heavy line at the end of the period, but the amplitudes are static. The bottom row shows a mix of energy levels 0 and 1, for which the amplitude now oscillates.

The probability amplitudes are also reminiscent, though, of a random walk with added noise, as in figure 2.2. In finance, this could represent the price as it evolves through a sequence of transactions. However, instead of diffusing without limit, the price is constrained by the dynamics to remain within the boundaries of the box.

3.4 Standing Waves

We can calculate the mean and standard deviation of position as

$$\langle x \rangle = \frac{2}{L}\int_0^L x \sin^2 \frac{(n+1)\pi x}{L} = \frac{L}{2} \tag{3.32}$$

and

$$\langle x^2 \rangle = \frac{2}{L}\int_0^L x^2 \sin^2 \frac{(n+1)\pi x}{L} = L^2 \frac{2(n+1)^2\pi^2 - 3}{6(n+1)^2\pi^2}. \tag{3.33}$$

The variance is therefore

$$\Delta x^2 = \langle x^2 \rangle - \langle x \rangle^2 = L^2 \frac{(n+1)^2\pi^2 - 3}{(n+1)^2\pi^2} - \frac{L^2}{4} = L^2 \frac{(n+1)^2\pi^2 - 6}{12(n+1)^2\pi^2}, \tag{3.34}$$

which depends on the energy number n.

The probability of a particle being observed in a particular location for any energy eigenstate depends on the wave function for that particular state. It might seem puzzling that for energy number n, there are n nodes (not including the endpoints) where the probability of observing the particle is zero. However, the situation can be compared with the vibration of a real, imperfect guitar string; in practice, the motion will involve a mix of modes and will not perfectly vanish at any point.

The wave functions for the energy eigenstates are standing waves rather than traveling wave packets, which raises the question of how they relate to momentum. One way to answer this is to note that the wave function can be written in the form

$$\psi_n(x) = \sqrt{\frac{2}{L}} \sin \frac{(n+1)\pi x}{L} = \sqrt{\frac{2}{L}} \frac{e^{i(k_n x - \omega_n t)} - e^{-i(k_n x + \omega_n t)}}{2i}, \tag{3.35}$$

where again, $k_n = (n+1)\pi/L$. The standing wave can therefore be represented as a superposition of two waves traveling in opposite directions, with momenta of $\pm\hbar k_n$. When the momentum is measured, it therefore has an equal probability of being found in one of these two states. In finance, where the momentum is related to a rate of drift, this points to an important difference between the classical and quantum approaches: The classical model assumes a fixed drift, whereas the quantum model works with a superposition of drifts.

The mean momentum is

$$\langle p\rangle = \frac{1}{2}\hbar k_n + \frac{1}{2}(-\hbar k_n) = 0, \tag{3.36}$$

and similarly,

$$\langle p^2\rangle = \frac{1}{2}(\hbar k_n)^2 + \frac{1}{2}(-\hbar k_n)^2 = \hbar^2 k_n^2, \tag{3.37}$$

so the variance is

$$\Delta p^2 = \langle p^2\rangle - \langle p\rangle^2 = \hbar^2 k_n^2 = \hbar^2 \left(\frac{(n+1)\pi}{L}\right)^2. \tag{3.38}$$

Combining with the equation for the variance of position then gives

$$\Delta x^2 \Delta p^2 = \frac{(n+1)^2\pi^2 - 6}{12}\hbar^2 \geq \frac{\hbar^2}{4}, \tag{3.39}$$

so $\Delta x \Delta p \geq \hbar/2$, as expected from the uncertainty principle.

Another property of the eigenstate wave functions is that they are orthonormal in the sense that

$$\int_{-\infty}^{+\infty} \psi_m^*(x)\psi_n(x)dx = \frac{2}{L}\int_0^L \sin(\frac{m\pi x}{L})\sin(\frac{n\pi x}{L})\,dx = \delta_{mn}, \tag{3.40}$$

where the Kronecker delta has $\delta_{mn} = 1$ for $m = n$ and 0 otherwise. We can therefore express an arbitrary state as a linear combination of these orthonormal eigenstates.

Finally, although the amplitudes are constant for energy eigenstates, the system can show more complicated behavior when they are combined. The lower row in figure 3.2 shows the wave function and amplitude for the state

$$\Psi_n(x,t) = \frac{1}{\sqrt{2}}\Psi_0(x,t) + \frac{1}{\sqrt{2}}\Psi_1(x,t) \tag{3.41}$$

$$= \frac{1}{\sqrt{L}}\left(\sin(\frac{\pi x}{L})e^{-i\omega_1 t} + \sin(\frac{2\pi x}{L})e^{-i\omega_2 t}\right). \tag{3.42}$$

The $1/\sqrt{2}$ weighting of each term is chosen to satisfy the normalization requirement. As seen also in the next chapter, when the solution involves a mix of energy states, the resulting behavior is dynamic, with the amplitude in this case bouncing back and forth in time, rather like a ball bouncing off the walls.

3.5 The Schrödinger Equation

We found the above solution for the infinite well problem using only the constraints that the wave function had to satisfy. In general, though, if a particle were associated with a wave, then it followed that the wave should represent the solution to some kind of equation. Newton had shown that classical mechanics obeyed his three laws of motion. In 1926, even before Born had identified the wave function with a kind of probability wave, Erwin Schrödinger came up with a quantum version of a law of motion, which described now how the wave function evolved in time.

For a particle of mass m and total energy E, the equation in one spatial dimension is

$$-\frac{\hbar^2}{2m}\frac{\partial^2 \Psi}{\partial x^2} + U\Psi = E\Psi, \tag{3.43}$$

where $U = U(x)$ is the potential energy of the particle. The equation was similar in structure to the equations already used by physicists to describe things like sound waves or electromagnetic waves, with the difference that the waves now represented a kind of probabilistic information about the system. As Schrödinger later wrote: "The psi-function . . . is now the means for predicting probability of measurement results. In it is embodied the momentarily-attained sum of theoretically based future expectation, somewhat as laid down in a catalog."[4] (The concept of theoretically based future expectation will sound familiar to anyone who works in finance.)

The equation cannot be proved from first principles any more than the law of gravity can, and its use in physics (or in finance) is ultimately justified by the fact that it can be used to solve problems. But perhaps the best way to understand the equation is to see it as a consequence or generalization of the premise that a system can be described by a linear superposition of waves of the form $\Psi = Ae^{i(kx-\omega t)}$. We can write

$$-\frac{\hbar^2}{2m}\frac{\partial^2 \Psi}{\partial x^2} = \frac{\hbar^2}{2m}k^2\Psi = \frac{p^2}{2m}\Psi. \tag{3.44}$$

However, the total energy is given by $E = p^2/(2m) + U$, so

$$E\Psi = \frac{p^2}{2m}\Psi + U\Psi. \tag{3.45}$$

Combining these gives the Schrödinger equation.

Since

$$i\hbar\frac{\partial \Psi}{\partial t} = \hbar\omega\Psi = E\Psi, \tag{3.46}$$

where we have used $E = \hbar\omega$, it follows that we can alternatively write the equation as

$$-\frac{\hbar^2}{2m}\frac{\partial^2\Psi}{\partial x^2} + U\Psi = i\hbar\frac{\partial\Psi}{\partial t}. \tag{3.47}$$

If we assume as here that the potential energy U is independent of time, then solutions are linear combinations of wave functions $\Psi = Ae^{i(kx-\omega t)}$ that have the property that they preserve total probability. Once a solution is normalized, it stays normalized. Wave mechanics therefore provides a consistent mathematical framework for talking about how probability evolves in time.

If we focus on standing waves, we can write the equation in its time-independent form as

$$-\frac{\hbar^2}{2m}\frac{d^2\psi(x)}{dx^2} + U\psi(x) = E\psi(x). \tag{3.48}$$

For the infinite well problem, since $U = 0$, the Schrödinger equation inside the box is just

$$-\frac{\hbar^2}{2m}\frac{d^2\psi(x)}{dx^2} = E\psi(x). \tag{3.49}$$

As a check, the solution we found earlier,

$$\psi_n(x) = \sqrt{\frac{2}{L}}\sin\frac{(n+1)\pi x}{L}, \tag{3.50}$$

has

$$-\frac{\hbar^2}{2m}\frac{d^2\psi_n(x)}{dx^2} = \frac{\hbar^2}{2m}\frac{(n+1)^2\pi^2}{L^2}\psi_n(x) = E_n\psi_n(x) \tag{3.51}$$

and so satisfies the equation as expected. The Schrödinger equation therefore gives us the same harmonic wave solutions that we found by assuming a general wave structure and imposing boundary conditions.

3.6 Discrete Finance

The solution for the infinite well problem is mainly based not on what we know about particles but on the requirement that the wave satisfies the conditions of a probability wave; it vanishes at the boundaries, and the total probability adds to unity. This is important because our aim ultimately is to apply the same formalism in finance, where the wave specifies the probability not of a particle's position but of an asset's price. The idea is to find a way to make the probabilistic wave move so that we can explore dynamic effects such as price impact.

Again, the reason for exploring quantum models in finance is not because we want to compare stocks with electrons; it is because we are looking for a way to model probability in situations where there is no fixed and stable equilibrium. Classical finance is essentially static and models price change using a normal distribution with constant volatility. Quantum techniques allow us to view the probability distribution as something that can move and be affected by forces. It would have seemed outrageous (it still does) when de Broglie proposed that matter could have wavelike properties. The idea that financial information can be modeled using wave equations seems tame in comparison.

Put another way, the classical approach assumes that the probability distribution of log price must follow some version of the static random walk depicted in figure 2.2. The quantum approach allows us to bring dynamics into the picture, but as seen in figure 3.2, the probability distributions retain much of the same character, so we are still on familiar ground.

Of course, the infinite well problem does not seem to have an obvious financial analogue, unless it is transactions where the price is bound above and below, for example, by trading restrictions, and there is no restoring force. As we will see, though, this simple model contains many key features that we will use later, and their interpretation is simple and intuitive.

The dynamics of the system are expressed in terms of physical quantities such as position, frequency, and energy, which of course have meaning outside of physics. The concept of energy, for example, goes back to Aristotle's *energeia*, which refered to a kind of activity. In finance, we will associate position with a measure of price change, and energy with a measure of transactions.

In the quantum model, energy is related to frequency. In finance, we can connect this with a turnover rate. Energy is also discrete, so the quantum number n serves as a kind of count. This is shown in the amplitudes for the infinite well problem, where n counts the number of peaks in the probability distribution. In finance, we can use the same number to represent a number of transactions (by a transacton), which also take place as discrete events.

In physics, the constant $\hbar$ has units of action, or energy multiplied by time, and depends on the units of measurement. In finance, energy is a transaction count, so we can set $\hbar = 1$.

Another useful property is the idea of a minimum uncertainty level. In physics, this was important because it provided a solution for the problem of the stability of atoms. In finance, a key plank of the classical approach is the so-called no-arbitrage principle, also known as the law of one price. This essentially states that any asset in a freely functioning market can have only one price because, otherwise, investors could profit by buying at the cheaper price and immediately selling at the higher. As Walras put it, any good "has only a single price in the market." Applying the no-arbitrage principle to option pricing leads to the Black-Scholes model, whose only parameters are a volatility and a risk-free rate.

However, an obvious empirical property of stock markets is what we might call the law of two prices. As discussed already in chapter 2, when you want to buy or sell an asset, you are always presented with an ask and a bid price. The first is the lowest price at which someone is offering to sell, and the latter is the highest price at which someone is offering to buy. There is always a difference between them, known as the spread.

The existence of the spread can be attributed to uncertainty: The price is never precisely known, so a buyer wants to be slightly below the best estimate, whereas the seller wants to be slightly above. However, its main empirical property is that it never seems to go away. A consequence is that trading shares always involves costs due to the spread, which acts like an irreducible level of energy. Any proof such as Black-Scholes that assumes that trading costs can be ignored is therefore on shaky grounds.

The no-arbitrage principle seems especially ironic given that the business model of much of the financial sector is explicitly based on arbitrage (e.g., hedge funds). Perhaps the simplest example of arbitrage is that of the market-maker, who buys a stock at the cheaper bid price and sells it on at the more expensive ask price. The reason they can do this is because they are patient. Prices fluctuate randomly within a band due to uncertainty, so a buyer or seller who needs to transact straight away will have to take whatever price is available. A market maker can wait to buy when the opportunity arises and then sell it on to someone in a hurry. In classical theory, the profit can always be explained away as compensation for the risk of holding onto the stock or for providing a service. But the risk is two sided (the stock might go up as well as down), and the billions of profits made annually by market-making firms such as Citadel Securities suggest a rather amazing level of service quality. A simpler interpretation is that although arbitrage may not be easy, it goes on all the time and is profitable especially for those firms that can exploit it at scale. We return to this topic in chapter 10.

Other empirical properties that elude classical analysis are q-variance and the volatility smile. As we will see, both of these properties are markers for a minimum quantum of variance that can be ultimately attributed to the law of two prices. In physics, the uncertainty principle presented a vision of the universe with uncertainty at its core, and the same applies in finance.

3.7 Summary

The infinite well problem shows many of the key properties of a quantum system, including the idea that energy can exist in discrete quanta. Interestingly though, there is very little physics involved because the main constraint is that the wave function vanishes outside the box, so only a discrete number of wavelengths can be accommodated. It isn't hard to see how the same approach can be applied to probabilistic problems more generally. Or put another way, nothing in the above treatment suggests that wave functions can only be applied to subatomic particles.

The "quantum leap" in finance therefore comes down to accepting the following:

- The classical equilibrium-based framework is inadequate for modeling observed effects related to variance.
- To address these issues, we wish to make the probability density function dynamic.
- We therefore switch to a framework based on quantum probability, which can be viewed as the next-simplest type of probability after the classical one.
- By quantizing an entropic force, we obtain (in chapter 5) a complex wave function whose dynamics are governed by the Schrödinger equation.
- The resulting behavior is consistent with probabilistic and dynamic principles, so, for example, the probability remains normalized.

The question then is whether this mathematical framework does a better job at modeling and predicting financial phenomena. That should be the only test. To be clear, you do not need to accept that stocks are ontologically united with electrons, that traders are quantum entangled, or that aligning yourself with the quantum nature of the universe will make you rich (though see chapter 10).

In fact, a prerequisite to making this quantum leap is to rid oneself of the notion that quantum methods are identified with physics. As Pasteur Institute biologist Antoine Danchin wrote, "The truth of the model is not the truth of the phenomenon. It is a common confusion between these two kinds of truth—the norm in magic—that sometimes sanctifies the model (which is regarded as part of the real world) and gives the scientist the role of priest."[5] Models are just tools; what counts is whether they are useful for understanding and predicting a system.

And of course, the quantum leap also means leaping out of the comfort zone of quantitative finance, which appears to be nineteenth-century equilibrium mechanics. And if things get a little counterintuitive, you sometimes have to trust the mathematics.

If this all sounds acceptable, then we are nearly ready to move on to the real model. The reason that the infinite well is so simple (even if the solutions can be quite ornate) is because the potential energy inside the box is zero, and the only dynamics are that the particle cannot stray beyond the boundaries. It is also a little too simple for our purposes because the idea of a price range with fixed limits and no restoring force does not map easily into the context of a stock market. In the next chapter, we consider what might be called the next most complicated system, where the force is a linear function of position.

4

The Quantum Spring

> The truth is, the science of Nature has already been too long made only a work of the brain and the fancy. It is now high time that it should return to the plainness and soundness of observations on material and obvious things.
>
> —Robert Hooke, *Micrographia*, 1665

> A fact rarely noticed is that the propositions of quantum physics which defy our common-sense view of material reality strangely echo another domain, that of language, of the symbolic order—it is as if quantum processes are closer to the universe of language than anything one finds in "nature"; as if, in the quantum universe, the human spirit encounters itself outside itself.
>
> —Slavoj Žižek, 2012

In chapter 2, we showed that the classical probabilistic model of transactions can be used to derive a linear entropic force. The apparently static model therefore already contains the seeds of a dynamical model. In order to make use of it, though, we need to make one change, which is to think of this force acting not on price but on the probability of price, which is not the same thing. In other words, the wave function is going to evolve with time, as in quantum mechanics. To model it, we will need what might be the next-simplest system after the infinite well, which is the quantum harmonic oscillator.

4.1 The Quantum Harmonic Oscillator

A classical harmonic oscillator involves an object of mass m oscillating around a central point with a spring-like restoring force given by Hooke's law $F = -kx$, where k is a constant and x is the displacement. The equation of motion can be written in terms of momentum p as

$$p = m\dot{x} \tag{4.1}$$

$$\dot{p} = F = -kx, \tag{4.2}$$

or equivalently, as $m\ddot{x} = -kx$. This has the oscillatory solution

$$x = A\cos(\omega t + \varphi), \tag{4.3}$$

where the phase φ depends on the starting point. The energy is given by

$$E = \frac{p^2}{2m} + \frac{1}{2}m\omega^2 x^2, \tag{4.4}$$

where $\omega = \sqrt{k/m}$ is the frequency of oscillation. The first term represents the kinetic energy, and the second term the potential energy.

To derive the quantum version of this system, known as the quantum harmonic oscillator, we apply the Schrödinger equation from the last chapter. For a particle of mass m, potential energy U, and total energy E, this again in time-independent form is

$$-\frac{\hbar^2}{2m}\frac{d^2\psi(x)}{dx^2} + U\psi(x) = E\psi(x). \tag{4.5}$$

Substituting the expression for potential energy then gives

$$-\frac{\hbar^2}{2m}\frac{d^2\psi(x)}{dx^2} + \frac{1}{2}m\omega^2 x^2\psi(x) = E\psi(x). \tag{4.6}$$

In the infinite well problem, the potential energy is zero inside the box and infinite outside it, so the location of the particle has a hard constraint. Here, the potential energy varies with x^2 and so approaches infinity for large displacements, but there is no fixed limit. We would therefore expect the wave functions to extend farther in space as their energy increases, but at low energy to be concentrated around the origin.

Suppose we therefore propose as a solution the wave function $\psi(x) = ce^{-ax^2/2}$, where c is a normalization constant. (This would also make sense given that the linear entropic force that we are quantizing was originally derived from a normal distribution.) Then

$$\frac{d\psi(x)}{dx} = -caxe^{-ax^2/2} \tag{4.7}$$

$$\frac{d^2\psi(x)}{dx^2} = -cae^{-ax^2/2} + ca^2x^2e^{-ax^2/2} = (a^2x^2 - a)\psi(x). \tag{4.8}$$

Plugging into the Schrödinger equation gives

$$-\frac{\hbar^2}{2m}(a^2x^2 - a)\psi(x) + \frac{1}{2}m\omega^2x^2\psi(x) = E\psi(x). \tag{4.9}$$

Since this must hold for all x, we need the terms to agree for all powers of x. For the x^2 term, this gives

$$-\frac{\hbar^2}{2m}a^2+\frac{1}{2}m\omega^2x^2=0, \tag{4.10}$$

so

$$a=\frac{m\omega}{\hbar}. \tag{4.11}$$

Doing the same for the constant term gives

$$\frac{\hbar^2}{2m}a=E. \tag{4.12}$$

The energy associated with this wave function is therefore

$$E=\frac{\hbar^2}{2m}a=\frac{\hbar^2}{2m}\frac{m\omega}{\hbar}=\frac{\hbar\omega}{2}. \tag{4.13}$$

It follows from this that the normalized wave function

$$\psi_0\left(x\right)=\left(\frac{m\omega}{\pi\hbar}\right)^{1/4}\exp\left(-\frac{m\omega}{2\hbar}x^2\right) \tag{4.14}$$

is a solution for the quantum harmonic oscillator.

4.2 Energy Eigenstates

We next claim that this state represents the lowest energy state. To see this, recall that the Heisenberg uncertainty relation states that the lower limit for the product of uncertainties in position and momentum is $\Delta x\Delta p=\hbar/2$. The energy of the oscillator must be at least

$$E_0=\frac{(\Delta p)^2}{2m}+\frac{1}{2}m\omega^2(\Delta x)^2, \tag{4.15}$$

so substituting $\Delta p=\hbar/(2\Delta x)$ from the uncertainty bound gives

$$E_0=\frac{\hbar^2}{8m(\Delta x)^2}+\frac{1}{2}m\omega^2(\Delta x)^2. \tag{4.16}$$

Minimizing the energy by setting the derivative to zero and solving for Δx then gives

$$\Delta x=\sqrt{\frac{\hbar}{2m\omega}}. \tag{4.17}$$

The minimum energy is therefore

$$E_0 = \frac{\hbar^2}{8m(\Delta x)^2} + \frac{1}{2}m\omega^2(\Delta x)^2 = \frac{\hbar\omega}{2}, \tag{4.18}$$

which is the same as what we found above, confirming that this is indeed the minimal energy state, known as the ground state.

The full wave function including the time-varying component for the ground state is

$$\Psi_0(x,t) = \exp(\frac{-i\omega t}{2})\psi_0(x), \tag{4.19}$$

which rotates around the real axis with an angular frequency $\omega/2$. The amplitude of this wave function is a normal distribution with standard deviation

$$\sigma = \sqrt{\frac{\hbar}{2m\omega}}, \tag{4.20}$$

which is the same as Δx.

The wave functions for higher energy states E_n are derived recursively and work out (consult one of the many textbooks or online sources) to be

$$\Psi_n(x,t) = \exp(-(n+\frac{1}{2}i\omega t))\frac{1}{\sqrt{2^n n!}}\psi_0(x)H_n\left(\sqrt{\frac{m\omega}{\hbar}}x\right), \tag{4.21}$$

where the functions H_n are the Hermite polynomials. The first of these are

$$H_0 = 1 \tag{4.22}$$

$$H_1 = 2x \tag{4.23}$$

$$H_2 = 4x^2 - 2 \tag{4.24}$$

$$H_3 = 8x^3 - 12x. \tag{4.25}$$

Figure 4.1 shows the first four energy eigenstates for a quantum harmonic oscillator. The plots on the left show the real component of the wave functions, and the plots on the right are the probability amplitudes. The eigenstates are similar to their infinite well counterparts, with the difference that probability is now constrained not by a hard barrier but by a linear restoring force. (The bottom row is discussed in the next section.) The energy eigenvalue of eigenstate n is given by

$$E_n = \frac{\hbar\omega}{2}(1+2n). \tag{4.26}$$

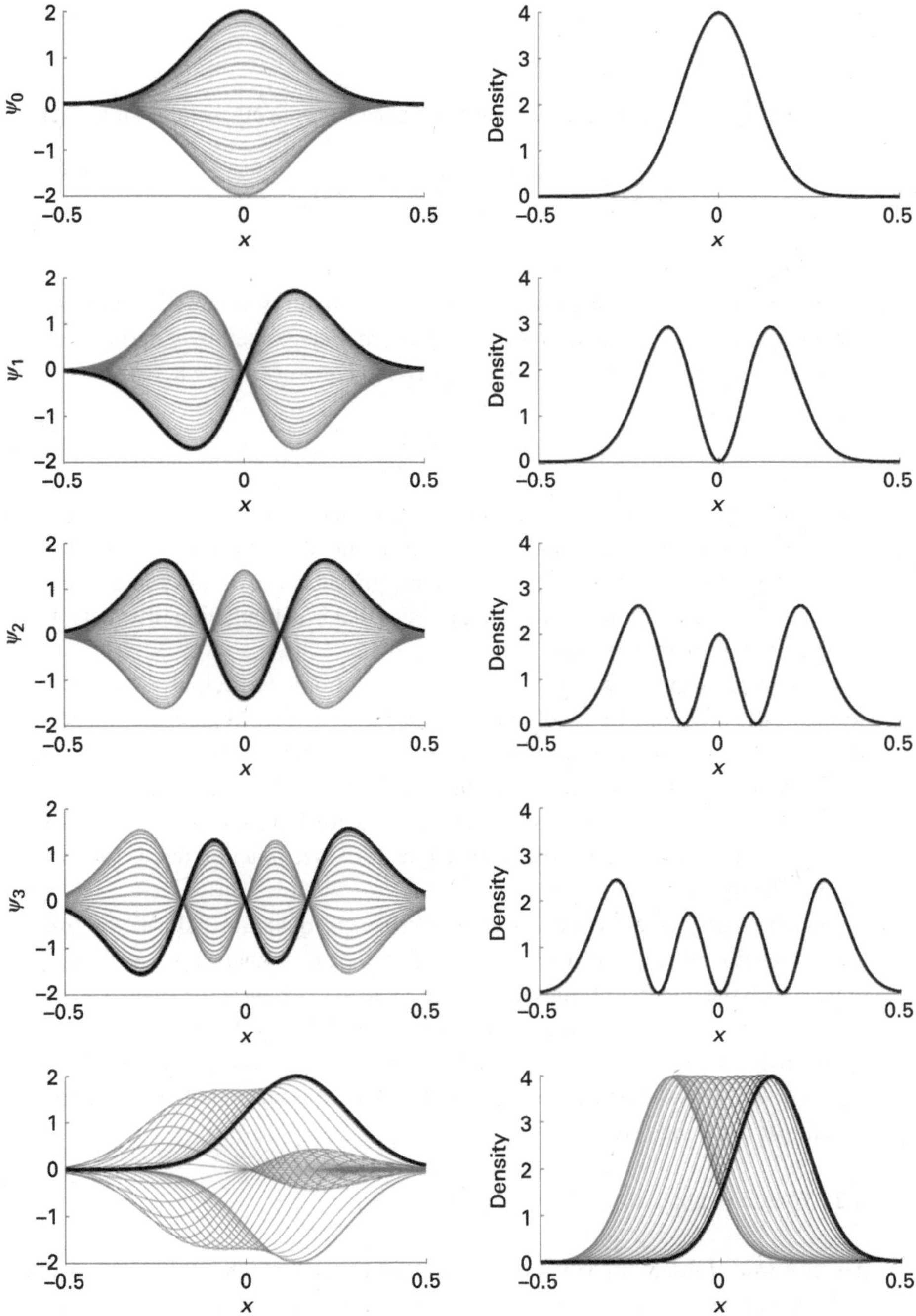

Figure 4.1

Figure shows real part of wave functions (left) and amplitudes (right) for the quantum harmonic oscillator. First four rows are energy eigenstates $n = 0$ to 3. The wave function rotates around the real axis with time, ending at the heavy line at the end of the period, but the amplitudes are static. The bottom row shows a coherent state, for which the amplitude now oscillates from side to side.

We can again calculate the mean and variance for each eigenstate. This gives

$$\langle x \rangle = 0 \tag{4.27}$$

$$\langle x^2 \rangle = \sigma^2(1+2n), \tag{4.28}$$

so it follows that the variance scales directly with the energy E_n.

A physical example of a quantum harmonic oscillator is a diatomic molecule, which behaves like a quantum version of two masses joined by a spring. The atoms resonate with a natural frequency given by $\omega = \sqrt{k/m_r}$, where

$$m_r = \frac{m_1 m_2}{m_1 + m_2} \tag{4.29}$$

is known as the reduced mass. Experiments show that the frequency is quantized with a minimum frequency known as the zero-point vibration. The quantum harmonic oscillator also plays a key role in many physical theories, in part because it is one of the few systems in quantum physics that is computationally tractable and has a closed-form solution.

In finance, its appeal is that by quantizing the entropic force, it offers us a way to make our probabilistic model of transactions dynamic. In classical finance, the base model is the normal distribution, like the one in the top right panel of figure 4.1. As seen in chapter 2, the problem with this model is that it is essentially static. The wave function version in the top left panel, however, views this distribution as being derived from a dynamic wave function that is rotating around the real axis.

Higher energy levels contain multiple peaks. In quantum field theory, the energy level n corresponds to a number of particles. In finance, we will associate n with the number of transactions for a particular transacton (which again represents a kind of virtual transaction for a unit of stock). Note that the peaks of the distributions on the right of the figure resemble a random walk of length n plus noise, with the difference that the distribution is shaped by the presence of a linear restoring force.

4.3 The Coherent State

The last row of figure 4.1 is known as a coherent state, which can be viewed as the result of displacing the oscillator by an amount x. As with a classical spring, this increases the potential energy by the amount

$$U(x) = \frac{1}{2} m\omega^2 x^2. \tag{4.30}$$

It can be shown that the wave function that results is not in a single energy eigenstate but consists of a mix of eigenstates

$$\Psi(x,t)=\sum_{0}^{\infty} w_n(\lambda)\Psi_n(x,t), \tag{4.31}$$

where

$$w_n(\lambda)=\frac{e^{-\lambda}\lambda^n}{n!} \tag{4.32}$$

is a Poisson weighting with

$$\lambda=\frac{m\omega x^2}{2\hbar}=\frac{x^2}{4\sigma^2}, \tag{4.33}$$

where we have used $\sigma=\sqrt{\hbar/(2m\omega)}$. Put another way, a displacement of x leads to a coherent state with an average energy of λ. The corresponding probability density function behaves like a ground state oscillating around the origin, in a manner similar to a classical oscillator with a frequency ω, as shown in the bottom right panel of the figure (basically, it is a normal distribution on a spring). Here, the displacement is set to $x=\sqrt{2}\sigma$, so $\lambda=1/2$. It compares with the infinite well case in the bottom row of figure 3.2, where a mix of two eigenstates also produced oscillatory behavior.

It can be checked that the variance in position of the coherent oscillation at any particular time is

$$\Delta x^2=\sigma^2=\frac{\hbar}{2m\omega}, \tag{4.34}$$

while the variance in momentum is

$$\Delta p^2=\frac{m\hbar\omega}{2}, \tag{4.35}$$

so $\Delta x\Delta p=\hbar/2$, and this is a minimal uncertainty state. However, because the coherent state oscillates from side to side, the total variance over a complete period is increased due to the variance of the oscillation, which is $x^2/2$, to give

$$\text{Var}=\sigma^2+\frac{x^2}{2}=\sigma^2(1+2\lambda). \tag{4.36}$$

Another way to look at this is to note that from equation 4.28, the variance of energy level n is $\sigma^2(1+2n)$, so taking the Poisson-weighted sum over all states gives a total variance of $\sigma^2(1+2\langle n\rangle)=\sigma^2(1+2\lambda)$. For the case here that $\lambda=1/2$ and $x=\sqrt{2}\sigma$, the variance is $\Sigma^2=2\sigma^2$.

The reader may have noticed the similarity between the expression $\sigma^2 + x^2/2$ and the q-variance relation equation 1.2. As seen in the next chapter, the prediction of q-variance is simply a consequence of using the quantum oscillator to model price because perturbing the price boosts volatility according to this equation.

4.4 Summary

The quantum harmonic oscillator is one of the simplest quantum systems, which shows a rich variety of complex behaviors but still involves only a small number of parameters that translate easily to finance.

Just as the energy number n in physics can represent a number of particles, in finance, we will use it to represent a number of transactions for a particular transacton, which again is a naturally discrete phenomenon. Classical finance—where there is no bid–ask spread, there is no arbitrage, and all price change is due to external events—is therefore consistent with the quantum model: It is just the special $n = 0$ case, where no transactions ever take place and the model is always in its ground state.

The standard deviation σ gives a base level of uncertainty in position. For physics, this describes our knowledge about the location of a particle; in finance, it concerns our knowledge about price, as reflected in the bid–ask spread (we make this relation more concrete in the next chapter).

In physics, the parameter ω represents the frequency of the wave function. For a particular energy eigenstate, it scales the rate at which the wave function rotates around the real axis. For a coherent state, it equals the frequency of the side-to-side oscillation, so one complete oscillation is performed in a time $T = 2\pi/\omega$. In finance, we will similarly use it to describe a rate of turnover for a transacton.

In the classical probabilistic model from chapter 2, the mass

$$m = \frac{\hbar}{2\omega\sigma^2} \tag{4.37}$$

measures the resistance to a change in price for a buyer or seller. In the oscillator model, the mass of a transacton is therefore similar to the inertial mass of a particle in physics, which is acted on by the entropic force.

The parameter $\hbar$ plays a hallowed and historic role in quantum mechanics because it relates quanta to a fundamental level of energy. Its dimensions correspond to energy multiplied by time, which in units of mass M, length L, and time T is ML^2T^{-1}. In finance, the parameter doesn't have the same meaning because the energy for a particular transacton is just a transaction count. It follows that we can simply set $\hbar = 1$ with no effect on the results.

In physics, the measurement of a particle's position leads somehow to the collapse of the wave function. But no one knows exactly what this means or how it occurs (and what happens to the wave function after being used). In finance, the oscillator is just a model, and the measurement is just the price, which spares us a lot of ontological worrying.

The oscillator's most useful feature for our purposes, though, is that it allows us to move from a zero-order model based on equilibrium, as in classical finance, to a first-order model with a linear restoring force. In particular, the link between energy and variance gives us a way to model the dynamics of variance, which is what underlies the three anomalies described in the opening chapter, that have long eluded a classical treatment. In the next chapter, we show how the oscillator model allows us to address the first two of these anomalies, which concern the effect of large transactions and imbalance in general.

5

Imaginary Oscillations

Just as we measure gravity by its effects in the motion of a pendulum, so we may estimate the equality or inequality of feelings by the decisions of the human mind. The will is our pendulum, and its oscillations are minutely registered in the price lists of the markets.

—William Stanley Jevons, *The Theory of Political Economy*, 1871

Whether you can observe a thing or not depends on the theory which you use. It is the theory which decides what can be observed.

—Albert Einstein (quoted in Salam, 1990)

Economists have long been drawn to the idea that markets experience oscillations between states of high and low activity, or between fear and greed. The neoclassical economist William Stanley Jevons argued in an 1878 paper that financial crises were driven by variations in sunspot activity, which affected global temperatures and therefore the price of wheat.[1] Jevons's contemporary, the French economist Clement Juglar, discovered what he believed was a boom/bust cycle in investment of nine to twenty-five years, which progressed through the four phases of prosperity, crisis, liquidation and recession. Other cycles identified by economists included the Kitchin cycle for inventory of 40 months; the Kuznets infrastructure cycle of fifteen to twenty-five years; and the Kondratiev technology wave of forty-five to sixty years.[2]

In 1933, during the Great Depression, the Norwegian economist Ragnar Frisch (who also coined the term econometrics) developed one of the first mathematical models of the business cycle. He was later awarded the first Nobel Memorial Prize in economics for this work, along with another econometric modeler the Dutch economist Jan Tinbergen.[3] The idea that the economy has regular cycles assumes the existence of a restoring force (Adam Smith's invisible hand) that tends to pull prices back toward a central equilibrium. The fact that oscillations are not perfectly regular could be accomodated by assuming that perturbations have a random quality and by including a degree of damping so that oscillations do not continue indefinitely.

Oscillator models fell out of favor during the postwar era and were inconsistent with the efficient market hypothesis.[4] This assumed that prices are restored to equilibrium immediately and viewed price changes as following a random walk with perturbations caused by external news. It therefore made no sense to model markets in terms of classical springs, unless perhaps the springs were infinitely stiff. The random walk picture was key to the Black-Scholes option-pricing algorithm, where it was assumed that asset prices fluctuate in a random fashion with a certain known volatility.

The quantum view of market oscillations is a little different because it assumes that it isn't prices that are oscillating, but it is the probability of price changes; and the oscillations are not real, but they occur in the imaginary plane. However, the effect of these oscillations on asset price behavior are very real and easily detected.

5.1 The Market Oscillator

Although it has not been a very active area of research, a number of versions of quantum oscillator models have been developed over the years. Perhaps the first paper to take this approach was Ye & Huang (2008). In their model, the quantum harmonic oscillator was in its ground state most of the time but had an additional oscillatory term so that the expected price swung between highs and lows. Meng et al. (2015) included a boundary condition on the wave function, while Meng, Zhang and Guo (2016) extended the approach to a stock index. Ahn et al. (2017) included additional damping terms, whereas Gao & Chen (2017) used quantum anharmonic oscillators to explore the dynamics introduced by different market participants such as momentum and fundamental traders, and Baaquie (2021) used the oscillator to price corporate bonds.

In all these studies, it was found that the quantum model could recreate the basic properties of financial statistics, which perhaps is not surprising since they contained enough tuneable parameters to fit the data. However, questions remained about whether the quantum approach was appropriate in the first place. If markets do not behave like classical oscillators, then on the surface at least they do not seem to resemble quantum oscillators either. For example, if the oscillator represents the market, then what does it mean to say that the market has discrete energy levels?

As with a classical random walk model, the properties of the wave function are the same in any quantum oscillator model, so what counts is how the techniques are applied. The unique features of the model discussed here are that it is based on quantization of an entropic force; focuses on transactions (real or potential) rather than the market as a whole; and uses coherent states to relate price change and volatility over a period.

To recap from the previous chapter, the wave function for the quantum harmonic oscillator can be described as a Poisson-weighted superposition of energy eigenstates. The mean of each eigenstate $\psi_n(x)$ is $\langle x \rangle = 0$, and the variance is $\langle x^2 \rangle = \sigma^2(1+2n)$.

The oscillator has a fundamental level of uncertainty that, at the level of individual transactions, is related to the bid–ask spread. For example, if the ask price is $\sigma_\tau/\sqrt{2}$, where $\sigma_\tau = \sigma\sqrt{\tau}$ is the volatility scaled to the time period τ of a single transaction, and the bid price is $-\sigma_\tau/\sqrt{2}$, then the spread is $\epsilon = \sqrt{2}\sigma_\tau$ and the standard deviation of these two points is σ_τ. Indeed, a study by Wyart et al. (2008) found empirically that

$$\epsilon = c\sigma_\tau \tag{5.1}$$

for c in the range of 1.2 to 1.6, which is consistent with the model. Note that, when we speak about the oscillator having a particular position such as $x=0$, this does not mean the price is precisely known, because it always subject to uncertainty. Similarly, a change in log price over a period T represents a shift in the central price estimate, which we model by displacing the oscillator.

If we perturb the oscillator by an amount x, this boosts the energy by an amount $U(x) = m\omega x^2/2$ and puts the system into an oscillatory coherent state (see figure 5.1) with an average energy number from equation 4.33 of

$$\langle n \rangle = \lambda = \frac{x^2}{4\sigma_\tau^2}. \tag{5.2}$$

Since we are identifying the energy level n with a transaction count, this is the same as assuming that the probability of a transaction occurring is λ (as in figure 2.2 for the classical case). If we consider a transaction across the spread, so $x = \epsilon = \sqrt{2}\sigma_\tau$, then

$$\lambda = \frac{x^2}{4\sigma_\tau^2} = \frac{1}{2}. \tag{5.3}$$

This value of λ also appears later when we consider the price change distribution.

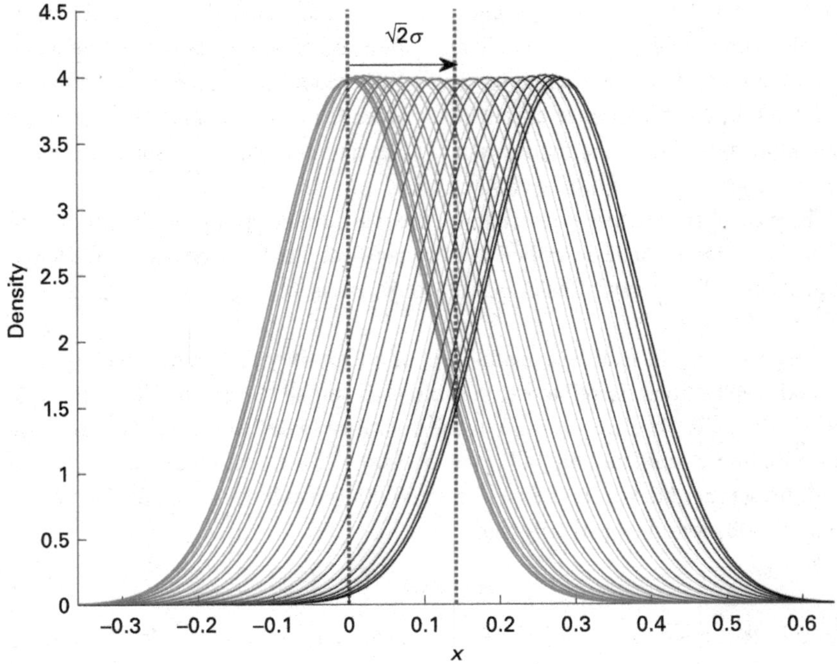

Figure 5.1
Following a perturbation of $\sqrt{2}\sigma$, the probability amplitude of a transacton with $\lambda = 0.5$ oscillates between $x = 0$ and $x = 2\sqrt{2}\sigma$ around its new equilibrium. The total variance over the period T is $\Sigma^2 = 2\sigma^2$. When the energy level is measured, the result follows a Poisson distribution with mean 0.5.

The mass

$$m = \frac{\hbar}{2\omega\sigma^2} \tag{5.4}$$

measures the degree of price flexibility or uncertainty, which are two sides of the same coin. The parameter $\hbar$ can be set to one if desired, whereas setting the frequency to

$$\omega = \frac{2\pi}{T} \tag{5.5}$$

means that each transacton goes through a complete cycle in a period of length T. The only free parameter in the model is therefore the ground state volatility σ. We now claim that these simple properties are enough to build a useful model of stock market transactions.

Before proceeding, we should note again that we have not made any assumptions that link the financial system to a physical one. The key assumption is that the propensity to transact can be modeled using a normal distribution. This corresponds to a linear entropic force and so can be viewed as a first-order approximation to the underlying dynamics. The frequency simply corresponds to a rate of turnover, whereas the mass relates to the inverse variance of the propensity curve. The energy depends on the eigenstate number and the frequency. All of these parameters and numbers have natural financial interpretations.

5.2 Price Impact Revisited

To demonstrate how the model can be used to address the anomalies reported in chapter 1, we begin with the problem of price impact. In chapter 2, a classical model was used to obtain a logarithmic formula for the price change due to a large order, whereas the empirical evidence favors a square root law. To derive the quantum model, we again define a transacton to be a unit of stock that is "in play" at a particular time. It therefore represents a potential transaction that can occur between a buyer and a seller. We also define the market imbalance as before to be $\iota = (N_b - N_a)/\min(N_b, N_a)$, where N_a and N_b are the numbers of buyers and sellers, respectively. We will assume for simplicity that price change over the period T is represented by a single representative transacton, and defer the case with multiple oscillators to the next chapter, where we consider the shape of the corresponding distribution.

If $N_a = N_b = N$, then the system is balanced. We associate this with the ground state, so the number of transactions is theoretically zero (a transaction would have the effect of changing the price and therefore the energy). In this model, for a transaction to take place, we therefore need a nonzero probability that another person will arrive or something will shift to break the deadlock.

If there are N available units for sale and the demand per unit increases over the time step by an amount $\Delta N = \iota N$, so $N_b/N_a = 1 + \iota > 1$, then this will boost the probability of a transaction occurring during that step. This increase in energy is equivalent to the amount gained by increasing the average energy number of the oscillator by $\Delta E/E_0 = \iota$. Comparing $E_n = (1+2n)E_0$, it follows that for an oscillator in energy level n, we have $\iota = 2n$.

However, if we displace a ground state oscillator centred at position 0 by an amount x, the energy increases by an amount

$$\Delta E = \frac{1}{2} m\omega x^2 = E_0 \frac{m\omega x^2}{\hbar} = E_0 \frac{x^2}{2\sigma^2}. \tag{5.6}$$

Comparing these, it follows from energy balance that a price change $x = \sigma\sqrt{2\iota}$ is the amount required in order to restore the oscillator to its original frequency, so the rate of purchases slows down to match the usual rate of sales.

A similar argument for the case where the number of suppliers changes shows that, in general,

$$x = \pm\sigma\sqrt{2|\iota|}, \tag{5.7}$$

where again the sign depends on the sign of ι (compare equation 2.6 from chapter 2). For example, if there are twice as many buyers as sellers, then $\iota = 1$, whereas if there are twice as many sellers as buyers, $\iota = -1$. The corresponding price perturbations are plus/minus $\sqrt{2}\sigma$ as in figure 5.1.

If the excess size of the trade is Q and the daily volume is V_d, then the imbalance over the period T can also be written as

$$\iota = \frac{Q}{V_d T}, \tag{5.8}$$

so

$$x = \pm\sqrt{2}\sigma\sqrt{\frac{Q}{V_d T}} = \pm\sqrt{2}\sigma_d\sqrt{\frac{Q}{V_d}}, \tag{5.9}$$

where σ_d is the daily volatility. As discussed later, the observed daily variance Σ is higher than the oscillator ground state variance by a factor $\sqrt{2}$. The result is therefore consistent with, and indeed predicts (or rather "postdicts" since the answer was known), the so-called "square root" law for price impact, which states that

$$x = \pm Y\Sigma\sqrt{\frac{Q}{V_d}}, \tag{5.10}$$

where Y is of order unity.[5]

5.3 Effect on Variance

Note that in this treatment, T represents an arbitrary period, and we are not dividing time into infinitesimal steps. It doesn't matter if we are considering the timescale of an individual transaction across the bid–ask spread, or an imbalance that plays out over hours or days. This will immediately confuse anyone who is used to classical finance, but it is a consequence of adopting quantum probability to model imbalance.

A related feature of the quantum formalism is that a quantum system is interrogated by making measurements that collapse the system down to one of its eigenstates. In finance, we can measure the price change over a period, or the energy of the system in the period, but we can't model the exact price trajectory during the period. Put another way, it is true that markets are always measuring the price as they go along; but the aim of the model is to predict the probabilistic outcome of multiple simulations at a set time T, and for this, measurement must be postponed until the end. Since the period T can be adjusted like a sliding scale, this proves to not be a limitation, though again for those steeped in classical finance, it may create a degree of cognitive dissonance (we return to this in the final chapter).

We can sum this up with the following measurement protocol. In order to model a price change distribution over a period T, we don't measure multiple points as in the classical model because this would involve splitting the period into discrete time steps or transactions. Instead, we measure the energy of the system as a whole and use that to deduce information about the distribution.

An example of this measurement protocol is the calculation of variance. In the quantum model, a large order does not just perturb the price, but it also increases the energy of the system. We again can't measure the variance in the usual way by taking the squared standard deviation of many points; however, we can infer it from the energy level. Suppose an imbalance ι persists over a period T such as one day. The variance over this period is then

$$\mathrm{Var} = \sigma^2 + \sigma^2|\iota| = \sigma^2 + \frac{x^2}{2}, \tag{5.11}$$

where x is the corresponding price change and σ is daily volatility.

This formula assumes that the imbalance holds over the entire day. However, if the imbalance only persists for a time $T_\iota < 1$ day, then the formula needs to be adjusted. The first term becomes $\sigma^2 T_\iota$, which is smaller than σ^2. However, the second term concerns, not the final degree of price change, which is unknown, but rather the experienced rate of change. If this is assumed to continue over the full day, then the second term $x^2/2$ needs to be boosted by a factor $1/T_\iota$, which gives

$$\mathrm{Var} = \sigma^2 T_\iota + \frac{x^2}{2T_\iota}. \tag{5.12}$$

In other words, a large order that takes place over a short period such as an hour induces more price uncertainty than one that takes place over a full day.[6] Since even for the largest transactions we still have $\iota < 1$, this boosting effect would only apply to times less than a day because at that time, the price fluctuation due to the transaction becomes comparable in magnitude to the imbalance seen with normal daily price changes.

As an example, suppose that a large excess order equivalent to the daily volume takes place over the course of a day, so $\iota = 1$. If we look just at the first half day so $T_\iota = 0.5$ days, then in the classical model, the variance would be $\sigma^2 T_\iota(1+\iota) = \sigma^2$. In the quantum model, the large order is experienced as a rate change, and at time 0.5, the end point is not known. Instead of increasing throughout the day, the component of volatility due to the order makes a kind of quantum jump to a level of σ^2 straight away, so the total is $1.5\sigma^2$. As anyone who has experienced a heart-in-mouth moment knows, uncertainty doesn't steadily diffuse, and sometimes it just shows up.

The top panel of figure 5.2 reprises figure 1.1 from chapter 1, which plotted variance as a function of Q/V instead of $Q/(VT_\iota)$. For a period T_ι of 345 minutes, or about one trading day, the line is nearly flat. The reason is that the imbalance for these points is very low with $\iota < 1$, so there is little effect on variance. As discussed in the next chapter, this level of imbalance is similar to the background rate. However, the line for $T_\iota = 3.5$ minutes has a much steeper slope, but the maximum contribution to variance for the highest level of imbalance is still small relative to the daily variance. When the data is plotted against $Q/(VT_\iota)$ as in the lower panel, the graphs have slopes that are much more similar.

Figure 5.3 ties these results together for price impact over a period of 345 minutes, or roughly a trading day, so Q/V is the same as the imbalance ι. The graph shows that price change x roughly follows the square root law (dashed line) but with some variation. The shaded area covers plus/minus one standard deviation as calculated from the variance formula. This graph can be viewed as a kind of supply/demand diagram for the markets. In conventional models of supply and demand, the lines of supply and demand are drawn separately, the equilibrium price is assumed to be the point of intersection, and there are no uncertainty bands. In the quantum version, what counts is not supply or demand in isolation, but rather the ratio of the two. When demand exceeds the usual rate of supply, the price increases and so does the variance. Note that unlike in classical models, the only free parameter in this model is the volatility σ.

To summarize, the quantum oscillator model is inherently dynamic and can be used to account for effects such as price impact using only a minimal set of parameters. It is based on a linear restoring force and so can be viewed as a first-order approximation to the underlying dynamics. An interesting feature is that both price change and variance over a particular period are related to a degree of imbalance. In the next section, we extend this idea to periods of any length.

5.4 Q-Variance

Classical finance is based on the idea that prices are at equilibrium but are perturbed by random shocks. There is therefore no role in this picture for persistent imbalances between buyers and sellers (which is one reason that modeling

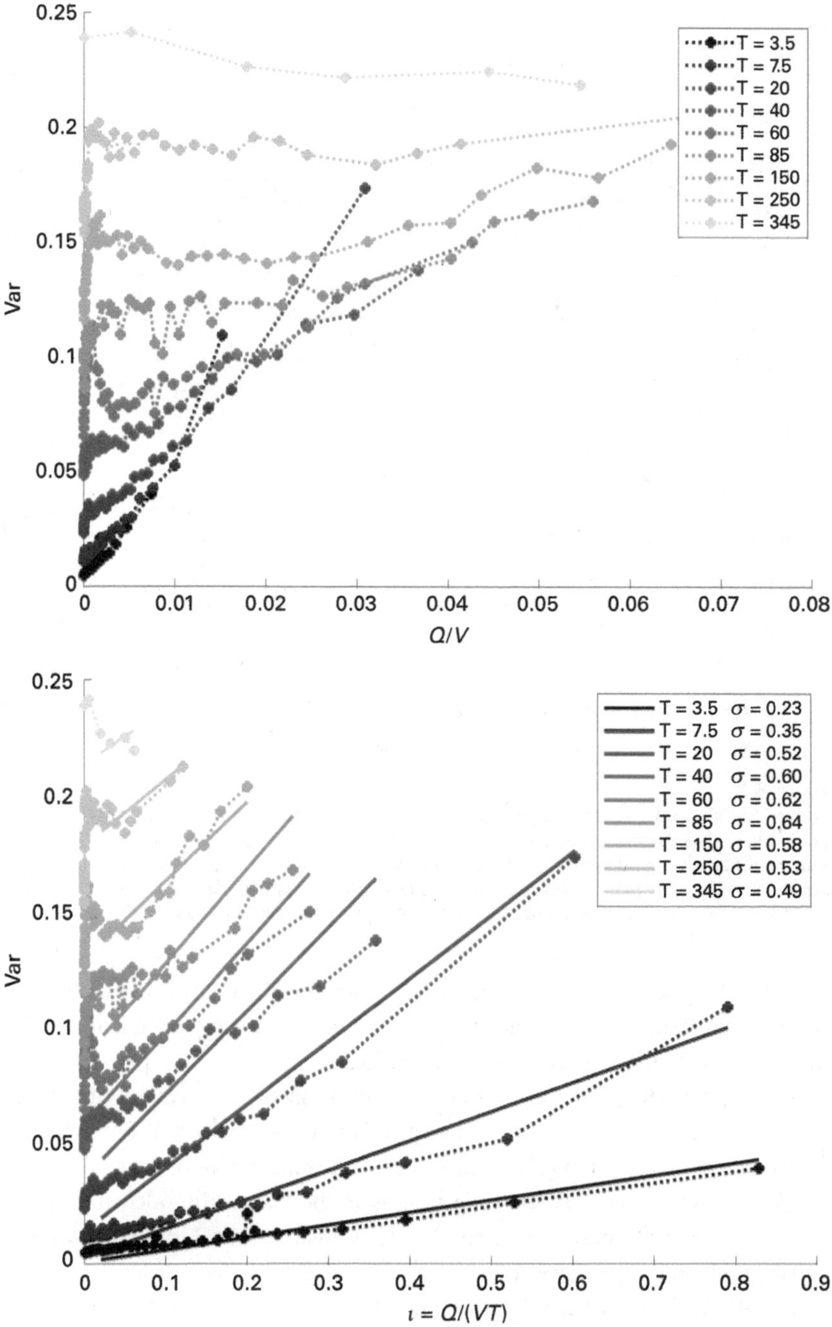

Figure 5.2
Plots of variance as a function Q/V (top) and $\iota = Q/(VT_\iota)$ (bottom) for large orders. Durations are binned into ranges with midpoints varying from 3.5 minutes (dark gray) to 345 minutes (light gray). The top panel is the same as figure 1.1 in chapter 1. Data digitized from Bucci et al. (2019).

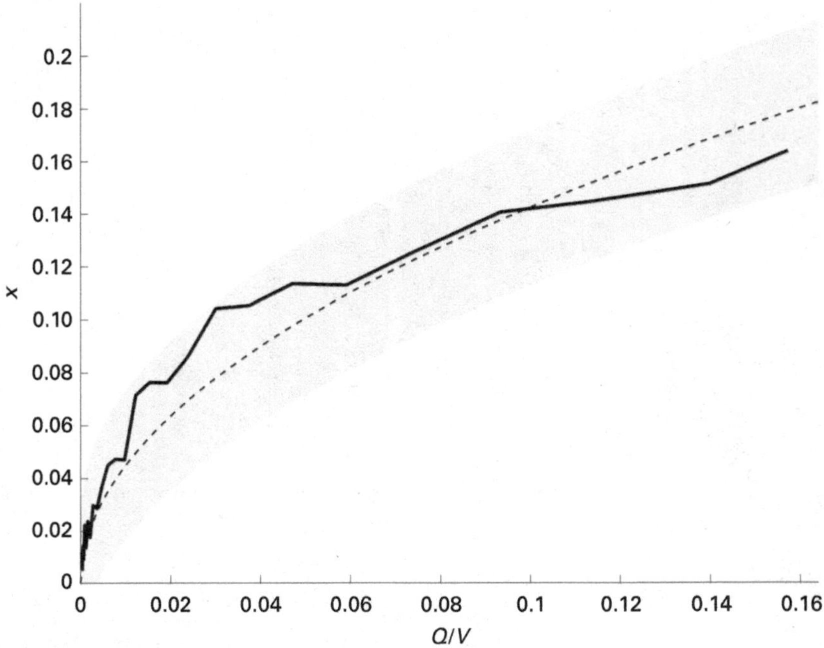

Figure 5.3
Dashed line shows a quantum supply-demand curve of log price change x versus daily imbalance Q/V, where Q is the size of the excess order and V is the average daily volume. Solid line shows estimated market impact from large transactions occurring over periods of 300–390 minutes, so about one trading day (data digitized from Bucci et al. (2019)). The shaded area, representing price uncertainty from the quantum model, corresponds to plus or minus one standard deviation.

the effect of price impact is problematic). Quantum finance allows us to move beyond this static model by incorporating a linear restoring force that acts in a probabilistic fashion on the price distribution.

In the quantum picture, the system is viewed as being always out of balance. We can therefore extend the model of price impact to periods of any length T. Because forces are assumed to play out over the entire period, we again do not break time down into discrete intervals, as in the classical model, but instead need to look at the period as a whole. Also, instead of asking what variance corresponds to a given level of imbalance caused by a large order, we change the question slightly to ask what variance corresponds to a given change in price.

Suppose that the log return over a period T is given by x. From equation 5.11, the variance over the same period is

$$\mathrm{Var} = \sigma^2 + \frac{x^2}{2}, \tag{5.13}$$

Table 5.1
Table shows two weeks of data for Microsoft (MSFT) for a period T of five trading days (one week).

	Date	S	y	x	z	v
1	1992-01-02	2.375	0			
2	1992-01-03	2.35417	−0.00881			
3	1992-01-06	2.42708	0.0305			
4	1992-01-07	2.5	0.0296			
5	1992-01-08	2.58854	0.0348	0.08305	0.58959	0.08128
6	1992-01-09	2.65104	0.02386			
7	1992-01-10	2.60938	−0.01584			
8	1992-01-13	2.64844	0.01486			
9	1992-01-14	2.67188	0.00881			
10	1992-01-15	2.73958	0.02503	0.05368	0.38108	0.05553

which we also encountered in chapter 4 (equation 4.36). The volatility σ is here computed for the period T, so normalizing to the units of T (such as a day or year) gives

$$\mathrm{Var} = \sigma^2 + \frac{x^2}{2T} = \sigma^2 + \frac{z^2}{2}, \tag{5.14}$$

where $z = x/\sqrt{T}$. This is the property we have called q-variance.

The procedure for testing q-variance is illustrated by table 5.1, which gives two weeks of data for a stock (MSFT). The column S is the daily price data, and y is daily log price change. For each period of $T = 5$ days, the value of x is determined by summing the daily log price changes over the period to give the total log price change. To remove the effect of drift (usually a small effect, which we account for in chapter 7), we subtract the mean drift over a week, which here is 0.00304. Finally, the annualized variance over the period is computed in the usual way from the daily log price changes.

Before proceeding to examples, a useful corollary to the q-variance equation is that the total variance is approximately equal to $\Sigma^2 = 2\sigma^2$, where again, σ is a minimum volatility that is experienced over periods where the price change is small. To see this, suppose we divide the z axis into M bins of width Δz centered at z_k. If each bin k has M_k points, for a total N data points, then the variance of z can be written (again ignoring drift) as

$$\text{Var} = \frac{1}{N}\sum_{i=1}^{N} z_i^2 = \frac{1}{N}\sum_{k=1}^{M}\sum_{j=1}^{M_k} z_j^2 = \frac{1}{N}\sum_{k=1}^{M} M_k z_k^2 \tag{5.15}$$

since $z \approxeq z_k$ within bin k. However, from q-variance, the expected variance in bin k is

$$V_k = \sigma^2 + \frac{z_k^2}{2}. \tag{5.16}$$

The total expected variance is therefore the weighted sum

$$\text{Var} \approxeq \frac{1}{N}\sum_{k=1}^{M} M_k V_k = \frac{1}{N}\sum_{k=1}^{M} M_k(\sigma^2 + \frac{z_k^2}{2}) = \sigma^2 + \frac{1}{2N}\sum_{k=1}^{M} M_k z_k^2 \tag{5.17}$$

$$\approxeq \sigma^2 + \frac{1}{2}\text{Var}. \tag{5.18}$$

Since the bin size Δz can be arbitrarily small, it follows that

$$\text{Var} \approxeq 2\sigma^2. \tag{5.19}$$

In the calculations above, we have been ignoring the effects of drift on price. In the classical approach, as discussed later, the drift term is often associated with the risk-free rate and so tends to be treated in a precise manner as a known quantity (even though there is no such thing as a completely risk-free asset). In the approach used here, the drift cannot be computed in advance and so is handled only as an approximate offset that is tied up with other effects such as skew.

5.5 A Gallery of Smiles

It is interesting to note that the smile-shaped q-variance property, predicted by the quantum model, appears to hold quite generally, at least as a first-order approximation. Figure 1.2 in chapter 1 illustrated the property for the S&P 500 index. Figure 5.4 shows the same for a range of separate periods T, using data from 1992 to 2024. Periods are nonoverlapping, so there are fewer points for longer periods.

Another way to visualize the property is through heatmaps, as in figure 5.5, which compiles data from different periods to compare the S&P 500, Dow Jones Industrial Average, and Financial Times Stock Exchange indexes, along with a classical random walk. The three indexes show the same q-variance property, whereas the classical model does not. In fact, as discussed further

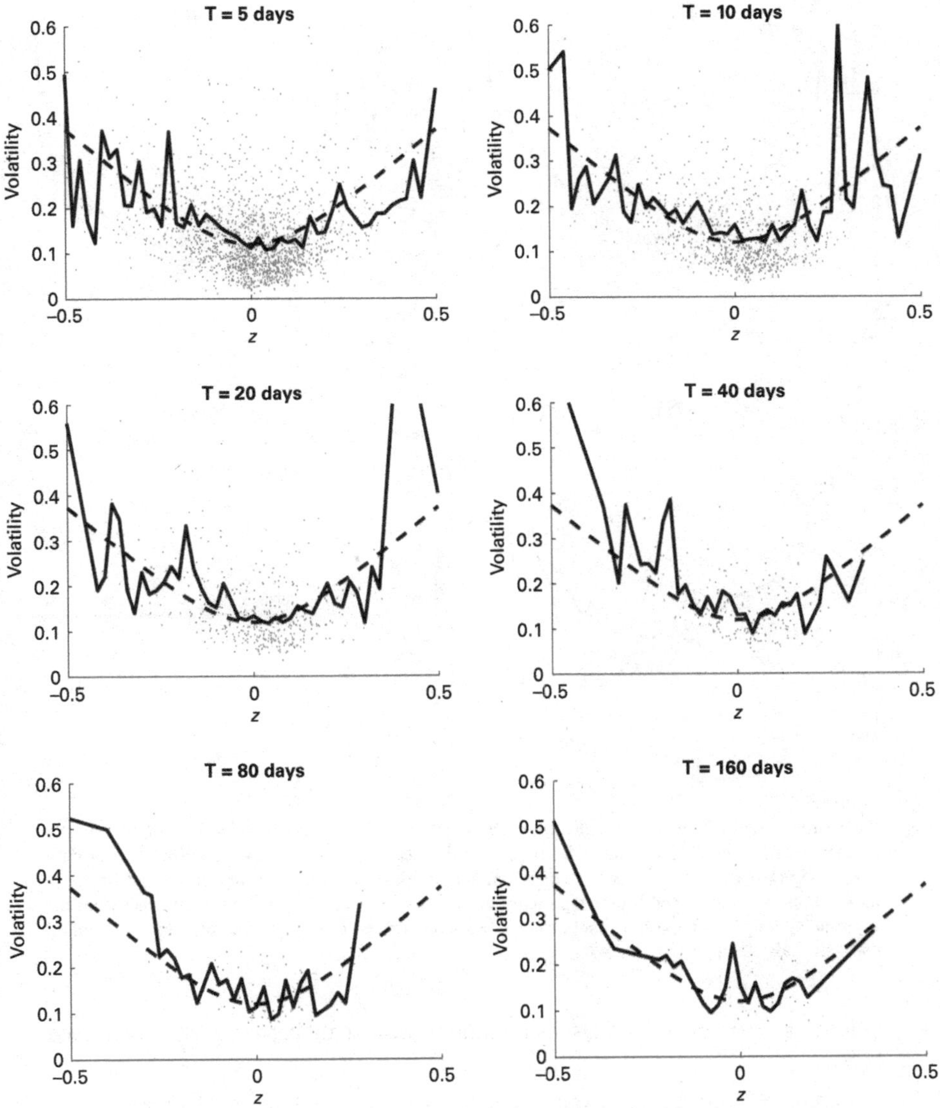

Figure 5.4
Plots of volatility (gray points) as a function of normalized log price change $z = x/\sqrt{T}$ over the same period, for S&P 500 index (1992–2024). Black line is average, and dashed line is the q-variance curve. Periods are one, two, four, eight, sixteen, and thirty-two weeks, with no overlapping.

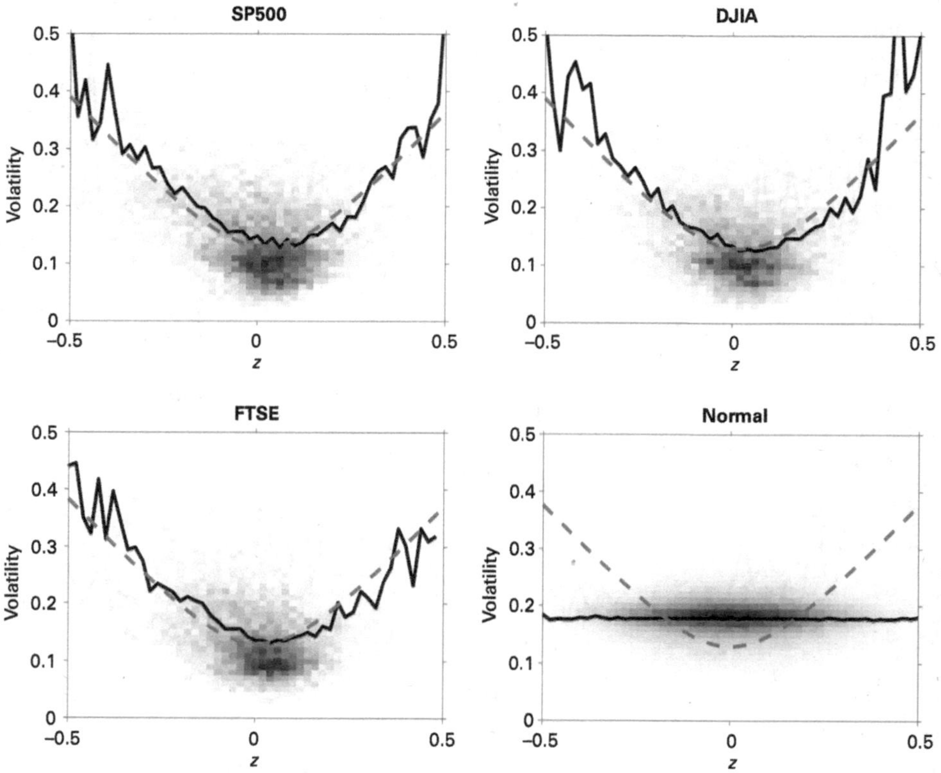

Figure 5.5
Plots show volatility versus z for the S&P 500 index, the Dow Jones Industrial Average, and the Financial Times Stock Exchange 100 Index for the years 1992–2024, along with artificial data from a lognormal time series for comparison. Black lines show the volatility computed from the mean variance, and dashed line is the quantum model with a small horizontal shift to account for asymmetry. The heatmap in the background shows the density of points. The results are computed using periods of one to fifty weeks.

below, no version of a classical random walk can produce the q-variance behavior.

Figure 5.6 repeats the experiment for a random selection of major stocks for the years 2007–2024, along with GLD, which is an exchange-traded fund that tracks the gold price. Of the twelve plots shown here, GLD appears to be the least strong fit, although the data is affected by the fact that volatility is relatively low and there are fewer points at higher values of z. Currencies including crypto are also not immune to q-variance, as shown by figure 5.7. Note the larger scale for the BTC-USD exchange rate needed to accommodate the high level of volatility.

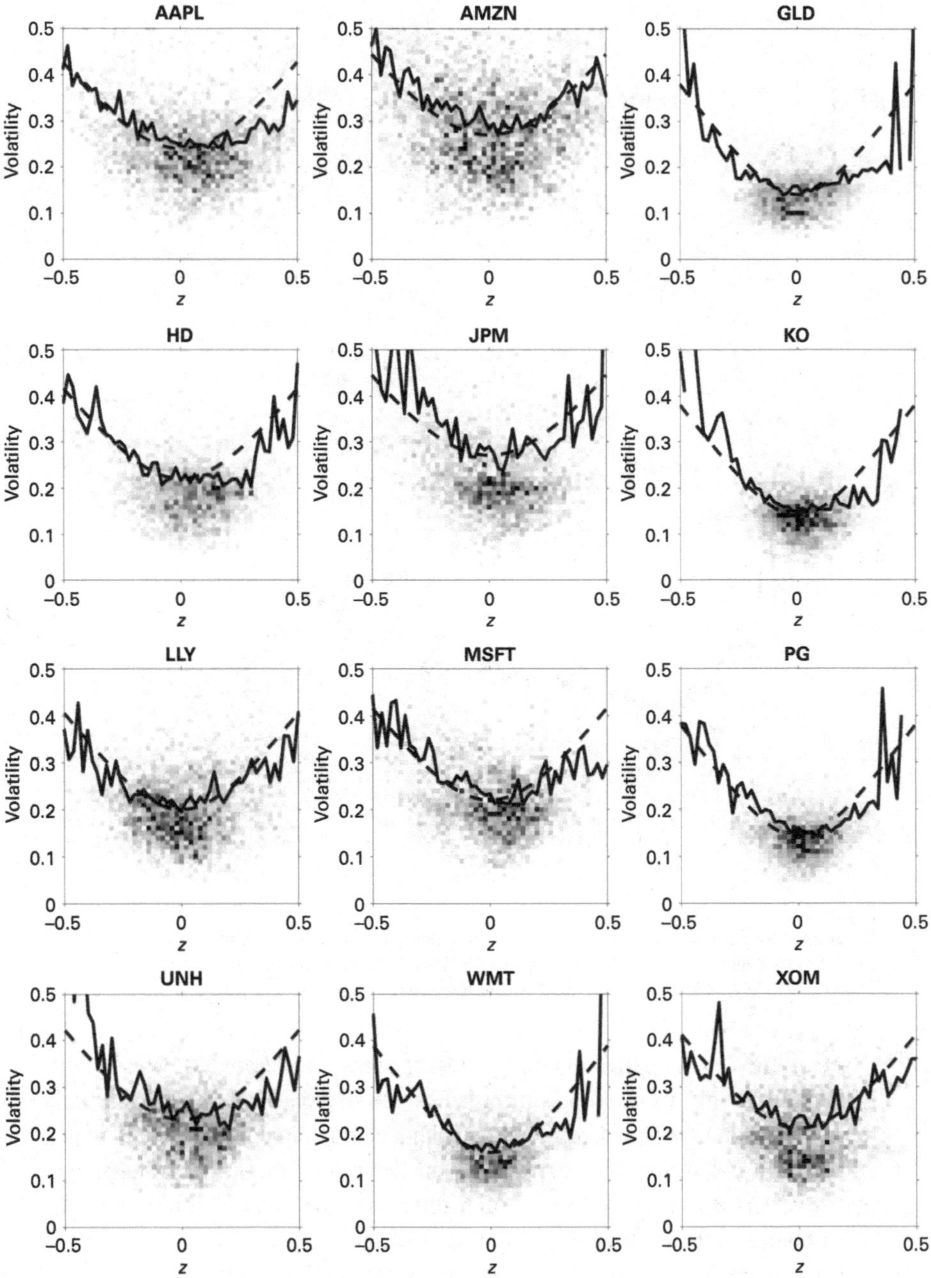

Figure 5.6
Plots show q-variance for a random selection of large companies (2007–2024), along with the exchange-traded fund GLD, which tracks the gold price.

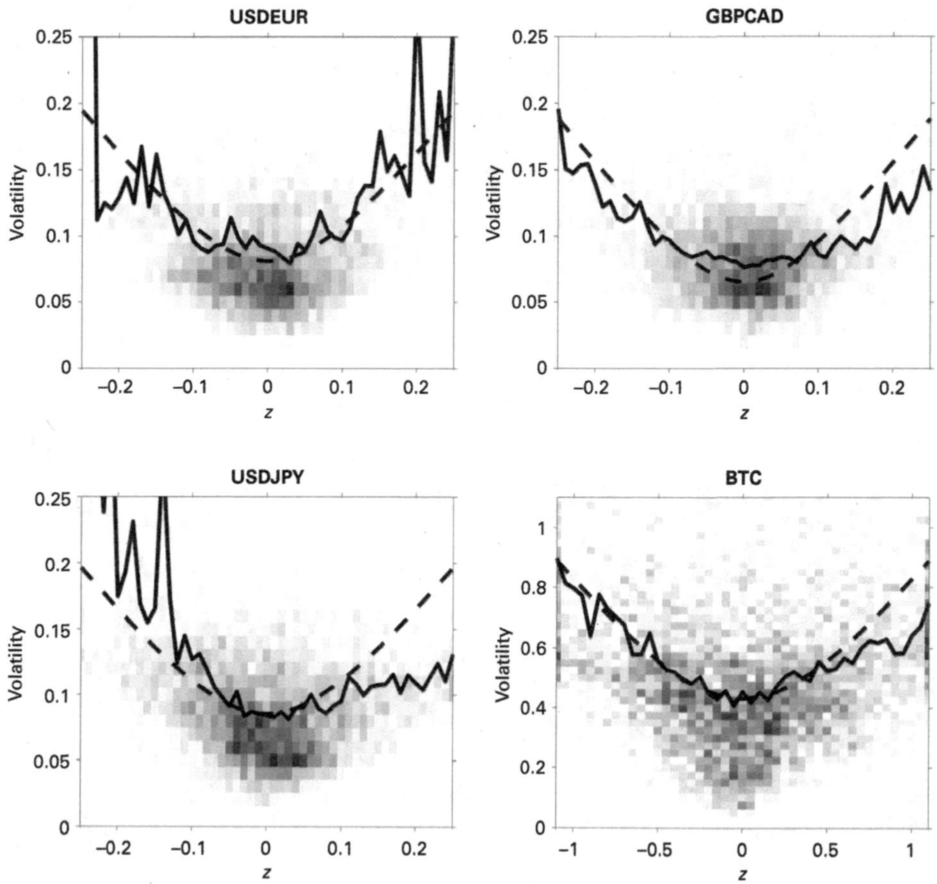

Figure 5.7
Q-variance for various currency pairs (2009–2024) and the BTC-USD exchange rate (2014–2024). Note the horizontal and vertical scales are smaller for currencies than for stocks due to lower volatility, with the exception of Bitcoin, which has higher volatility.

Q-variance even applies to bond yields, as shown by figure 5.8. Bond yields behave differently from returns on assets since they cannot grow indefinitely but remain bound within a certain range. This is illustrated by figure 5.9, which compares bond yields with the returns on Bitcoin. It might seem surprising that q-variance can apply to two such different time series, though note the resemblance in the plots of log daily price changes.

The best evidence for q-variance occurs when you look at the average over a large number of stocks, which filters out some of the noise. Figure 5.10 shows q-variance for the 350 stocks that have been in the current S&P 500 for at least

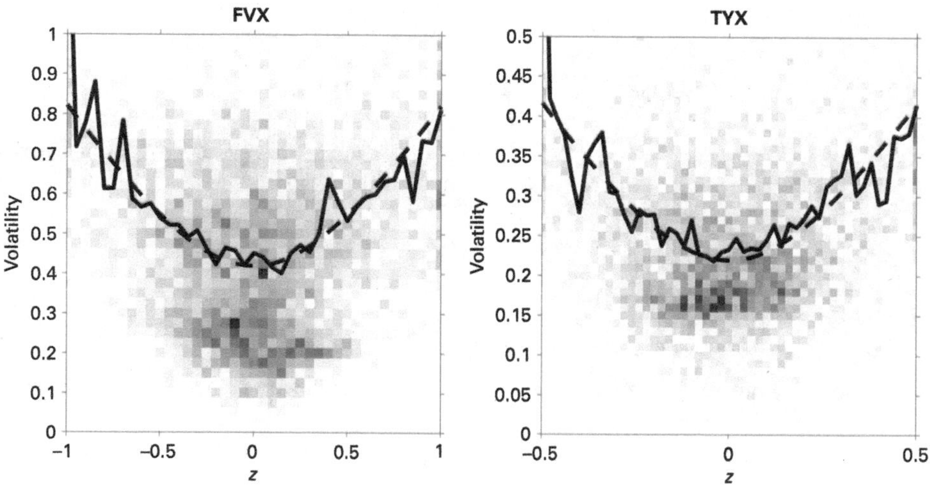

Figure 5.8
Q-variance for the five-year Treasury bond yield (FVX), and the thirty-year yield (TYX), 2007–2024. Note the different volatility scales.

50 percent of the period from January 1975 to November 2025 (so about 25 years). The vertical axis in this plot is variance rather than volatility. The advantage of plotting variance here is that a stock's minimum variance corresponds to a vertical shift, so the plots are roughly offset curves. The quantum model (dashed line) is a good fit to the average (black), with a small horizontal shift that can be attributed to effects such as skew. Note that the mean variance curve is a better fit here than for the index itself because it represents an average of variances rather than the variance of an average price (which tends to be smaller and more noisy).

We should note though that q-variance is based on a first-order approximation to the dynamics of market behavior, so performance will vary. Figure 1.2 from chapter 1 showed the q-variance property for the S&P 500 index since 1927. Figure 5.11 divides the same data up into three periods. The quantum model (dashed line) is a good fit for the average (solid black line). In theory, the curves for the three periods should be shifted versions of the quantum curve; however, the period 1960 to 1992 (circle symbols) is flatter than the others. In general, the model seems to perform better when the minimum volatility is higher than around 0.15, which is usually the case for individual stocks. Effects due to low volatility will be more of a problem for an index, which averages out some of the price variation, and statistics will also be affected by correlations between individual stocks.

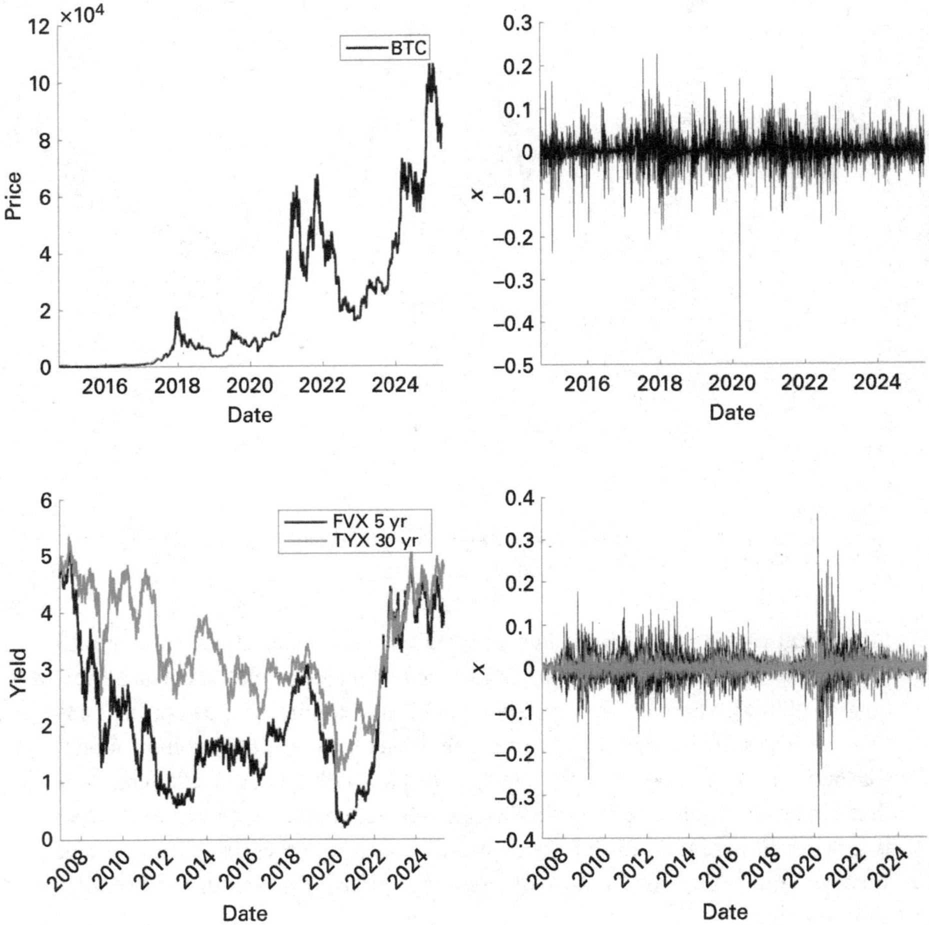

Figure 5.9
Comparison of Bitcoin and bond yields. Bond yields (bottom left) are constrained within a certain range and behave in a very different fashion from Bitcoin (top left), although the daily log price changes do bear some resemblance (right column). Black line in bottom plots is the five-year Treasury bond yield (FVX), gray line is the thirty-year yield (TYX), which is less volatile.

In general, it seems surprising that the q-variance property holds as well as it does for a variety of different assets and periods. However, although q-variance is a common property of financial data, one should note that it doesn't apply more widely to other areas because a prerequisite is that annualized volatility should be roughly constant when measured over different time periods. This tends not to be the case when say data has a degree of regular periodicity. For example, the sunspot data that Jevons saw as a driver for economic cycles has

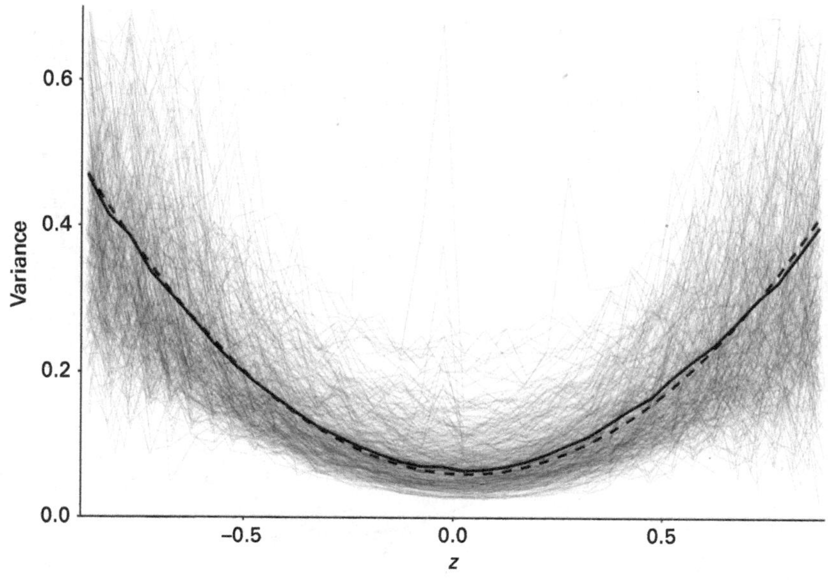

Figure 5.10
Plot shows q-variance for 350 stocks of the 500 in the current composition of the S&P 500. Data is for the period January 1975 to November 2025. The criterion for a stock's inclusion is that price data must be available for 50 percent of the period, so about 25 years. Black line shows square root of average variance, and dashed line is quantum model with minimum variance $\sigma^2 = 0.060$ and a small offset of 0.033 to account for skew. Variance is shown rather than the volatility because the curves for different stocks roughly follow the same quadratic shape with different vertical offsets.

an average period of about eleven years, and the annualized volatility measured over that period is roughly half that measured over an annual period, so q-variance does not apply.

5.6 Summary

The q-variance property is a striking and powerful phenomenon for a number of reasons. One is that it involves no parameter other than a minimum volatility, and yet it applies to a range of assets and indexes and time periods ranging from a couple of days to over a year (shorter time periods have not been investigated in detail here other than for the question of price impact).

A related reason is that because the quadratic term in q-variance has no adjustable parameter, it represents a falsifiable prediction. This is extremely rare—or as Paul Wilmott put it, "almost unique"—in finance, where the emphasis is usually on either making simple models that are useful but do not fit the data well (e.g., because they assume constant volatility) or on fitting

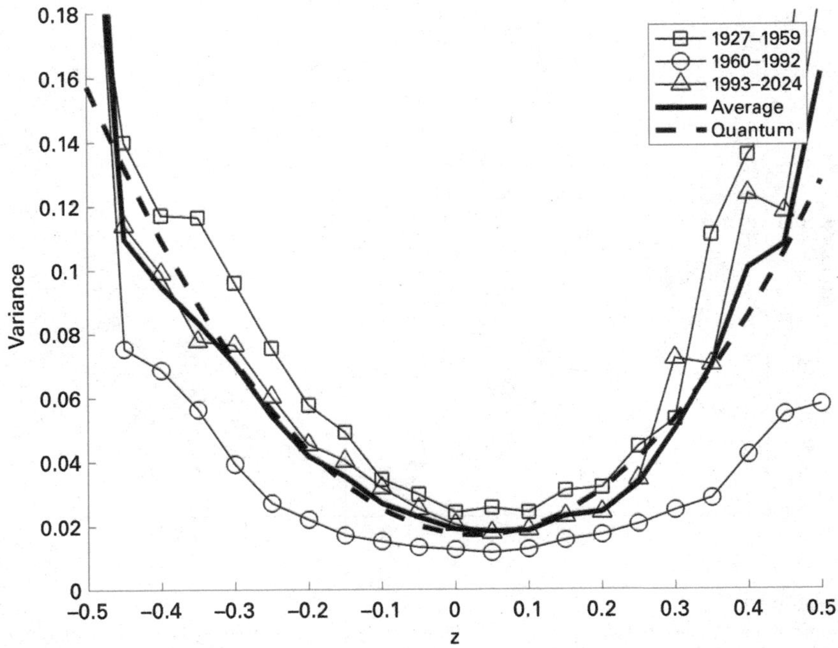

Figure 5.11
Plot shows variance as a function of z computed over periods T ranging from one to fifty weeks for the S&P 500 index 1927–1959, 1960–1992, and 1993–2024. The black line shows the average variance, and dashed line shows the quantum model. One factor is that q-variance for an index is the variance of an average, which is lower and more noisy than the average of the variance of individual stocks as in figure 5.10.

complicated models to data.[7] After a while, I realized that the reason many people found the result hard to understand was that they simply hadn't encountered anything like it before—formulas in finance don't have terms like $z^2/2$ where there is no control knob to make them fit, so they just assume that the $1/2$ is a fit too.

Another reason the property is unusual is that it is both large and extremely easy to check once you know what to look for. Unlike in physics, no special equipment—no observatory or particle accelerator—is required to detect it. And yet as mentioned in chapter 1, it apparently went unnoticed for decades, even though the data has long been publicly available and despite the fact that the topic of volatility is one of interest to both academics and practitioners, with related research output in the form of journal articles, specialized books, and conference papers being enough to fill a small library. In fact in financial terms at least it is hard to think of another area of mathematical modeling which has seen greater investment than the models of asset price behavior used by banks and hedge funds. We return to this in the final chapter.

Finally, the property is a powerful one because it is incompatible with the random walk and therefore has implications for mainstream models. Indeed, although it is certainly strange that the property was not previously reported, it would have been even stranger if it had been known about all along but not followed up on, since as we'll see, it does imply that we have to rethink much of quantitative finance. In the next chapter, we look at how the q-variance property affects option pricing, using a model based on quantum jumps.

6

Quantum Jumps

Natura non facit saltum (Nature makes no sudden leaps)
—Epitaph of Alfred Marshall's 1890 *Principles of Economics*.
It remained there until the final edition of 1920.

If all this damned quantum jumping were really here to stay, I should be sorry, I should be sorry I ever got involved with quantum theory.
—Erwin Schrödinger (1926), as reported in Heisenberg (1971)

A main objective of quantitative finance is to provide a probabilistic model of the price distribution at some future time. For example, any theory of option pricing is based ultimately on a model of how the asset price will evolve over the option period, which is what determines the expected payout. Since the time of Bachelier, this has been based on some version of a random walk.

The French mathematician Abraham de Moivre, a friend of Isaac Newton, had shown in 1733 that the distribution of a random walk would converge to the so-called normal distribution. Scientists including Pierre-Simon Laplace, and particularly Carl Friedrich Gauss, used the method to analyze the errors in astronomical data (which is why its other name is the Gaussian distribution). One of the technique's greatest advocates was the Victorian polymath Francis Galton, who described it as a "wonderful form of cosmic order" and the "supreme law of Unreason." He would demonstrate it using a pinball-like device he invented called a quincunx, in which balls released from the top would bounce down through rows of evenly spaced pegs to collect in bins at the bottom.

Mathematical justification for the ubiquity of the normal distribution came with the central limit theorem, which proved that the normal distribution could be used to model the sum of any random processes, provided that a number of conditions were met. In particular, the separate processes had to be independent and identically distributed.

It was therefore a natural step for Bachelier to apply the random walk model to the stock market. However, although the model had many mathematical advantages, in finance, a problem in practice has long been that log price returns are not perfectly normal; for example, their distribution exhibits so-called fat tails, where the likelihood of extreme events is larger than predicted by the classical model.[1] Economists have therefore devised a number of more complicated alternatives to the normal distribution. An early example was the Merton jump-diffusion (MJD) model, which assumes that asset price is subject to two kinds of volatility: the normal sort represented by σ and a second kind that is caused by discontinuous jumps.

In this chapter and the next,[2] we take a step back to revisit the MJD model and explore some of its properties before using it as motivation for a quantum model that can be viewed as being jumps all the way down.

6.1 Jumping Markets

In classical models such as the Black-Scholes-Merton (BSM) model, log price changes are assumed to be the result of a Brownian process in continuous time. If the stock price $S(t)$ follows the stochastic differential equation

$$dS = \mu S dt + \sigma S dX \tag{6.1}$$

with an initial value of $S(0) = S_0$, then applying Itô's lemma, we can write the resulting probability distribution for $x = \log(S/S_0)$ after a period T as

$$F(x, \mu, \sigma, T) = f\left(x, (\mu - \sigma^2/2)T, \sigma\sqrt{T}\right), \tag{6.2}$$

where f is the probability density function for the normal distribution (the $\sigma^2/2$ adjustment to the drift occurs because we are working in terms of x rather than S).

A limitation of the model was that, being based on Brownian motion, it didn't allow for the sort of extreme, discontinuous changes that occur often in markets due, for example, to news or a sudden shift in sentiment. In a 1976 paper, Merton proposed an alternative model that incorporated such jumps.[3] The stochastic differential equation became

$$dS = \mu S dt + \sigma S dX + (J - 1) S dq, \tag{6.3}$$

where dq is a Poisson process with associated probability $\lambda\, dt$ and J is a random process that we assume to be normal. The resulting distribution of log price change over a period T then becomes a Poisson-weighted sum of Gaussians. For the case where the jumps have mean zero (otherwise another parameter is needed) and standard deviation δ, the distribution can be written

$$F(x, \mu, \sigma, \lambda, \delta, T) = \sum_{n=0}^{\infty} w_n(\lambda T) f(x, \mu_n, \sigma_n), \tag{6.4}$$

where $w_n(\lambda T) = e^{-\lambda T}(\lambda T)^n/n!$ is a Poisson weighting, and $f(x, \mu_n, \sigma_n)$ is the normal distribution with drift $\mu_n = \mu T - \sigma_n^2/2$ and standard deviation $\sigma_n = \sqrt{\sigma^2 T + \delta^2 n}$.

One advantage of the MJD model, arguably, was that it could be calibrated to give a better fit to data than the normal model (although this was offset by the fact that it had more parameters). However, there was a problem, which was that the effect of the jumps tended to wash out with time.

Figure 6.1 shows the distribution of normalized log price change $z = x/\sqrt{T}$ for the S&P 500 index over different periods T from one to thirty-two weeks. The dotted line, showing the MJD model, fits the observed distribution for periods of one week but has nearly converged to a normal distribution for periods of thirty-two weeks. (The choice of parameters is discussed below; note the effect of drift is small over these timescales.) The effect of jumps is therefore important over short timescales, but not over the long term.

As seen in the figure, though, the actual returns data don't show any sign of becoming more normal—in fact, the shape seems quite stable. One option would be to recalibrate the model for each period length; however, common sense suggests that it would be preferable to use a model with a single set of parameters for all periods, as with the dashed lines.

A related question concerns the property of q-variance, which can be written in terms of volatility as

$$\sigma_z = \sqrt{\sigma^2 + \frac{z^2}{2}}. \tag{6.5}$$

Figure 5.4 from the previous chapter showed the volatility for the S&P 500 index over the same periods T of one to thirty-two weeks. As discussed there, for each T, the points are obtained by taking the daily returns over a sequence of such periods and computing the variance and the total returns for each. A Brownian process of the sort used in the BSM model clearly does not satisfy q-variance because the volatility is constant. In the MJD model, because the Poisson process is independent from the diffusion process, the variance in z can be shown to be[4]

$$\mathrm{Var} = \sigma^2 + \lambda(\mu^2 + \delta^2), \tag{6.6}$$

where parameter units are scaled to the period of interest as usual.

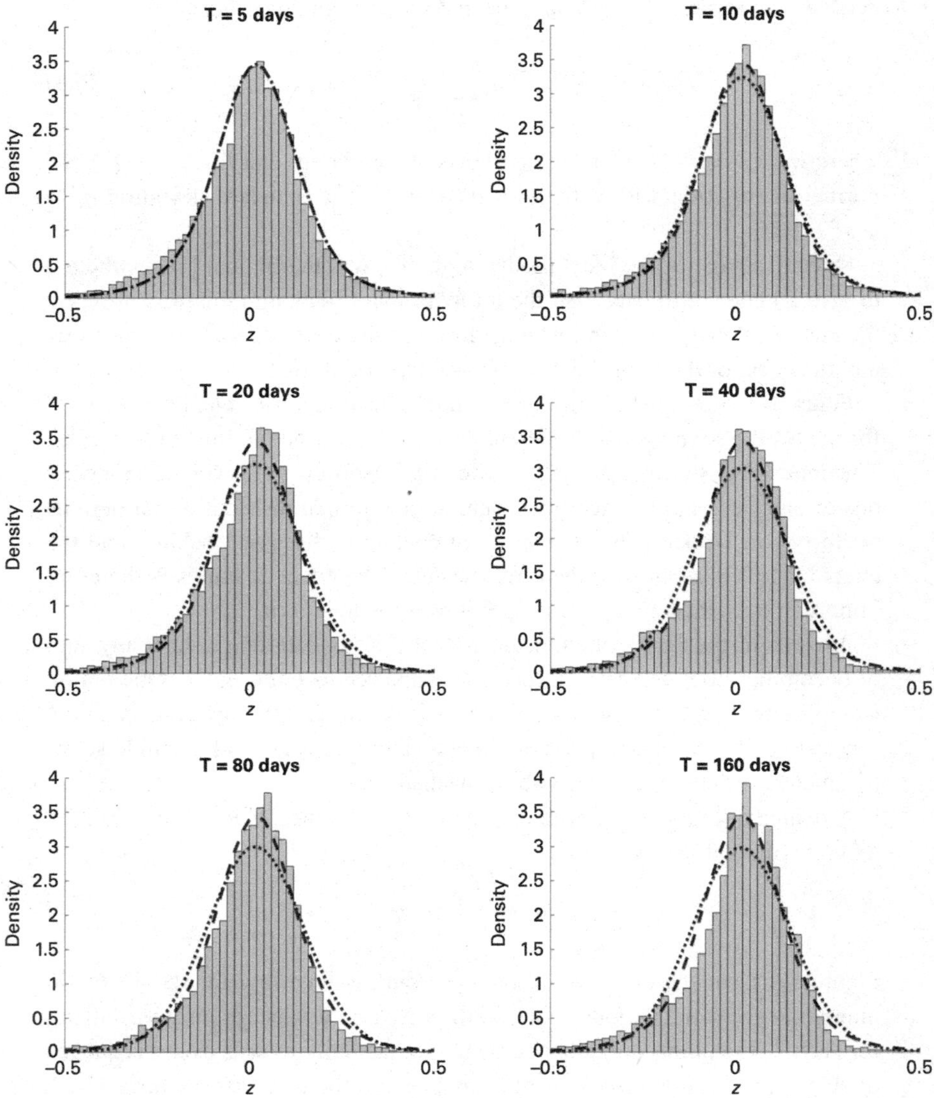

Figure 6.1

Plots of normalized log price change $z=x/\sqrt{T}$ for S&P 500 index (1992–2024) over different periods T_n of $n=1$, 2, 4, 8, 16, and 32 weeks, corrected for drift. Periods are overlapping. Dotted line is MJD, and dashed line is the quantum model, with a small horizontal offset of 0.025 to account for skew. The MJD model parameters are set to $\sigma=0.095$, $\mu=0$, $\delta=\sqrt{2T_1}\sigma$, and $\lambda=0.5/T_1$, so the model agrees with the quantum jump (QJ) model for time T_1 (one week) but is nearly Gaussian at T_{32}.

Suppose we assume that $\mu = 0$ and the displacements z are caused primarily by jumps of size δ, which will be true at least for larger jumps. Comparing with equation 6.5 for q-variance, we should then set $\lambda = 0.5$. (Note again that the quadratic coefficient of $1/2$ in q-variance is not a parameter but comes directly from the energy balance of equation 4.36.) For consistency with the corollary to q-variance that the total variance is $2\sigma^2$ (see equation 5.19), we also set $\delta = \sqrt{2}\sigma$.

It can be checked numerically that when thus calibrated, the MJD model approximately satisfies equation 6.5 for a particular period T. This is shown by figure 6.2, which repeats the experiment in figure 5.4, but this time using an artificial time series generated using the MJD model rather than actual index data. When again calibrated to a period of five days (one week), the MJD model agrees quite well with equation 6.5 (black line in first panel), and indeed the individual data points (black dots) resemble the oberved index data for the same period (first panel of figure 5.4). The MJD model therefore comes close to capturing the relationship between volatility and price change over this period. However, the result holds only for the period of a week, and at thirty-two weeks, the volatility is essentially constant, which makes sense since the corresponding distribution in figure 6.1 is nearly normal.

To summarize, it seems that we can use the MJD model to simulate data that approximates the correct behavior in terms of both log price change (the distribution in z) and volatility (q-variance) over a certain period; however, this breaks down over longer periods. The same would apply to other models based on a random walk.

Suppose, for example, that we use a model to calculate daily price change and obtain a distribution that is not Gaussian. If we then want to extend the model to look at price changes over a year, then we might think that we can randomly draw the daily price changes from the daily distribution and add these up to get the final distribution (this is essentially what the MJD model does). However, if we do so, the result will be nearly Gaussian, which would be incorrect (we are assuming the initial distribution is reasonably well behaved, so the central limit theorem applies). Similarly, the q-variance property of equation 6.5 would not hold since it fails when the distribution is normal.

Since an obvious requirement of a model to be used for pricing options is that it be able to capture the basic properties of asset price behavior, including q-variance, it follows that we need a new model. Put another way, the empirical evidence (e.g., figure 5.5 for volatility and figure 6.1 for probability density) shows that any model based on a random walk as in equation 6.1 is missing important information. We therefore need a different interpretation of the underlying dynamics—in other words, what we mean by a jump.

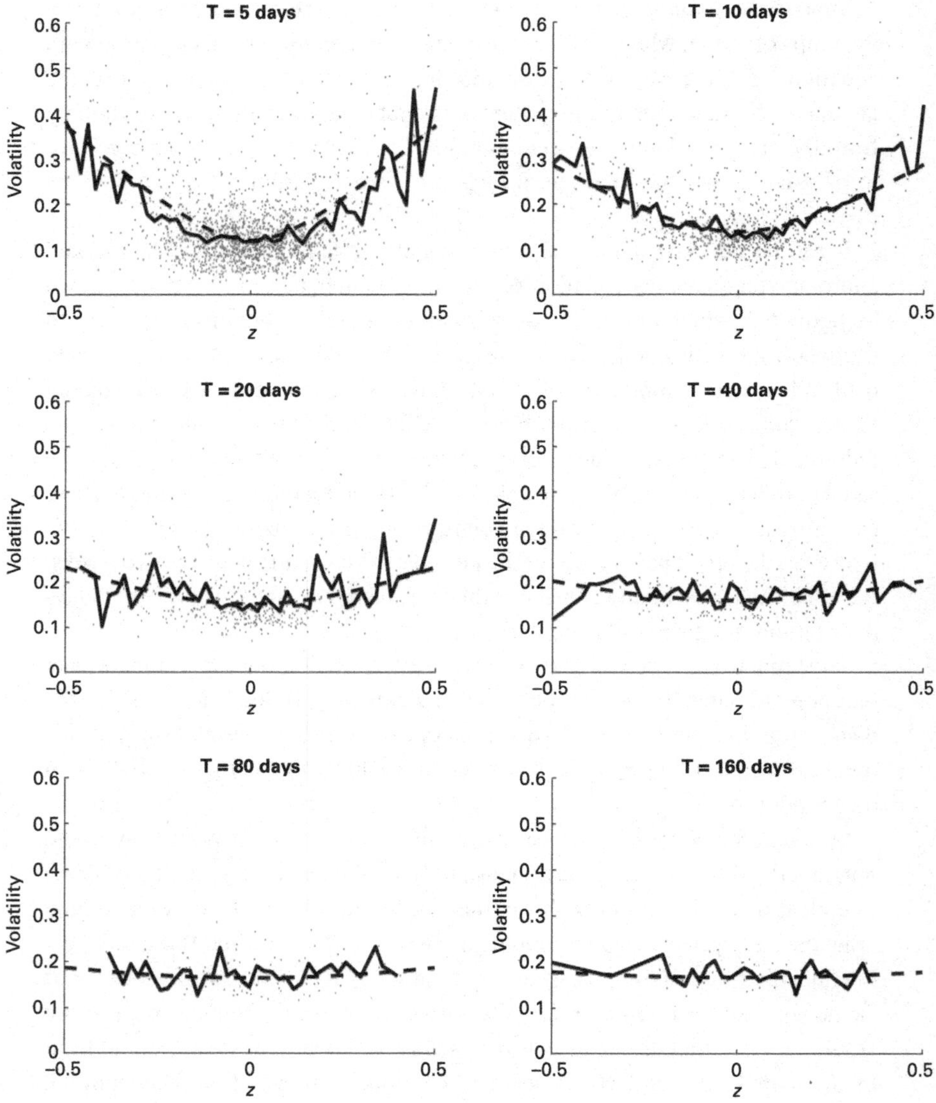

Figure 6.2

Plots of volatility (gray points) as a function of normalized log price change $z=x/\sqrt{T}$ over the same period for artificial data generated using the MJD model with no drift. Black line is average, and dashed line is the variance curve scaled for the MJD model. Periods are one, two, four, eight, sixteen, and thirty-two weeks, without overlapping. The result is a good match for q-variance at one week but becomes increasingly flat at higher times.

6.2 The Q-Distribution

We earlier defined a transacton to be a representative unit of stock that is for sale on the market. The seller has an ask price, and the buyer a bid price, and they are not the same. The transacton is therefore like a microcosm of the market. Since each transacton describes a single potential transaction over the time T, we set the frequency to $\omega = 2\pi/T$ as in equation 5.5 so that each transacton goes through a complete cycle independent of the period length. Note that the uncertainty in position x of an oscillator in its ground state is then given by

$$\Delta x^2 = \frac{\hbar}{2m\omega} = \frac{\hbar T}{4\pi m}, \tag{6.7}$$

so the variance of each oscillator grows linearly with T. The effect, therefore, is the same as increasing the number of transactions over time (which is an alternative way to provide the same scaling).

As discussed in chapter 5 (see equation 5.3), transactions across the bid–ask spread perturb the oscillator and put it into a coherent state, whose energy number when measured follows a Poisson distribution with average $\lambda = 0.5$. That chapter used a single representative oscillator to analyze price change and variance due to a given level of imbalance (since position and energy are both additive, a classical analogue would be representing a number of springs in series, with a single large spring). We now want to consider multiple transactons in order to calculate the nature and shape of the price change distribution over a period for the general case.

If M classical springs are acting in series then the total standard deviation scales with $\sqrt{M}$ (see equation 2.17). Suppose then that we have M identical transactons of ground state standard deviation $\sigma/\sqrt{M}$, for a total standard deviation σ, where the number will depend on the average volume. In order to determine the volatility of the market over a single period, as mentioned in chapter 5, we can't make multiple measurements of position as in the classical model since this would collapse the wave function. Nor will it work to make single measurements of position for each transacton since dividing the period into separate, sequential transactions in this way would again lose information about dynamics and just give a number of independent measurements from the same distribution, resulting in a normal distribution that we know is incompatible with q-variance. And the continuous-time stochastic calculus used to derive the BSM and MJD models is right out.

As with variance, we instead need to follow the measurement protocol described in section 5.3, in which the distribution is determined by interrogating the energy level of the system as the dynamics play out over a complete period (this is consistent also with the model of q-variance where we used a single oscillator to represent all transactions over the period). When the energy is measured, the model is collapsed down to an energy eigenstate, where the total price change can be computed as the classical sum over M transactons. The distribution in any energy state n will therefore be normal, with a variance that corresponds to that state. The total price change distribution, however, will be the weighted sum of these normal curves.

To express this mathematically, we treat our ensemble of M identical oscillators as entangled, which here just means that they all share the same energy state n, that can be determined using a single measurement (otherwise each oscillator would require a separate measurement, contradicting our protocol of measuring the system as a whole).[5] The number n can therefore be viewed as representing the energy state of the market system.[6] Ignoring the small drift terms for simplicity, the position wave function of the system can be written

$$\Psi(z_1, \ldots, z_M) = \sum_{n=0}^{\infty} \sqrt{w_n} \cdot \prod_{m=1}^{M} \psi_n(z_m), \tag{6.8}$$

where ψ_n is the wavefunction of a quantum harmonic oscillator in energy state n, and

$$w_n \equiv w_n(0.5) = \frac{e^{-0.5} 2^{-n}}{n!} = \frac{1}{\sqrt{e}\, 2^n n!} \tag{6.9}$$

is the Poisson weighting. Measuring the energy level n of the system collapses the entire ensemble into

$$\Psi_n(z_1, \ldots, z_M) = \prod_{m=1}^{M} \psi_n(z_m) \tag{6.10}$$

with probability w_n. After energy measurement, we measure the position z_m of each oscillator and compute the total

$$z = \sum_{m=1}^{M} z_m. \tag{6.11}$$

The probability distribution of z, conditioned on n, is the distribution of the sum of m independent samples from $|\psi_n|^2$. This can be written as the M-fold convolution of

$$P(z|n) = \left|\psi_n^2\right|^{(*M)}(z). \tag{6.12}$$

Averaging over all possible n gives

$$P(z) = \sum_{n=0}^{\infty} w_n \cdot \left|\psi_n^2\right|^{(*M)}(z). \tag{6.13}$$

In the large-M limit, each term becomes approximately Gaussian with standard deviation σ_n, so

$$\left|\psi_n^2\right|^{(*M)}(z) \cong f(z, \mu_n, \sigma_n), \tag{6.14}$$

which gives what we will refer to as the q-distribution:

$$F_Q(z, \mu, \sigma) = \sum_{n=0}^{\infty} w_n f(z, \mu_n, \sigma_n). \tag{6.15}$$

As shown by the dashed lines in figure 6.1, the agreement of this q-distribution with observed price change data is quite good, apart from details such as the effect of skew. Unlike the MJD model, the parameters are now independent of period T, and the jumps take place in z instead of in x, which is consistent with the scaling seen in figures 6.1 and 5.4 for both price change and volatility.

If we again ignore for simplicity the effect of drift, the variance is the Poisson-weighted sum

$$\mathrm{Var} = \sum_{n=0}^{\infty} w_n \sigma_n^2 = \sum_{n=0}^{\infty} w_n \sigma^2(1+2n) = \Sigma^2, \tag{6.16}$$

where $\Sigma = \sqrt{2}\sigma$ is the total volatility, and we have used the Poisson distribution properties $\sum_{n=0}^{\infty} w_n(\lambda) = 1$ and $\sum_{n=0}^{\infty} w_n(\lambda) n = \lambda$, where here $\lambda = 0.5$.

The mean for $\mu = 0$ is

$$\langle z \rangle = -\sum_{n=0}^{\infty} w_n \frac{\sigma_n^2}{2} = -\sigma^2 = -\frac{\Sigma^2}{2} \tag{6.17}$$

The mean and the variance are therefore the same as for the classical model with standard deviation Σ. The variance is also consistent with the result obtained from q-variance (equation 5.19), which confirms that the value of σ used in the q-distribution is the same as the minimum volatility in q-variance (although in practice, when fitting market data as opposed to simulated data, they will usually differ somewhat).[7]

To obtain the corresponding log price change over a period T, we can write the quantum jump (QJ) model as

$$x = G\sigma\sqrt{T}(1 + P\sqrt{2}), \tag{6.18}$$

where G is Gaussian and P is drawn from a Poisson distribution with rate constant $\lambda = 0.5$. The model applies to price change over a period, but we can appoximate the daily log price change over the period by using the same equation scaled to one day. A subtle difference between this model and the calibrated MJD model is that the latter involves two Gaussian terms, along with the Poisson term, so the behaviors are very close but not identical. The MJD model fits the q-distribution but does not perfectly capture q-variance. The QJ model with $\lambda = 0.5$ gives an improved fit to q-variance, and the distribution is almost the same. Equation 6.18 depends on T and so needs to be regenerated for different period lengths (this is what distinguishes it from a classical random walk); however, it is useful for graphing purposes as seen in figure 6.3.

The top panel of figure 6.4 shows how the q-distribution is composed by adding the contributions from the separate eigenstates, with only the first three states contributing significantly. Compared to a normal distribution with the same variance (bottom panel), the q-distribution has the same mean but is more sharply peaked and has fatter tails.

The q-distribution can be generated numerically using an ensemble of M independent random walks

$$R_{T,m} = \sum_{j=1}^{T} y_{j,m}, \qquad m = 1, \ldots, M, \tag{6.19}$$

where for each walk m the standard deviation is $\sigma_m = \sigma\sqrt{2n_m + 1}$, and n_m is chosen from a Poisson distribution with $\lambda = 0.5$. The ensemble can therefore be viewed as a scenario-based probabilistic forecasting technique, where the scenarios correspond to energy levels n_m. It can be checked that the ensemble average does not exhibit q-variance (the simulation lacks the dynamics of the quantum model) but instead shows a flattened version of the quadratic curve, similar but not identical to the implied volatility curve seen in the next chapter.

To be clear, the claim is not that the q-distribution can provide a perfect fit to markets—for example it doesn't do skew or bimodality, as seen with some stocks—but only that it improves on the equilibrium-based classical model and is consistent with q-variance. This is illustrated in figure 6.5 for the 350 stocks from figure 5.10, where in the lower panel, z for each stock is normalized to match the average in terms of standard deviation. Although there is some variation for individual stocks, the q-distribution is a good fit for the mean. Galton had described the normal curve as the "supreme law of Unreason" because of the way it appears as if by magic from the chaos of random processes, but what emerges from the market data, strangely enough, are the harmonics of a quantum oscillator.

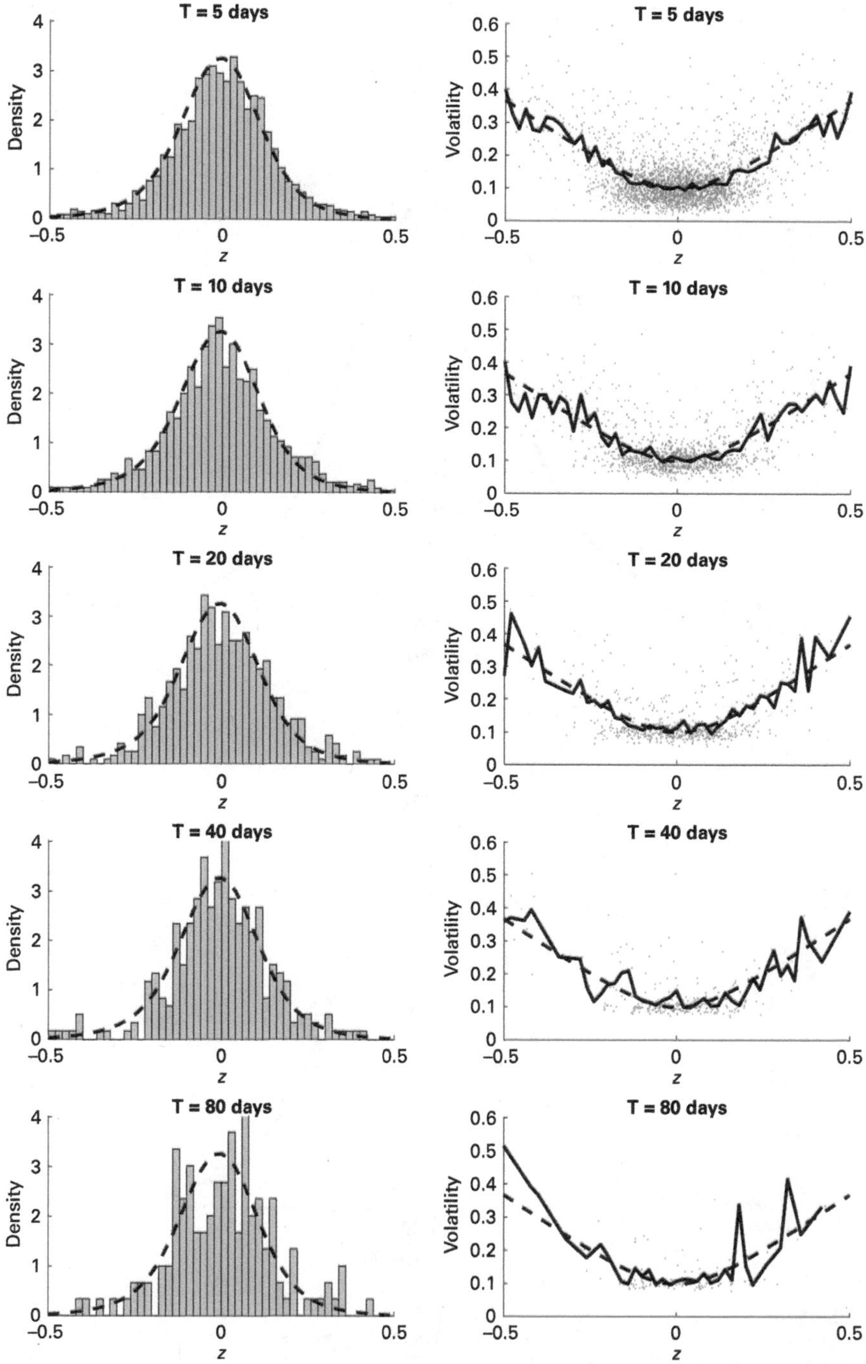

Figure 6.3
Plots showing probability density (left) and q-variance (right) for the QJ model with $\sigma = 0.1$, for nonoverlapping periods T of 1, 2, 4, 8, and 16 weeks. Compare figures 6.1 and 5.4, which show the same for the S&P 500 index.

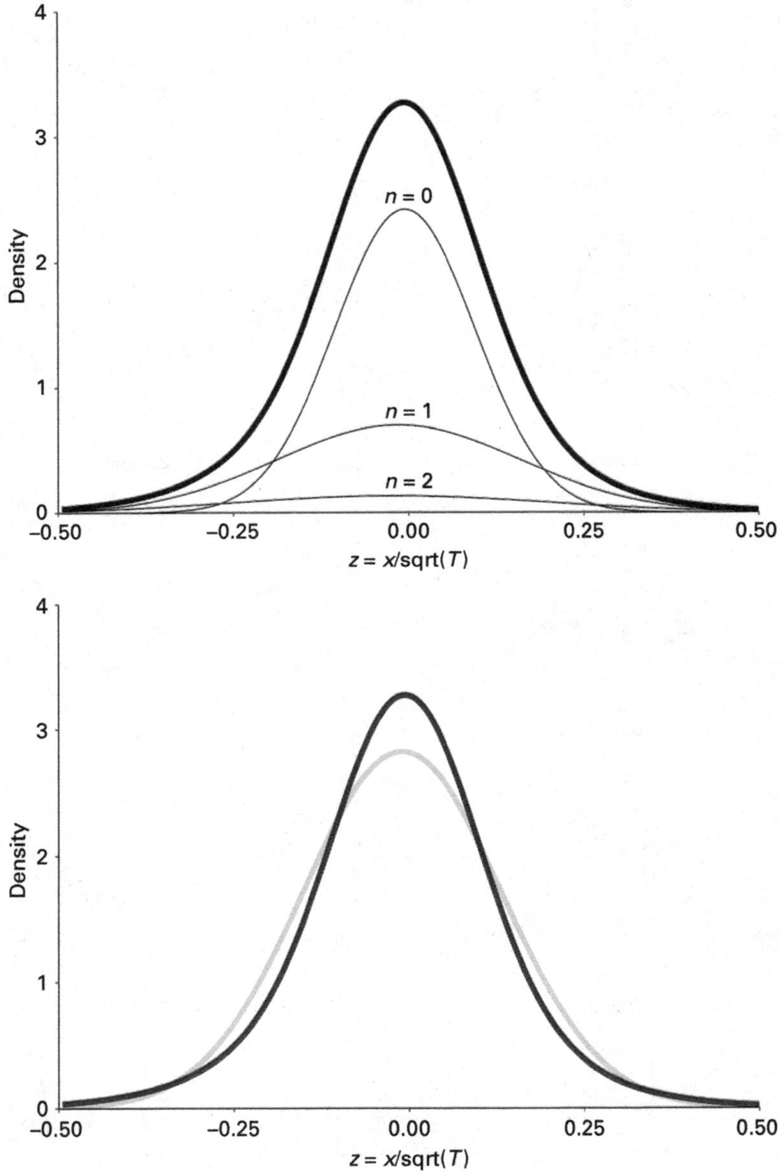

Figure 6.4
Top panel shows how the q-distribution (heavy black line) is composed of normal distributions with different standard deviations. Bottom panel compares with a normal distribution (gray), which has the same variance. The q-distribution is more peaked and has fatter tails.

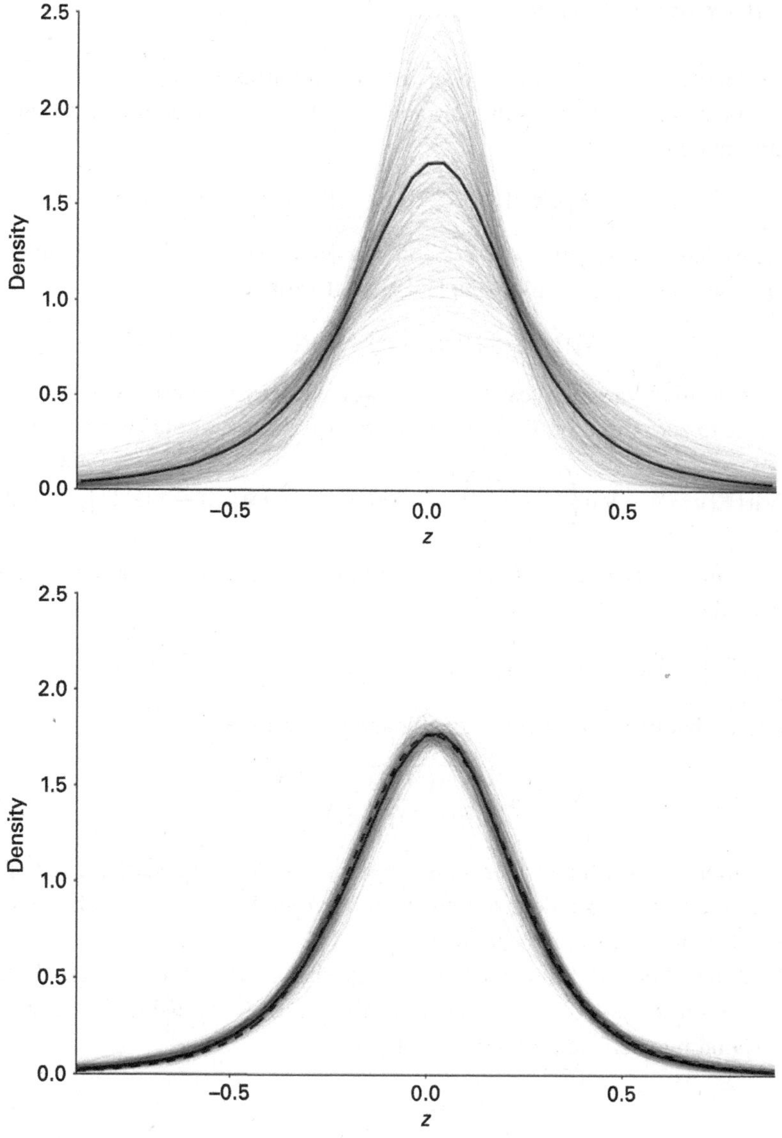

Figure 6.5
Thin gray lines in top panel show the distribution of z for the 350 stocks from figure 5.10. The mean is shown by the solid line. In the bottom panel, for each stock, z is scaled so the width of the curve matches that of the mean, but the shape is otherwise unchanged. The q-distribution (dashed line) has $\sigma = 0.185$ and a small horizontal offset of 0.038 to account for the effects of skew.

6.3 The Variance of Variance

If we denote the variance of z over a time period as $v = v(T)$ then as seen above its expected value for the QJ model is $\mathbb{E}[v] = 2\sigma^2$. The fourth moment, conditional on n, is

$$\mathbb{E}[z^4 \mid n] = 3\sigma^4 \mathbb{E}[(2n+1)^2] = 18\sigma^4 \tag{6.20}$$

where we have used $\mathbb{E}[n] = \lambda = 1/2$ and $\mathbb{E}[n^2] = \lambda^2 + \lambda = 3/4$. To compute the variance-of-variance, we apply the law of total variance,

$$\mathrm{Var}(v) = \mathbb{E}[\mathrm{Var}(v \mid z)] + \mathrm{Var}\big(\mathbb{E}[v \mid z]\big). \tag{6.21}$$

The first term $\mathbb{E}[\mathrm{Var}(v \mid z)]$ can be viewed as a measurement error which should converge to zero for large T. For the second term, from q-variance we can write

$$\mathrm{Var}\big(\mathbb{E}[v \mid z]\big) = \mathrm{Var}\left(\sigma^2 + \frac{z^2}{2}\right) = \frac{1}{4}\mathrm{Var}(z^2) = \frac{1}{4}\left(\mathbb{E}[z^4] - \mathbb{E}[z^2]^2\right). \tag{6.22}$$

Substituting the moments of the q-distribution, the variance-of-variance therefore satisfies

$$\mathrm{Var}(v) \geq \mathrm{Var}\big(\mathbb{E}[v \mid z]\big) = \frac{1}{4}\left(18\sigma^4 - 4\sigma^4\right) = 3.5\sigma^4. \tag{6.23}$$

It follows that the dimensionless coefficient of variation

$$\mathrm{CV}(T) \equiv \frac{\sqrt{\mathrm{Var}(v(T))}}{\mathbb{E}[v(T)]} \geq \sqrt{\frac{3.5}{4}} \approxeq 0.94 \tag{6.24}$$

has a lower bound which is constant across time scales. The variance $v(T)$ for the QJ model therefore does not concentrate around its mean as T increases, and no law of large numbers applies.

This lower bound for the coefficient is shown as the horizontal dotted line in figure 6.6. A similar calculation for the BSM model shows that the corresponding coefficient of variation is given by

$$\mathrm{CV}(T) = \sqrt{\frac{2}{T}}, \tag{6.25}$$

where here T is the number of days, which appears as the downwards-sloping dotted line in the log-log axes. The variance-of-variance in this case purely reflects measurement error of an underlying stable quantity, and so approaches zero for longer periods.

The coefficient for the MJD model (dashed line) has a higher initial value than the random walk, but follows the same trajectory. The coefficient for the

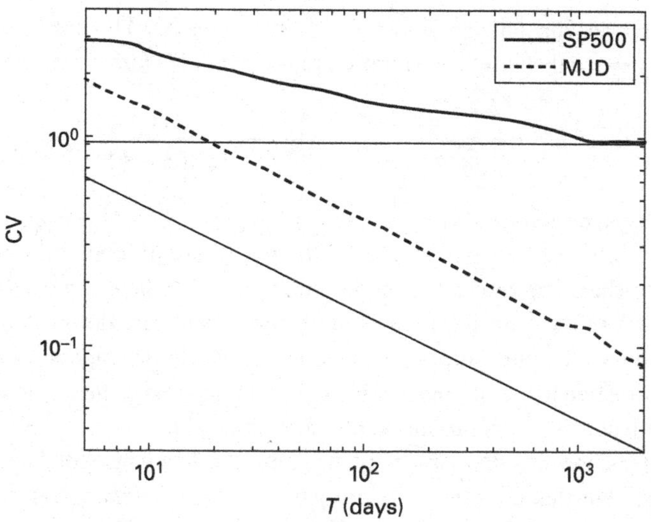

Figure 6.6
Solid line shows the coefficient of variation CV(T) for the S&P 500 index 1927–2025, for periods T of 5 to 1000 days. Dashed line is the MJD model, horizontal dotted line is the lower bound from the QJ model, downwards-sloping dotted line is the BSM random walk case.

S&P 500 index (solid line) is higher still but approaches the QJ model for large T, consistent with equation 6.24.

More sophisticated models of volatility commonly used in quantitative finance extend the classical Brownian-motion model to the concept of variance. The variance over a time interval is represented as a temporal average of an underlying local variance

$$v(T) = \frac{1}{T}\int_0^T \sigma_t^2\, dt, \tag{6.26}$$

where σ_t^2 is a stationary process with finite second moment. Of course, this local variance can never be measured directly because variance is only defined over a finite time period.

If we assume that returns over a period T are conditionally Gaussian, with variance v drawn from a density $p(v)$, then applying Bayes' formula gives

$$\mathbb{E}[v \mid z] = \frac{\int_0^\infty v p(z \mid v) p(v)\, dv}{\int_0^\infty p(z \mid v) p(v)\, dv} = \frac{\int_0^\infty v^{1/2} e^{-z^2/(2v)} p(v)\, dv}{\int_0^\infty v^{-1/2} e^{-z^2/(2v)} p(v)\, dv}. \tag{6.27}$$

If $p(v)$ decays exponentially or faster, then $\mathbb{E}[v \mid z]$ grows subquadratically in z, and exact q-variance cannot hold. Assume though that the density of v has a regularly varying tail, so $p(v) \sim Cv^{-1-\alpha}$ as $v \to \infty$. For $z \neq 0$, changing variables $v = z^2 u$ then yields quadratic growth $\mathbb{E}[v \mid z] \sim k(\alpha)\, z^2$ where

$$k(\alpha) = \frac{\int_0^\infty u^{-\alpha-1/2} e^{-1/(2u)}\, du}{\int_0^\infty u^{-\alpha-3/2} e^{-1/(2u)}\, du} = \frac{1}{2(\alpha - \frac{1}{2})}. \tag{6.28}$$

Exact q-variance requires $k(\alpha) = 1/2$, implying $\alpha = 3/2$. However, for a tail $p(v) \sim Cv^{-1-\alpha}$, the second moment $\mathbb{E}[v^2]$ is finite if and only if $\alpha > 2$. Q-variance therefore forces the model into a regime where the coefficient of variation $\mathrm{CV}(T)$ diverges. Averages at all time scales are dominated by rare volatility bursts. Or put another way, q-variance makes such models blow up (in fact this is related to the 'moment explosions' studied in the stochastic volatility literature, where a model produces infinite moments[8]).

Of course it is always possible to fit data after-the-fact when you have enough parameters; but this does help explain why the 2025 *Wilmott* magazine challenge, to match q-variance using a classical continuous-time model with no more than three parameters, failed to produce a winning candidate.[9] Several of the entries attempted to fit the q-variance curve by drawing variance from an inverse-gamma distribution with shape factor 3/2, in order to explicitly match the $\alpha = 3/2$ power-law requirement for the variance process; however the resulting models were unstable and did not converge over reasonable time scales.

The relative constancy of $\mathrm{CV}(T)$ across time scales seen in stock market data also provides a structural explanation for the empirical phenomenon of volatility clustering. Because variance does not self-average, periods of high or low volatility persist under aggregation: a high-variance window is statistically likely to contain subwindows that are also high variance. Clustering therefore arises not from slow mean reversion of an underlying volatility process, or from some kind of fractal pathway process, but from the scale-invariant fluctuations of $v(T)$ itself.[10]

6.4 Summary

In this chapter, we motivated the QJ model of price change by comparing it with a suitably calibrated version of the MJD model from 1976. For any given T, the q-distribution equation 6.15 is just the MJD distribution equation 6.4 with a particular choice of parameters. Put another way, the model log price change distributions agree after the MJD model has been calibrated to fit the empirical data—in particular, q-variance. It might therefore seem that these are just two versions of the same thing; however, their underlying structures are completely different. The MJD model is based on the random walk idea that as time flows forward, price is subject to a sequence of perturbations and is solved numerically by discretizing in time. Equation 6.15, however, treats the time period T as a whole and instead features a discrete number of transactons. The BSM model, meanwhile, can be made to agree with data if we recalibrate the "constant" volatility to give the correct answer for any situation (hence, the implied volatility curve, discussed below), but then the same could be said of just about any model.

If the BSM model is a zero-order approximation to market dynamics that assumes equilibrium and constant volatility, then the QJ model is a first-order approximation that allows for imbalance and assumes a linear restoring force acting on probability. The constraints imposed by q-variance and the oscillator model mean that the only parameters are a drift rate μ and a base volatility σ, which are the same as for the classical case, although as discussed further below, their interpretation is different.

The q-distribution for price change was derived by summing the contributions of transactons over a complete period T in a manner that is consistent with q-variance. This property, in turn, is described by the equation relating volatility and displacement for a quantum harmonic oscillator. Volatility is treated not as a process, but as a measurement. Just as q-variance appears to be a newly discovered property, it also seems that the q-distribution has not previously been used in finance, probably because, although it may offer a good fit to data over a range of timescales, it again doesn't fit with the classical random walk picture. (When scale-invariant distributions are used in finance, they typically take the form of stable Lévy processes such as a Cauchy process, which has fat tails but also undefined variance.[11])

Finally, the fact that the q-distribution is expressed in terms of z, is constant in period T, and is consistent with the bid–ask spread also gives us a very different perspective on the nature of volatility. Rather than being caused by investor reactions to "news" as in the efficient market picture, volatility when measured over a day, month, or year is essentially a reflection of underlying uncertainty as measured by the gap in perceived value between a buyer and a seller— almost as if time is standing still (a different kind of infinite moment). In the next chapter, we show how the same fundamental uncertainty manifests itself in the pricing of options.

7

Option Pricing

After the discovery of Bachelier's work there suddenly came to the mind of all the eager workers the notion of what the Holy Grail was. There was the next step needed. It was to get the perfect formula to evaluate and to price options.
—Paul Samuelson, quoted in the 1999 BBC film *The Midas Formula*

It's only a model.
—Monty Python and the Holy Grail, 1975

The question of how to price financial options is one of the oldest in finance. As mentioned in the first chapter, Bachelier argued in his 1900 doctoral thesis that prices followed what we now call a random walk, with an average return that he took to be zero. The price of an option therefore depended only on the variability of the stock's price, which he referred to as its "nervousness" (today, we call it the volatility). In this chapter, we explain why option prices exhibit a nervous smile.

7.1 Black-Scholes and the Holy Grail

Bachelier's approach was ahead of its time and initially received little attention. However, some sixty years later, Samuelson rediscovered it and, hoping it would point the way to what he called the "Holy Grail" of option pricing, arranged for a translation.

The translator of the paper was the University of Chicago doctoral student Arthur James Boness, who also developed his own model.[1] Following Samuelson, he replaced price with its logarithm, so price changes were proportional and price itself always remained positive.

The expected payout from a call option with expiration after a period T is given by

$$C = \langle \max(S-K,0) \rangle = \int_{S=K}^{\infty} (S-K) f(S) dS, \tag{7.1}$$

where $f(S)$ is the probability density of price S after time T. If the stock price followed a lognormal process with expected rate of return μ and volatility σ (we assume for simplicity that there are no dividends), then Boness calculated that the correct price of the call option, normalized by the share price S, was

$$C_B(\mu, \sigma, T, S, K) = F(h) - \frac{K}{S} e^{-\mu T} F(h - \sigma\sqrt{T}), \tag{7.2}$$

where T is time to expiry, K is the strike price, S is the current value of the stock, F is the cumulative normal distribution, and

$$h = \frac{-\log(\frac{K}{S}) + (\mu + \frac{1}{2}\sigma^2)T}{\sigma\sqrt{T}}. \tag{7.3}$$

This formula is simply the expected payout from a call option whose underlying stock follows a lognormal price distribution. The result was therefore similar to that of Bachelier except that it involved log price instead of price, and the rate of return μ was an estimated constant instead of being zero.

Since the option price depended on a subjective growth estimate, the model was still not a completely objective formula, which is why, as Gatarek (2023) observed, it "is mentioned only in books about history of finance." The key step was taken in 1973 with the publication of the BSM model. Its elegant proof relied on the argument that by holding the option and constantly buying and selling units of the underlying stock in response to price changes, one can construct a risk-free portfolio whose return—according to a no-arbitrage assumption—had to equal the risk-free rate r that could be obtained on something like a Treasury bond (although, of course, bonds are not really zero risk, and their price can fluctuate in a crisis). A consequence was that, as with Bachelier, the expected return μ dropped out of the equation—but instead of being zero, it was replaced by r.

The BSM model met with immediate success and helped kick off an explosive growth in options trading. Ross (1987) described it as "the most successful theory not only in finance, but in all of economics." In his 1990 book *Continuous-Time Finance*, Merton wrote that the model, "virtually on the day it was published, brought the field to closure," while in the forward, Samuelson added that "one of our most elegant and complex sectors of economic analysis—the modern theory of finance—is confirmed daily by millions of statistical observations." Rubinstein (1994) called it "the most widely used formula, with embedded probabilities, in human history." The Nobel Prize Committee—who awarded Black and Scholes their prize in 1997—agreed that "thousands of traders and investors now use this formula every day to value stock options in markets throughout the world." Bodie (1999) compared its discovery to that of DNA in the way that the latter "gave birth to a new field of immense practical importance—genetic engineering," while BSM "gave birth to the important field of financial engineering."[2]

These are heady accolades for what is essentially a zero-order model based on equilibrium and a particular choice for the growth rate. But as with many successful products—say, Coca Cola—the real value lies less in the formula than in the story it told.

7.2 No Risk

The great attraction of the BSM model, or rather its proof, lies in the hedging process that in theory could, according to Merton, "eliminate all of the risk" by substituting a subjective and uncertain estimate (μ) with an objective measurement (r).[3] Or as economist Stan Jonas told the BBC in 1999, "Up until the time that they came up with their insight, the world was full of uncertainty and risk, uncontrollable and un-analyzable. And then in a moment of tremendous clarity they realized that two risky positions taken together can effectively eliminate risk itself."[4]

The net result for option pricing was exactly the same as the Boness model with $\mu = r$. One could therefore come to the same conclusion more simply by saying that the option price was the expected payout, subject to the assumption that the relevant drift rate was the risk-free one. However, this would miss the point, which was to prove that μ and r are the same by constructing a risk-free portfolio. As Simons (1997) wrote, "The Black-Scholes model is different from a statistical model. It is an analytical formula" with which in theory, "one can determine the value of the option exactly." And by putting options trading onto an apparently objective and rational basis, the result was to effectively transform options trading from something akin to gambling to a scientific form of risk management.

As a simple demonstration of the hedging method, suppose that instead of an option on a stock, a dealer sells a derivative contract whose value D_T at expiration T is equal to the price S_T at that time of one unit of the stock. If the initial price of the contract is D_0, then the risk to the dealer is that the stock price will go up, so to hedge against that, he buys a unit of stock himself. At time T, he can sell that for the price $D_T = S_T$, so there is no risk.

The dealer holds a portfolio that is short one certificate, long one unit of stock, and totally risk free for an initial cost of $S_0 - D_0$. It therefore has the same value as another portfolio consisting of a deposit of the same initial amount in a risk-free account. The final value of the first portfolio (stock minus option) at time T is $S_T - D_T = 0$, whereas the final value of the second portfolio (deposit account) is $e^{rT}(S_0 - D_0)$. Since these should be equal, it follows that $e^{rT}(S_0 - D_0) = 0$ and $S_0 = D_0$. However, $D_T = S_T = e^{rT} S_0$. In other words, the value of a contract whose payout D_T depends on a random variable S_T can be priced in a deterministic fashion by hedging the risk away and comparing with a risk-free account.

Of course, this is a trivial example; however, it does show how with hedging, there is no need to account for subjective ideas about whether the value of the stock is going to increase or decrease over the time period. You just need to balance the portfolio so that the price changes cancel out. When the derivative D is an option, the value is a nonlinear function of the stock price, which makes the solution more complicated. As the price evolves in time, the balance between the stock and the option in the risk-free portfolio has to be constantly adjusted. If the stock price changes by one dollar, then it can be checked that the option price changes by Δ_t dollars, where

$$\Delta_t = \frac{\partial D_t}{\partial S_t} = F(h). \tag{7.4}$$

At any time t, the hedged portfolio is therefore $\Delta_t S_t - D_t$.

Valuing this portfolio and equating to the risk-free rate is one way to derive the BSM theorem. As a concrete example of how it can be applied, consider a one-year at-the-money call option (so the strike price K equals the current stock price S) where the risk-free rate is zero and the volatility is $\sigma = 0.2$. Then equation 7.3 gives $h = \sigma/2 = 0.1$, so $\Delta_t = F(h) = 0.54$. This might explain why Nelson (1904) wrote, long before BSM, that "Sellers of options in London as a result of long experience, if they sell a Call, straightway buy half the stock against which the Call is sold; or if a Put is sold; they sell half the stock immediately."[5]

Returning though to the simple example of buying a certificate tied to the value of a stock, it is clear that the whole problem is unrealistic. For one thing, why would someone buy a derivative whose payout is equal to that of the stock? Wouldn't it be simpler just to buy the stock? And why would the dealer go to the effort of offering this contract if the return is the same as the risk-free rate? What would the point be?

The answer, of course, is that the trader who sets up the contract and the client who purchases it are only doing so because they hope to make money on the deal. And the only way that they can both think this at the same time is if there is uncertainty about the value of the stock. The client buying the certificate thinks the price will go up, so the certificate will be worth more than they paid, whereas the dealer selling it thinks its value will go down.

Obviously, this is a contrived situation, but for the case with options, a similar logic applies. Why would a dealer sell an option and then go through the rigamarole of dynamic hedging only to recover the risk-free rate? What about transaction costs or the overhead for selling and maintaining the contract in the first place? Again, the reason is that the seller and purchaser have different views on the future price of the asset. In other words, the market for derivatives only exists in the first place because of uncertainty.

With the quantum model, we can make this a little more precise. Recall that in the oscillator model, the volatility reflects the uncertainty that is measured by the bid–ask spread (see also equation 5.1). Assuming that transaction costs are zero is the same as assuming that uncertainty, and therefore volatility, are also zero.

As shown by q-variance, volatility is also related to price change over a period, and therefore drift. We therefore can't make the assumption that volatility is constant as in the Black-Scholes model, or even amenable to a continuous-time approach. Equation 6.1 for Brownian price change states that $dS = \mu S dt + \sigma S dX$, but what is the value of σ?

Of course, hedging is still useful as a risk management tool; you just can't build a naive mathematical proof around it. This points to a larger problem, which is that classical quantitative finance lives in a kind of Platonic world where such considerations don't come into play. Models are often justified by saying that they represent a simplified case that captures the main properties. Things like transaction costs are details that can be ignored. An analogy is often made with physics, where the laws of motion can be used to compute, say, the arc of a projectile with effects such as friction and air resistance added in later if necessary. However, modeling options is more like flying a kite; you can't ignore the air because that is the very thing keeping it aloft.

7.3 Might as Well Jump

Of course, although models may live in a Platonic world, traders have long been aware that the real world does not conform perfectly to models—and they have to make a living. Just as empirical studies showed that price changes were not perfectly lognormal, so the prices actually paid for options therefore departed from the BSM model. The implied volatility, defined as the number that gives the observed price when used as input to the BSM model, turned out to depend on the strike price K. When implied volatility was plotted against strike price, it tended to follow a smile shape, which seemed inconsistent with the classical model.

This led to a number of refined models of volatility,[6] including that based on Merton's jump diffusion. As described in the previous chapter, the price change distribution given by equation 6.4 for the MJD model is a Poisson-weighted sum of normal distributions. It therefore follows that the expected value of a call option is the Poisson-weighted sum of the corresponding BSM prices for each term:

$$C_{MJD}(r,\sigma,\lambda,\delta,T,S,K)=\sum_{n=0}^{\infty} w_n(\lambda T)C_{BSM}(r,\sigma_n,T,S,K), \qquad (7.5)$$

where $C_{BSM}(r,\sigma_n,T,S,K)$ is the BSM price with volatility $\sigma_n=\sqrt{\sigma T+\delta^2 n}$.[7]

Compared with the BSM model, the MJD model had a number of disadvantages, which limited its use: It involved more parameters, whose values can be sensitive to noise in the data; it was harder to solve numerically (less of a problem today); and finally, the existence of jumps in the underlying meant that it was impossible to do perfect risk-free hedging even in theory.[8] As discussed already, the hedging argument also does not apply in the quantum framework (indeed, it is completely incompatible), but as with the MJD model, or the original Boness model, for that matter, we can still determine the appropriate price of an option based on expected payout, conditional on a particular choice of parameters. The corresponding option price in the quantum jump (QJ) model is then

$$C_{QJ}(\mu,\sigma,\epsilon,T,S,K)=\max\left(\sum_{n=0}^{\infty} w_n C_{BSM}(\mu,\sigma_n,T,S,K),\epsilon\right), \qquad (7.6)$$

where now $\sigma_n=\sigma\sqrt{1+2n}$, $w_n=(\sqrt{e}\,2^n n!)^{-1}$ is the Poisson weighting with rate parameter $\lambda=0.5$, and we have included a minimum cost for an option of ϵ, which, as discussed below, becomes relevant for extreme strikes.

This model can therefore be described as an ensemble (or many-worlds, if you like) model, where option prices are determined by a convex averaging over scenarios characterised by different (but constant) volatilities σ_n. (Since the no-arbitrage arguments behind Black-Scholes are robust to this averaging, the same arguments could apply in theory to the quantum model, were it not for that bid-ask spread.) Classical models assume that volatility is described by some kind of dynamic process, which in the case of Black-Scholes is constant. Unlike price, however, the volatility process cannot be fully hedged, and the quantum model simply makes this explicit. Note also that more complicated options, such as barrier options where payoff depends on whether the price of the underlying asset reaches a predetermined level at any point during the life of the option contract, can be modeled numerically using the ensemble approach described by equation 6.19.

Again, whether one uses the MJD model or the QJ model to compute option prices may seem to be irrelevant since the two agree once the former is recalibrated to fit the data for a particular period T. What counts is the probability distribution. However, there are two important differences. One is that in the MJD model, the drift parameter is usually set equal to the risk-free rate r, following the BSM model. In the QJ model, the drift μ is a free parameter, which is not generally equal to the risk-free rate. The second difference is that the QJ model incorporates the scaling $z = x/\sqrt{T}$, which again is inconsistent with the classical approach but becomes important as seen below (note x is now not corrected for drift as it was in chapter 5 to plot q-variance).

7.4 Model-Implied Volatility

We can simplify equation 7.6 by asking what volatility should be used in the BSM model to achieve the same result. This is like the concept of implied volatility, with the difference that instead of estimating it from market prices, we estimate it from the q-distribution (equation 6.15). We first compute the payout from call or put options given this theoretical distribution. The cost of the option is then set to the expected payout, or the small minimal cost ϵ that applies at extreme strikes. We then derive the implied volatility for each strike. This can be done numerically or can be approximated using a Taylor expansion around the origin. The latter gives

$$\sigma_q^2 = 2q^2\sigma^2 + (1 - q^2)z^2, \tag{7.7}$$

where again, $z = x/\sqrt{T}$, but the log price change x is now interpreted as log moneyness $x = \log K/S$, and

$$q = \frac{1}{\sqrt{2}} \sum_{n=0}^{\infty} w_n \sqrt{2n+1} = \frac{1}{\sqrt{2e}} \sum_{n=0}^{\infty} (2^n n!)^{-1} \sqrt{2n+1} \approxeq 0.95. \tag{7.8}$$

The proof is given below. A similar calculation for the MJD model modifies this constant to a function of period:

$$q_M = \frac{1}{\sqrt{2}} \sum_{n=0}^{\infty} w_n(\lambda T) \sqrt{\delta^2 n/T + 1}. \tag{7.9}$$

The quantum option pricing model can therefore be expressed approximately as

$$C_{QJ}(\mu, \sigma, \epsilon, T, S, K) \approxeq C_{BSM}(\mu, \sigma_q, T, S, K), \tag{7.10}$$

where again, μ is an estimated drift rate, and the volatility σ_q is given by equation 7.7 and so is strike dependent. (The MJD version sets $q = q_M$.)

Finally, the implied volatility computed above is the volatility that matches expected payouts. It can be viewed as a flattened version of the q-variance curve equation 7.6, which has the same form as equation 8 but with $q = 1/\sqrt{2}$, so we can think of it as q-variance for options (loosely speaking, option payouts integrate over the probability density, which explains the flattening effect). Of course, this "quantum-implied volatility" is not the same as the choices of options traders, so it is interesting to compare the two.

Figure 7.1 compares the model with actual implied volatility for a range of SPY options over a six-month period, with times to expiry of one, two, four, eight, sixteen, and thirty-two weeks (compare figure 5.4). The curves for different periods are very similar, again suggesting that a single model should be used for all. Although the model captures the main features, it is not a perfect match to the implied volatility used by traders. However, the aim of the model is not to perfectly fit the data—any fitting routine can do that without telling you anything new—but to capture the key properties using a minimal set of parameters. Also, as discussed further in the next few chapters, there is no reason (efficient market notions aside) to expect that the prices paid by traders perfectly reflect their expected payout. In other words, the model suggests places where there are opportunities for arbitrage. The main point, though, is that the implied volatility smile can be largely explained by saying that it reflects an attempt by traders to bring the BSM model into alignment with the observed properties of volatility.

Although the difference between the QJ and MJD distributions in figure 6.1 may seem relatively subtle, the two models give very different answers when used to estimate implied volatility. The quantum model accurately reflects the scaling of implied volatility with expiration time. In contrast, the MJD model becomes increasingly Gaussian in behavior, so the implied volatility at longer timescales is essentially flat. The BSM approach, of course, would model this curve as a straight line with a single strike-independent volatility. Any methods that use the BSM framework to estimate volatility will therefore be attempting to fit a quadratic variance with a constant, which, as discussed later, can lead to problems.

7.5 The Quantum Smile

We now derive the equation for the smile curve given above. The expected payout from an option with expiration after a period T can again be written as

$$C = \langle \max(S-K,0) \rangle = \int_{S=K}^{\infty} (S-K) f(S) dS, \tag{7.11}$$

where $f(S)$ is the probability density of price S after time T. Taking the derivative with respect to strike K gives

$$\frac{dC}{dK} = \int_{S=K}^{\infty} \frac{d}{dK}(S-K) f(S) dS \tag{7.12}$$

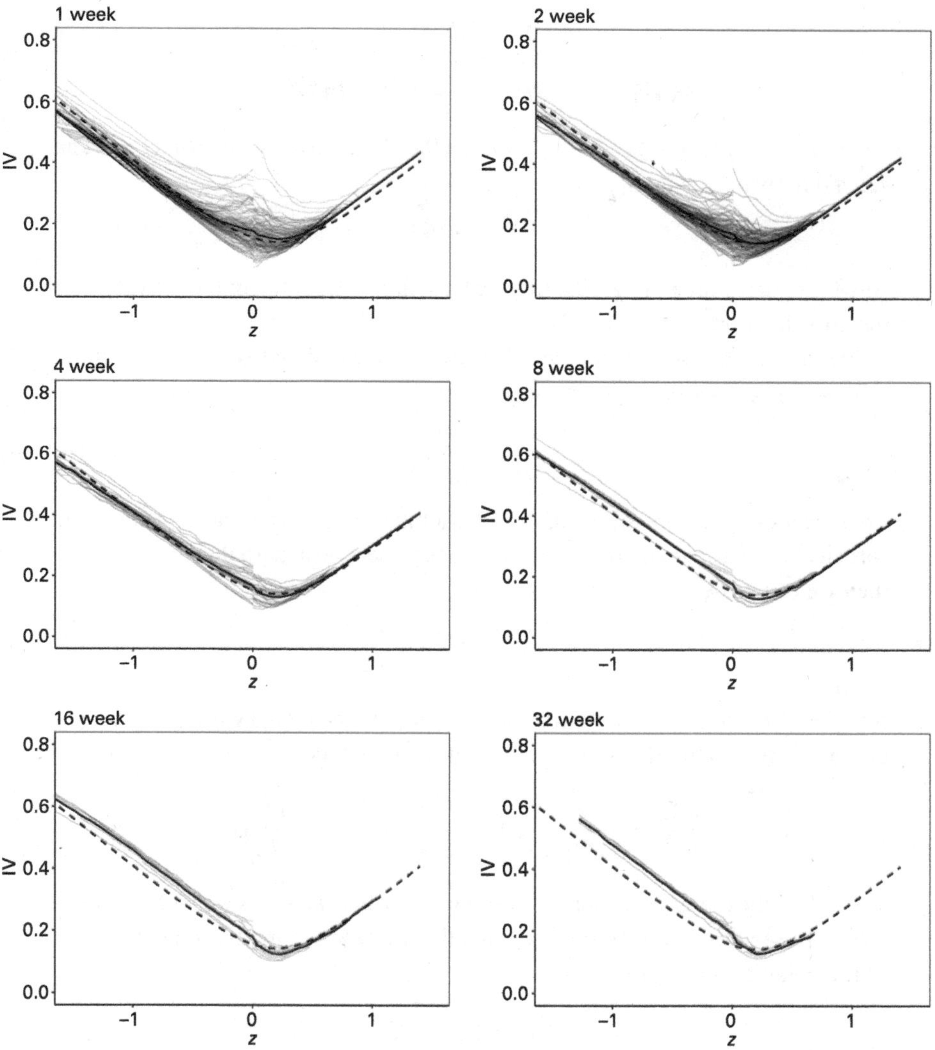

Figure 7.1
Gray lines show implied volatility for SPY options purchased over the first six months of 2023, with expirations of one, two, four, eight, sixteen, and thirty-two weeks. Put options are used for $z \leq 0$, and call options are used for $z > 0$. The model given by equation 7.7 (dashed line) with a horizontal offset of 0.2 serves as a good first-order approximation to the average implied volatility (black) and correctly captures the scaling with time. The MJD version with $q = q_M$ (not shown) agrees with the quantum model at one week, but the distribution is nearly normal at thirty-two weeks, so the implied volatility is nearly flat.

$$= -\int_{S=K}^{\infty} f(S)dS \tag{7.13}$$

$$= -f(S > K) = F(K) - 1, \tag{7.14}$$

where $F(K) = f(S \leq K) = 1 - f(S > K)$ is the cumulative density function. The second derivative is then

$$\frac{d^2C}{dK^2} = f(K), \tag{7.15}$$

so we can determine the probability density function knowing the curvature of the cost function.

For simplicity, we will assume that price is normalized so $S = 1$. Defining $z = \log(K)/\sqrt{T}$ as above, we have

$$\frac{dz}{dK} = \frac{1}{K\sqrt{T}}. \tag{7.16}$$

Let σ_z represent the volatility curve that is a function of z. If we assume the same form as for the usual volatility smile, with the linear term zero due to symmetry, then we can write

$$\sigma_z = \left(\sigma^2 + \frac{Y^2 z^2}{2}\right)^{\frac{1}{2}}. \tag{7.17}$$

Now let $C(K)$ be the cost function for a call option associated with this volatility curve. We first claim that the curvature of the cost function is given by

$$\frac{d^2C}{dK^2} = \frac{1}{\sigma\sqrt{2\pi T}}\left(1 + \frac{Y^2}{2}\right) = f_0\left(1 + \frac{Y^2}{2}\right), \tag{7.18}$$

where f_0 is the maximum value of a normal distribution with standard deviation $\sigma\sqrt{T}$. To see this, it can be checked that the first and second partial derivatives of the volatility curve are

$$\frac{\partial \sigma_z}{\partial K} = \frac{Y^2 z}{2K\sigma_z\sqrt{T}} \tag{7.19}$$

and

$$\frac{\partial^2 \sigma_z}{\partial K^2} = \frac{Y^2}{2K^2\sqrt{T}}\left(-\sigma_z^{-3}\frac{Yz^2}{2\sqrt{T}} + \sigma_z^{-1}\left(\frac{1}{\sqrt{T}} - z\right)\right), \tag{7.20}$$

where we have used

$$\frac{\partial}{\partial K}\left(\frac{z}{K}\right) = \frac{1}{K^2}\left(\frac{1}{\sqrt{T}} - z\right). \tag{7.21}$$

Evaluating at $K=1$ so $z=0$ and $\sigma_z=\sigma$ gives

$$\frac{\partial^2\sigma_z}{\partial K^2}=\frac{Y^2}{2\sigma T}. \tag{7.22}$$

Now, for $C(K)$ defined again as the cost of a call option at strike K, we have

$$\frac{dC}{dK}=\frac{\partial C}{\partial K}+\frac{\partial C}{\partial \sigma_z}\frac{\partial \sigma_z}{\partial K}. \tag{7.23}$$

Taking the derivative again and using the product rule for the second term gives

$$\frac{d^2C}{dK^2}=\frac{\partial}{\partial K}\left(\frac{\partial C}{\partial K}+\frac{\partial C}{\partial \sigma_z}\frac{\partial \sigma_z}{\partial K}\right)+\frac{\partial}{\partial \sigma_z}\left(\frac{\partial C}{\partial K}+\frac{\partial C}{\partial \sigma_z}\frac{\partial \sigma_z}{\partial K}\right)\frac{\partial \sigma_z}{\partial K}. \tag{7.24}$$

When evaluated at the minimum point, we have $\partial\sigma_z/\partial K=0$, so the second term is zero, and the first term is

$$\frac{d^2C}{dK^2}=\frac{\partial^2 C}{\partial K^2}+\frac{\partial^2 C}{\partial K\partial\sigma_z}\frac{\partial \sigma_z}{\partial K}+\frac{\partial C}{\partial \sigma_z}\frac{\partial^2 \sigma_z}{\partial K^2}=\frac{\partial^2 C}{\partial K^2}+\frac{\partial C}{\partial \sigma_z}\frac{\partial^2 \sigma_z}{\partial K^2}. \tag{7.25}$$

The term $\partial C/\partial\sigma_z$ is known as vega and at $z=0$ is given by

$$\frac{\partial C}{\partial \sigma_z}=\sqrt{\frac{T}{2\pi}}\exp\left(\frac{-\sigma^2 T}{8}\right)\approx\sqrt{\frac{T}{2\pi}}, \tag{7.26}$$

and similarly, it can be checked that

$$\frac{\partial^2 C}{\partial K^2}=\frac{1}{\sigma}\sqrt{\frac{1}{2\pi T}}\exp\left(\frac{-\sigma^2 T}{8}\right)\approx\frac{1}{\sigma}\sqrt{\frac{1}{2\pi T}}. \tag{7.27}$$

Using this and the formula for $\partial^2\sigma_z/\partial K^2$ from above, we obtain

$$\frac{d^2C}{dK^2}=\frac{\partial^2 C}{\partial K^2}+\frac{\partial C}{\partial \sigma_z}\frac{\partial^2 \sigma_z}{\partial K^2} \tag{7.28}$$

$$\approx\frac{1}{\sigma}\sqrt{\frac{1}{2\pi T}}+\sqrt{\frac{T}{2\pi}}\frac{Y^2}{2\sigma T} \tag{7.29}$$

$$=\frac{1}{\sigma\sqrt{2\pi T}}\left(1+\frac{Y^2}{2}\right) \tag{7.30}$$

$$=f_0\left(1+\frac{Y^2}{2}\right), \tag{7.31}$$

where again, f_0 is the maximum value of a normal distribution with standard deviation $\sigma\sqrt{T}$. It follows that if the volatility is given by the smile curve

σ_z, then the curvature of the associated cost function is boosted by a factor $1+Y^2/2$, as claimed.

The next step is to find the volatility for which a normal distribution gives the same expected payout as for the quantum model (i.e., the model-implied volatility). The expected payout for a lognormally distributed price change with standard deviation $\Sigma=\sqrt{2}\sigma$ (so equal to that of the quantum model) is approximately equal to

$$C_0=\int_0^\infty zf(z)dz=\frac{\Sigma}{\sqrt{2\pi}}=\frac{\sigma}{\sqrt{\pi}}, \tag{7.32}$$

where $f(z)$ is the normal distribution with standard deviation Σ (more correctly, we should express the payout in terms of the normalized strike price $K=e^x$, but the answers are nearly identical). The expected payout from the q-distribution, however, is

$$C_q=\sum_{n=0}^\infty w_n\frac{\sigma_n}{\sqrt{2\pi}}=\frac{\sigma}{\sqrt{2\pi}}\sum_{n=0}^\infty w_n\sqrt{2n+1}=qC_0, \tag{7.33}$$

where

$$q=\frac{1}{\sqrt{2}}\sum_{n=0}^\infty w_n\sqrt{2n+1}\approxeq 0.95. \tag{7.34}$$

The model-implied volatility at $z=0$ for the q-distribution is therefore equal to $q\Sigma=q\sqrt{2}\sigma$. The peak probability density associated with this normal distribution is $f_0/(q\sqrt{2})$.

The peak of the probability density for the q-distribution is

$$f_q=\sum_{n=0}^\infty w_n\frac{1}{\sigma_n\sqrt{2\pi T}}=\frac{1}{\sigma\sqrt{2\pi T}}\sum_{n=0}^\infty w_n\frac{1}{\sqrt{2n+1}}=pf_0, \tag{7.35}$$

where

$$p=\sum_{n=0}^\infty w_n\frac{1}{\sqrt{2n+1}}\approxeq 0.821. \tag{7.36}$$

To sum up, the normal distribution that matches the quantum payout at $z=0$ has a cost function curvature equal to $f_0/(q\sqrt{2})$, whereas the q-distribution has curvature pf_0. In order for a cost function with the smile curve to match, we need to boost the volatility by a factor equal to the ratio of these, which is $pq\sqrt{2}$. We therefore set

$$1+\frac{Y^2}{2}=pq\sqrt{2}\approxeq 2-q^2, \tag{7.37}$$

where we have used $q^2 + pq\sqrt{2} \approxeq 2$, which can be checked numerically.[9] The equation for the payout-implied volatility as a function of z is therefore

$$\sigma_z^2 \approxeq q^2 2\sigma^2 + (1 - q^2)z^2 \approxeq 1.8\sigma^2 + 0.10z^2. \tag{7.38}$$

The top panel of figure 7.2 shows the curve σ_z (dashed) compared with the implied volatility calculated directly from the q-distribution (black). The dashed line, which is based on a second-order approximation, is accurate in a range of about $\pm 2\sigma$. The fit improves significantly if we add a small transaction cost, which becomes important for extreme strikes, as in the lower panel where this cost is set equal to 0.0003 of the current asset price. The next chapter explains the reason for this effect, which is due to another kind of quantum—namely, the smallest charge for a contract.

7.6 Summary

The main innovation of the BSM model was that it used a hedging technique to derive the cost of an option. However, the result was equivalent to that obtained by assuming that the price change distribution is normal with a drift equal to the risk-free rate. The MJD model elaborated on this by allowing for discontinuous jumps but meant that the hedging argument no longer applied. The QJ model goes further by providing a specific alternative to the normal distribution, the q-distribution, which still only involves two parameters—the drift and the volatility—but respects q-variance.

The idea from BSM that the only growth rate that matters in option pricing is the risk-free rate is obviously deeply attractive from a theoretical perspective. The hard part of valuing an option is exactly knowing the expected return of the underlying asset, so it would be nice if you can magically delegate this job to the market for Treasury bonds.[10] However, one does suspect that reality may be more complex and uncertain.

When the physicist Richard Feynman tried in a 1963 lecture to summarize the main finding of physics in a single sentence, his answer, which echoed the Greek philosopher Democritus, was that “all things are made of atoms.”[11] In a 2025 lecture entitled “A Stylized History of Quantitative Finance,” the quantitative finance expert Emanuel Derman proposed a version for finance: “IF you can hedge away all correlated risk, AND you can then diversify over all uncorrelated risk, THEN you should expect to earn only the riskless rate. This sentence leads to modern finance.”[12]

But what if none of those things hold? (The quantum version perhaps would be “Prices emerge from transactions,” which doesn’t have quite the same ring

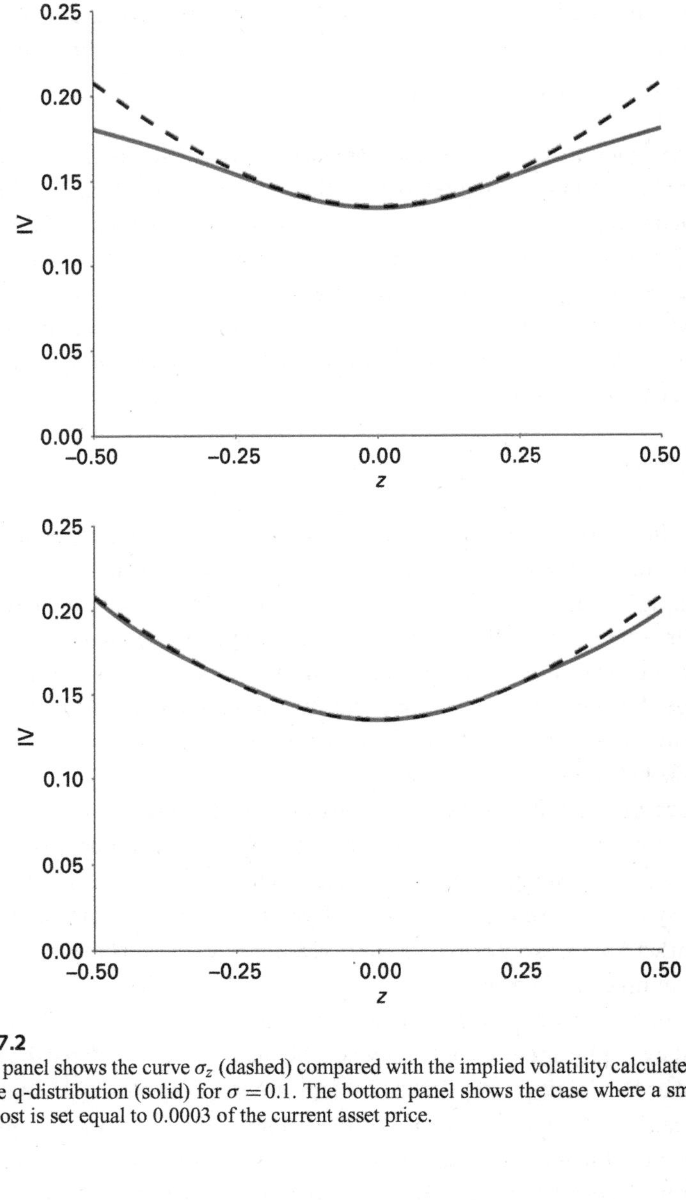

Figure 7.2
The top panel shows the curve σ_z (dashed) compared with the implied volatility calculated directly from the q-distribution (solid) for $\sigma = 0.1$. The bottom panel shows the case where a small transaction cost is set equal to 0.0003 of the current asset price.

of revolutionary genius.) The quantum model does not offer the IF/THEN determinism of classical logic, the security of engineering perfectly risk-free portfolios, or what Samuelson called the "Holy Grail" of a "perfect formula to evaluate and to price options."[13] On the bright side, it does at least get the volatility smile.

Interestingly, Derman ended his talk with a warning: "Be careful. Models often become widely embraced. The model, whose use should cause only a ripple of trading on the sea of the market, can become the sea itself. When a simplistic model is proved to be inaccurate by the behavior of the market, systemic market collapses can occur." To quantum ears, that sounds a bit like BSM and the associated equation $\mu = r$, which, as discussed in chapter 11, played a starring role in the 2007–2008 financial crisis.

Although q-variance and the q-distribution appear to be new, in the sense that they have not previously been used or reported in finance, both phenomena are pivotal to the question of implied volatility. In particular, the quantum option pricing model was derived by computing the model-implied volatility, which follows from the q-distribution, and can be viewed as a flattened version of q-variance. The next chapter shows how the same approach can be used to model and predict implied volatility surfaces over a wide range of periods and strikes.

8

Extreme Strikes

> A discovery must be, by definition, at variance with existing knowledge. During my lifetime, I made two. Both were rejected offhand by the popes of the field.
> —Albert Szent-Gyorgyi, *Dionysians and Apollonians* (1972)

> Nature loves to hide.
> —Heraclitus, *Fragment 123*

Given that the field of quantitative finance is in large part about finding ways to put a price on risk, a common question that comes up is how to price options with extreme strikes. In classical finance, the no-arbitrage condition means that the price of an option with an extreme strike price should approach zero because the chance of receiving a payout also approaches zero. For example, a put option betting that the S&P 500 index will halve in the next week should be practically free because according to random walk theory, the odds of that happening are miniscule. If the annual volatility is estimated to be 0.2, then the weekly volatility is about 0.028, so a collapse of 50 percent represents a 25-sigma event,[1] which has a probability of about one part in 10^{137}.

Obviously, that could never happen. However, in 2007, David Viniar, Goldman's chief financial officer, did complain that "We were seeing things that were 25-standard deviation moves, several days in a row," which suggests either very bad luck or a problem with the model.[2]

In quantum finance, this no-arbitrage argument does not apply, so option prices have a nonzero floor, which is also the case in actual markets. One reason is that there is always a degree of uncertainty attached to unknown events such as a freak disaster. Another is that there are transaction costs associated with arranging and maintaining the options in the first place. To account for such factors, options markets usually have a minimum cost on an option, which will typically represent a few hundredths of a percent of the underlying asset. This effect becomes important for options with strikes that are far above or below the currrent price.

8.1 Yes Arbitrage

Let C be the price of a call option for current price $S = 1$ and strike price $K = e^x$. It can then be shown[3] that

$$\lim_{x\to\infty} \frac{\log C}{x^2} = \frac{-1}{2\sigma^2 T}. \tag{8.1}$$

Setting $z = x/\sqrt{T}$, it follows that for large z,

$$\log C \approxeq \frac{-z^2}{2\sigma^2}. \tag{8.2}$$

The top panel of figure 8.1 shows this approximation for the case with $\sigma = 0.15$. The equation applies for constant σ; however, if we set

$$\sigma = mz, \tag{8.3}$$

where

$$m = \sqrt{-1/(2\log\epsilon)}, \tag{8.4}$$

and ϵ is a small constant number, then it can be checked numerically that the formula holds approximately so $C \approxeq \epsilon$. Put another way, if we set $C = \epsilon$, then the implied volatility is approximately equal to a linear function of z with slope around m.

However, the quantum model equation 7.38 states that

$$\sigma_z^2 \approxeq 1.8\sigma^2 + 0.10z^2, \tag{8.5}$$

which asymptotes to $0.10z^2$ for large z. It follows that a plot of σ_z versus z asymptotes for large $|z|$ to a line with slope

$$|m| = \sqrt{0.1} = 0.32. \tag{8.6}$$

As shown in the lower panel of figure 8.1, the costs due to a small constant amount behave in a manner similar to the quantum model at extreme strikes.

This model is inconsistent with classical bounds on implied volatility, which are based on the no-arbitrage principle. For example, a commonly cited result[4] states that the large-strike tail of implied volatility is bounded above by $\sqrt{2|x|/T}$. The quantum model, in contrast, says that the implied volatility in the wings is linear in $|z| = |x|/\sqrt{T}$, so the predicted behavior is fundamentally different.

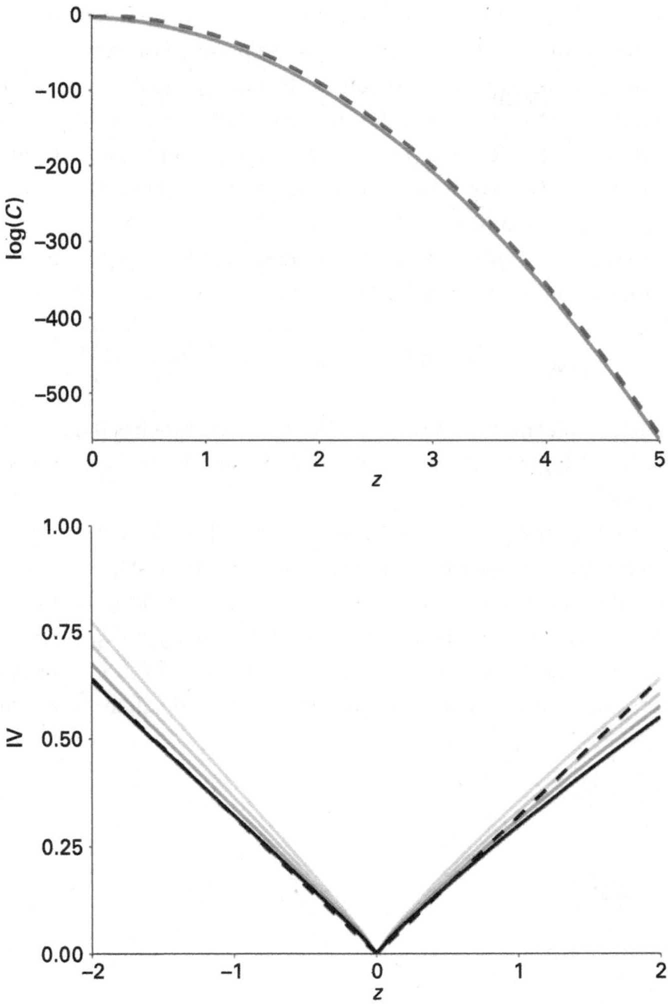

Figure 8.1
Top panel shows logarithm of option cost C (solid line) compared with the approximation (dashed line) for the case where $\sigma = 0.15$ is constant. Bottom panel shows implied volatility for options where the price is set equal to a small positive number $\epsilon = 0.00005$ (black), 0.0001 (dark gray), 0.0002 (medium), and 0.0004 (light). Dashed line is quantum model.

The proof of the classical result is claimed to be "model independent" but in fact, it relies on the usual core classical assumptions. For example, it conflates the present value of expected payouts, with the cost of options, and similarly defines implied volatility to be equal to the volatility, which, when used in the Black-Scholes model, gives a price equal to the present value of the expected payout. As we will see in this chapter and the next, these assumptions break down in the quantum model, or the real world.

Many models of implied volatility are designed to respect the no-arbitrage bounds. An example is the stochastic volatility inspired (SVI) model given by

$$\sigma_{SVI} = \sqrt{\left| a + b\left(\rho(x-m) + \sqrt{(x-m)^2 + \sigma^2}\right)\right|}. \tag{8.7}$$

For large $|x|$, this formula scales with $|x|^{1/2}$ and therefore has the desired asymptotic behavior.[5] Figure 8.2 shows the results using the parameter values taken from a paper.[6]

The quantum-implied volatility (QIV) and SVI models are therefore again very different, in terms of both complexity and results. The QIV model provides an approximate fit to the entire surface in z and T using only a base volatility σ, and the fit can often be improved by introducing a degree of horizontal shift to account for effects such as drift. In contrast, the SVI model uses five parameters, along with a complex and unusual nested square root structure, to

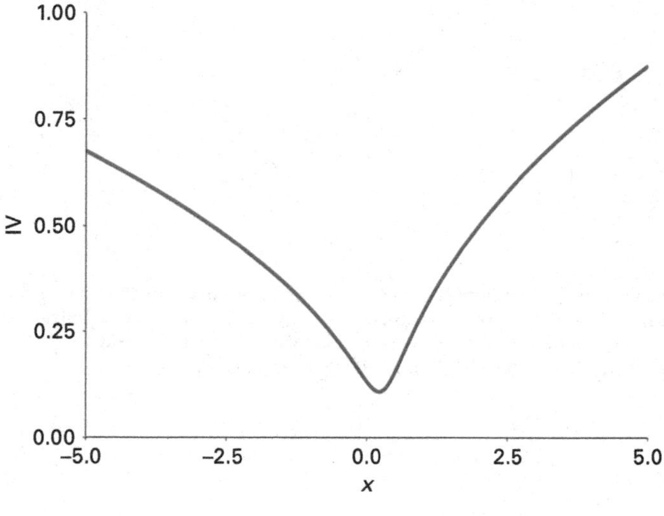

Figure 8.2
Implied volatility calculated using the SVI formula, with parameters $(a, b, m, \rho, \sigma) = (-0.0410, 0.1331, 0.3586, 0.3060, 0.4153)$ and $T = 1$ from Gatheral & Jacquier (2014). Note the negative curvature in the wings.

fit a single period (so the surface requires a different parameter set for each period).[7] Although this means that it can fit at-the-money options to a high level of accuracy, the no-arbitrage assumption forces it to scale with $|x|^{1/2}$ in the wings, which means that the implied volatility there is lower than seen with either the quantum model or the actual data. From equation 8.2, the corresponding option cost scales with $\exp(-|x|)$ and for large $|x|$ would be effectively zero, so smaller than any minimum tick size.

From a mathematical modeling perspective, it seems strange that a theoretical concept (no-arbitrage) takes priority over an obvious empirical reality (minimum option cost) when calibrating models. As we have already seen with things like price impact, a recurrent but somewhat surprising feature of quantitative finance is that key concepts are not always carefully tested against empirical data.

8.2 A Bird's-Eye View

Implied volatility is complicated by a number of behavioral and other effects,[8] so the situation actually becomes clearer when we stand back and take a bird's-eye view of a large range of strikes and expirations as in the top row of figure 8.3, which shows implied volatility as a function of T and x (left), or $z = x/\sqrt{T}$ only (right). The data, shown by the gray points, is derived from SPX options during the period 2004–2020 (it is the same as shown earlier in figure 1.3). The option prices are averaged over each strike and expiration (from five days to six months), and the implied volatility is then computed.

The dashed line in the right plot is the quantum implied volatility model, shown also in the middle row. The fact that, over a large range of strikes and expirations, the agreement with observed data is good suggests that investors expect the market to have the same non-lognormal characteristics, even up to the slope magnitude of about 0.32 from equation 8.6 (which again is a number, not a tuneable parameter). In other words, although from a classical perspective the implied volatility curve seems to be a puzzling and illogical anomaly, it is best viewed as a numerical anachronism that results from a normal model being used to model a non-normal system. Instead of being a sign that market participants are illogical, it is a marker of model error—or rather of an attempt to correct model error.

To make this claim more precise, the standard deviation of the points shown in the top right panel is found to be 0.312. Since the classical model assigns a constant volatility, this can be viewed as the standard deviation of the error for a volatility equal to the mean. The same calculation for the quantum model gives errors whose standard deviation is 0.052. One can therefore say that the quantum model accounts for 83 percent of the error for the implied volatility surface using only a single parameter.

Of course, what really counts is not whether the quantum model agrees with implied volatility (i.e., the behavior or traders) but whether it agrees with the actual expected payout (i.e., the behavior of asset prices). The bottom row of figure 8.3 changes the question to ask what the payout-implied volatility is. This is computed by taking the average payout (as opposed to costs) for SPX options with different strikes, and assuming a minimum option cost with $\epsilon = 0.00005$. In other words, instead of computing the implied volatility from option prices, we are asking what volatility should be used to correctly price options so their cost equals the expected payout. As seen in the right panel, the quantum model again captures the overall structure. The mismatch at the center is because the payout for at-the-money call options with $x = 0$ is higher than the payout for put options with $x = 0$ and reflects the fact that the average growth rate is higher than the risk-free rate used by the Black-Scholes model to calculate option prices. We return to this in chapter 10, when we consider a trading strategy designed to exploit the difference between implied volatility (what traders pay) and payout-implied volatility (what they get back).

Comparing the various volatility plots in figure 8.3, the reason for the striking resemblance noted in chapter 1 between the implied volatility and the quantum model surfaces is that they are both trying to approximate the same thing—namely, the payout-implied volatility (bottom row). Or put another way, the stock market shows quantum behavior, and traders are using a quantum model. They just don't know it.

An advantage of using index option prices and taking an average surface over years of data is that it reveals persistent features that may otherwise be lost in the noise. The quantum model can, of course, also be used to estimate implied volatility for individual stocks. Figure 8.4 shows 3D and 2D views of data for the firm AIG as part of a project to look at implied volatility for extreme strikes and long durations for a number of stocks.[9] It can be compared with the heatmaps previously shown for the index data. One finding was that for some stocks, the minimum volatility σ has a tendency to increase slowly with time; however, this is a fairly subtle effect that can be attributed in the quantum model to the way in which price changes are perceived.[10]

8.3 Finance, Falsified

The classical BSM option pricing model has remained the industry standard in quantitative finance for over five decades, in part because on the surface at least, it is easy to use and only a single parameter needs to be calibrated—namely, the

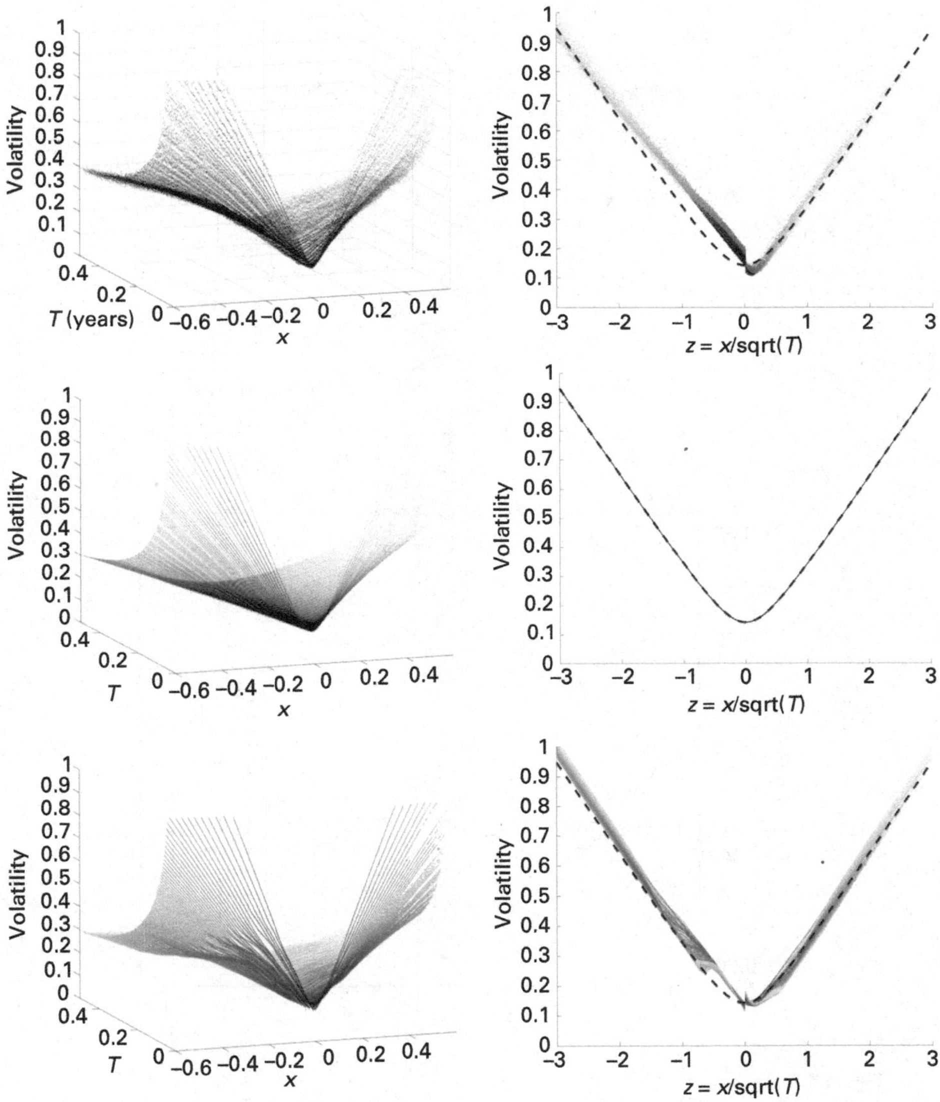

Figure 8.3
Top row shows implied volatility from SPX options 2004–2020, plotted as a function of x and T (left) and z only (right). Dashed line is the quantum model for implied volatility, which is independent of T, and asymptotes to a slope of about ± 0.32. Middle row shows the quantum model, and bottom row shows payout-implied volatility.

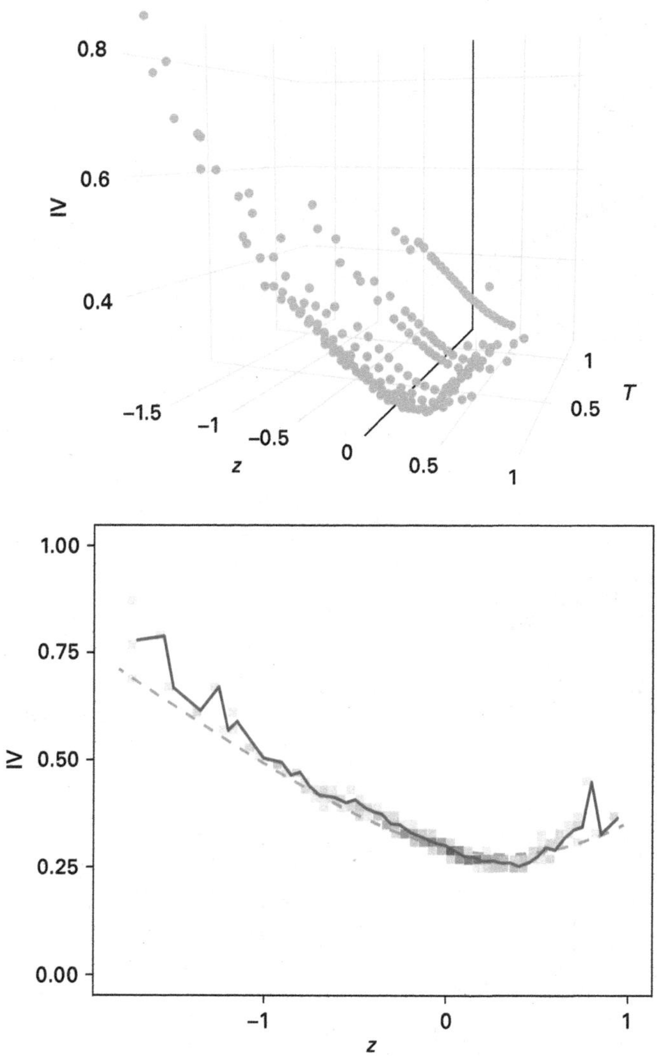

Figure 8.4
Top panel shows implied volatility for AIG stock as a function of z and T. Bottom panel shows average implied volatility (solid line) and quantum model (dashed line) with $\sigma = 0.28$ and a horizontal offset of 0.3. Data source: One William Street Capital Management.

volatility. The core assumptions of random walks and no arbitrage are applied to build models of implied volatility. However, the apparent simplicity is deceptive because the model effectively exports the complexity of option pricing to the user, who must estimate the correct volatility to use in the formula for a particular period and strike. And although the random walk model is serviceable as a zero-order approximation, the classical theory breaks down completely when it is applied to the question of volatility. In contrast, the implied volatility surface can largely be accounted for by assuming that prices follow the quantum model with no parameters other than a base volatility.

This points to a larger problem, which is that the apparent success of the BSM framework meant that most models are based on similar concepts. Although these assumptions have always been subject to criticism, the property of q-variance shows that they are fundamentally flawed.

Quants are often described as financial engineers. In my first professional job at an actual engineering firm, our team was working on a compact particle accelerator to be used for chip fabrication. We were beginning the construction of a prototype system when I found an error in the code for computing the magnetic fields. When I told the project manager, who was not usually given to moments of drama, I remember that the first thing he said was, "Do we need to stop construction?"

As it turned out, the problem could be handled because the errors mostly canceled out. The assumption in finance has long been that models aren't perfect, but at least they are simple, and the errors similarly come out in the wash.[11] However, q-variance is different because it goes right to the heart of the methods being used. The stability of the financial structure depends on a particular material called volatility, which it turns out responds to perturbations (it expands) in a way that models had not anticipated. Quants therefore need to take a leaf from real engineers and ask some hard questions about their theories and models:

- Does the theory assume random-walk/Brownian-motion behavior?
- Does the theory assume the bid–ask spread is zero?
- Does the theory assume that volatility over a period is independent of price change?
- Does the theory assume the absence of arbitrage?
- If the answer to any of these is yes, has the theory been properly tested against data?

The last question might seem redundant, but the reality is that classical theories have persisted for decades even when they are obviously incompatible with data. For example, the Black-Scholes model makes a number of simplifying assumptions and claims to correctly compute an option's expected payout using a constant volatility. The test of the model is therefore not whether "Thousands of traders and investors now use this formula every day," as the 1997 Nobel Prize Committee put it—which would be like awarding de Broglie a Nobel Prize, not because his theory made accurate predictions but because on the whole everyone was on board with it—but whether its assumptions and conclusions are correct. This can be checked.

Referring to the 1973 Black-Scholes paper, the main assumption is that "the stock price follows a random walk in continuous time with a variance rate proportional to the square of the stock price. Thus the distribution of possible stock prices at the end of any finite interval is lognormal. The variance rate of the return on the stock is constant." However, prices do not follow a random walk, volatility is not constant but follows q-variance, and the distribution is not lognormal but is better described as a q-distribution. The equations in the paper therefore do not apply.

Another assumption states that "there are no transaction costs in buying or selling the stock or the option." But transaction costs—including the bid–ask spread, which is key to the quantum model—do, of course, exist and become especially important for options at extreme strikes.

Finally, the main conclusion is that the option costs computed by the BSM model are appropriate in terms of expected payouts. There is a loophole here, which is that, in theory, at least the cost of an option reflects not just the payout but also the price of risk, and the hedging argument is supposed to account for this by moving the analysis to a risk-free playing field. Since volatility is not constant and transaction fees are significant, this argument breaks down, so we are left with the commonsense test that the option cost should be roughly equal to the expected payout (note this is not the same as the usual no-arbitrage argument, which ignores things like transaction costs).

This condition is easily tested, using historical market prices and a minimum option price, by comparing BSM costs and actual payouts, and as shown by the payout-implied volatility surface in figure 8.3, the model with constant volatility cannot work. (One can also do the test using the QJ model depicted in figure 6.3 where the risk-free rate is zero by design.) Again, this kind of experiment is a basic part of the scientific method, but it is also a first step in checking any kind of forecasting model such as a weather model. It also seems strange that the resemblance between this payout-implied surface and the usual implied volatility in the same figure has not been widely reported and discussed (at least, I couldn't find a reference), despite the fact that the data has long been available.

8.4 Summary

The BSM model relies on a number of core assumptions, including that price returns are lognormal and transactions costs are zero. These assumptions fail because of an irreducible level of uncertainty in financial markets, which affects both volatility and the minimum cost that applies at extreme strikes. The result is that option costs computed by the model include errors, which, compared to the quantum model, are both large and systematic. By any reasonable or serious standard, the BSM model is therefore falsified. The usual defense that the model is "good enough" does not work. Obviously, people can use it, just as they can use any other wrong model, but really, they shouldn't because it causes confusion. Also, further theoretical results should not be based on it.

Answering an audience question on quantum models at a 2025 conference, the quant who two years earlier had called them "too much of a stretch" gave an updated opinion: "It's certainly interesting. I guess the question is, do they make new predictions as opposed to just explaining old things like Black-Scholes which isn't really an achievement at this point." (Medieval philosopher to Galileo as he prepares to drop objects off the Leaning Tower of Pisa: "Your theory of motion is interesting, but isn't really an achievement if it only explains Aristotle.") (Not trying to compare myself with Galileo—it's a joke.) No, the quantum model cannot explain old things like Black-Scholes or support the counterintuitive story that markets are efficient and free of arbitrage so the only growth rate that matters is the risk-free rate. But neither can the data.

Of course, this does not mean that university economics departments will suddenly stop teaching BSM or similar models, or even apply updated warning labels to them. Indeed, it seems hard to think of an economic theory that has ever been falsified, and canonical ideas such as no-arbitrage or efficient markets, or models such as BSM that align with these principles, have proven especially enduring—which suggests either that they represent deep truths or that in economics, falsification is not considered to be a priority or even an acceptable goal. Economists tend to have a self-image of their field as being robust and open to criticism, but the reality as economist (and Nobel laureate) Paul Romer has noted is that to some at least, "neither facts that are false, nor predictions that are wrong, nor models that make no sense matter enough to worry about."[12] An editor of a journal informed me that one day, they would be able to "publish the truth," but in the meantime, they had to avoid alienating the mainstream economists who held sway in their department.

In other words, its track record suggests that the aim of the academy is not to hold theories up to the test of data but to protect them. This is one reason finance has not one or a few theories of volatility, but by some counts over thirty. However, economics is not going to move on to new ideas unless it discards some old ones. Perhaps the trick is to adopt more of an engineering perspective, and particularly the idea of ethical codes. In 2009, following the financial crisis, Derman and Wilmott published a "Modelers' Hippocratic Oath," whose pronouncements included that when using a model, "I will make explicit its assumptions and oversights."[13] Q-variance clearly qualifies as an important oversight, and a first step is to acknowledge its effect on models—and maybe even winnow the list down a bit.

We return to this topic in the final chapter. In the next chapter, we see that option prices violate the no-arbitrage principle on a truly industrial scale, in part because the methods used to measure volatility are not fit for purpose.

9

The Fear Gauge

The test of science is its ability to predict.

—Richard Feynman, *The Feynman Lectures on Physics*, 1964

In so far as a scientific statement speaks about reality, it must be falsifiable: and in so far as it is not falsifiable, it does not speak about reality.

—Karl Popper, *The Logic of Scientific Discovery*, 1959

Implied volatility, as usually understood, is a confusing topic because it involves the subjective decisions of traders, so it is hard to speak of it in objective terms. The advantage of model-implied volatility, as seen earlier, is that it relies only on a model distribution rather than the intricacies of market dynamics. Another kind of volatility is what we have called the payout-implied volatility, which is the number that gives the option price that corresponds to expected payout, based on a statistical analysis of historical returns.

Comparing these three different types of volatility allows us to determine, for example, the extent to which traders are influenced by markets or how closely their decisions align with actual outcomes. One problem about the BSM proof is that it conflated model volatility and payout-implied volatility. If the dynamic hedging argument was correct, then these two should be the same. In reality, as we have seen, the payout-implied volatility can only be determined by calculating the actual expected payouts based on historical data.

This issue affects not just the BSM model but also classical quantitative finance in general, where, for example, it is common practice to equate an expected payout with the market cost of a derivative. A good example of how these issues come together is the Cboe VIX index.

9.1 Fix the VIX

The 2019 VIX white paper[1] summarizes the development of the VIX index as follows: "In 1993, Cboe Global Markets, Incorporated® (Cboe®) introduced the Cboe Volatility Index® (VIX® Index), which was originally designed to measure the market's expectation of 30-day volatility implied by at-the-money S&P 100® Index (OEX® Index) option prices. The VIX Index soon became the premier benchmark for U.S. stock market volatility. It is regularly featured in the Wall Street Journal, Barron's and other leading financial publications, as well as business news shows on CNBC, Bloomberg TV and CNN/Money, where the VIX Index is often referred to as the 'fear gauge.' "

As the white paper explains, the VIX is based on an algorithm that computes a weighted sum of put and call options at different strike prices:

$$\sigma^2 = \frac{2}{T}\sum_i \frac{\Delta K_i}{K_i^2} e^{rT} Q(K_i) - \frac{1}{T}\left(\frac{I}{K} - 1\right)^2 . \tag{9.1}$$

Here, T is time to expiration, I is the forward index price derived from index options, K is the first strike below I, and r is the risk-free rate. K_i is the strike price of the ith out-of-the-money option Q, which is a call if $K_i > K$, a put if $K_i < K$, and the average of a call and a put if $K_i = K$.

The formula is derived by considering the returns of a hedged portfolio consisting of options with suitably chosen strikes. It is often said that the VIX is "model independent" because it only sums the price of options instead of explicitly attempting to calculate an implied volatility. Carr & Wu (2006), for example, write that the VIX index "is constructed from the price of a portfolio of options and represents a model-free approximation of the 30-day return variance swap rate." However, the formula takes it as given that prices follow a random walk so at each time, there is a single strike-independent volatility in the first place, and also that the relevant growth rate to use is the risk-free rate. Since the former was a main assumption of the Black-Scholes model, and the latter its main conclusion, the VIX index can be viewed as an extension or continuation of that theory, even if it is not evoked directly.

To see how the classical and quantum approaches differ, we will briefly sketch the proof of the VIX algorithm from first principles.[2] For simplicity, we will assume that the risk-free rate is $r = 0$. The argument begins with the standard assumption of Brownian motion, so the stock price S_t follows the stochastic differential equation

$$dS_t = \mu_t S_t dt + \sigma_t S dX_t, \tag{9.2}$$

where the t subscript indicates that the drift μ, volatility σ, and price S are all functions of time. Stochastic calculus[3] then allows us to write

$$S_t = S_0 \exp\left(\int_0^t \mu_s ds - \frac{1}{2}\int_0^t \sigma_s^2 ds + \int_0^t \sigma_s dX_s\right). \tag{9.3}$$

Taking the derivative of the logarithm gives

$$d(\log S_t) = \mu_t dt + \sigma_t dX_t - \frac{1}{2}\sigma_t^2 dt = \frac{dS_t}{S_t} - \frac{1}{2}\sigma_t^2 dt, \tag{9.4}$$

so

$$\frac{dS_t}{S_t} - d(\log S_t) = \frac{1}{2}\sigma_t^2 dt. \tag{9.5}$$

Now

$$\int_0^T d(\log S_t)dt = \int_0^T \mu_t dt + \int_0^T \sigma_t dX_t - \int_0^T \frac{1}{2}\sigma_t^2 dt \tag{9.6}$$

$$= \log S_T - \log S_0. \tag{9.7}$$

Since $r = 0$, it can be checked that

$$\mathbb{E}\left(\int_0^T \frac{dS_t}{S_t}\right) = 0, \tag{9.8}$$

where $\mathbb{E}$ denotes expected value. Combining equations 9.5, 9.7, and 9.8 gives

$$\sigma^2 = \mathbb{E}\left(\frac{1}{T}\int_0^T \sigma_t^2 dt\right) = -\frac{2}{T}\mathbb{E}\left(\log\left(\frac{S_T}{S_0}\right)\right), \tag{9.9}$$

where σ is the expected value of the variance over the period T.

Although the quantum model is not based on Brownian motion, so the above analysis does not apply, the associated distribution does give a similar result since as shown in equation 6.20, it satisfies

$$\mathbb{E}\left(\log\left(\frac{S_T}{S_0}\right)\right) = \langle z\sqrt{T}\rangle = -\frac{\Sigma^2}{2}. \tag{9.10}$$

Of course, the variance in the quantum model is always a function of z, so this only gives the total variance Σ^2 over the whole distribution. However, let's continue.

In classical finance, the proof of the Black-Scholes model relied on demonstrating the existence of a risk-free portfolio, where the option could be hedged by constantly buying and selling stocks. The net effect was simply to say that the value of the option was the expected payout, where the present value was calculated using the risk-free rate. However, the proof was misleading because it assumed, for example, that stocks could be bought and sold with no transaction fees. In the quantum model, this would mean that the bid–ask spread, and therefore the uncertainty and the volatility, were all zero. The VIX algorithm is based on a similar argument and, as we will see, suffers from the same lack of realism.

The above expression has given us the expected variance in terms of the expected log price. The idea then is to see if we can find a portfolio of options that has this payout. The expected variance is then just equal to the value of the portfolio. (If this all seems a very elaborate technique for estimating variance, that's because it is.)

The Carr-Madan formula tells us that we can write

$$x = \log\frac{S_T}{S_0} = \frac{S_T - S_0}{S_0} - \int_0^{S_0} \frac{\max(0, K - S_T)}{K^2} dK \tag{9.11}$$

$$- \int_{S_0}^{\infty} \frac{\max(0, S_T - K)}{K^2} dK. \tag{9.12}$$

Here, the expressions $\max(0, K - S_T)$ and $\max(0, S_T - K)$ are the payouts for put and call options. The formula is obtained by doing a Taylor expansion of $g(S_t) = \log(S_t)$ around the point $S_t = K$, where the second derivative is $g''(K) = -1/K^2$, and expressing the integral remainder in terms of the payout functions.[4]

Combining this with the previous result for variance, letting $C(K)$ and $P(K)$ be the price of call and put options and assuming that these costs equal the expected payouts, then gives

$$\sigma^2 = -\frac{2}{T}\mathbb{E}\left(\log\left(\frac{S_T}{S_0}\right)\right) \tag{9.13}$$

$$= \frac{2}{T}\int_0^{S_0} \frac{P(K)}{K^2} dK + \frac{2}{T}\int_{S_0}^{\infty} \frac{C(K)}{K^2} dK - \frac{2}{T}\mathbb{E}\left(\frac{S_T - S_0}{S_0}\right) \tag{9.14}$$

$$\approx \frac{2}{T}\sum_i \frac{\Delta K_i}{K_i^2} Q(K_i), \tag{9.15}$$

where the option prices Q are as defined above, we are approximating the integral numerically, and we have used $\mathbb{E}(S_T) = S_0$ since $r = 0$.

This is the same as the formula used in the VIX algorithm, equation 9.1, with the difference that we have made the simplifying assumption that $r = 0$. The second term in the VIX formula comes about because of the difference between the current and forward price of the index. (In the quantum model, of course, what counts for pricing options is not the yield on a bond but the expected growth rate of the underlying asset, so the concept of a "forward price" is somewhat nebulous.)

9.2 The Illusion of Accuracy

We should note here that the estimate for the variance is based on evaluating the difference between the means of log price change $x = \log(S_T/S_0)$ and fractional price change $(S_T - S_0)/S_0$, which is a fairly subtle effect, so the computation is prone to numerical error. This is important because the formula also makes the assumption—which is so common that it usually goes unremarked—that the expected value of the payout is equal to the cost of the options. This, in turn, is based on widely held ideas such as the no-arbitrage principle and efficient market theory, assisted by the BSM model, which implies that option prices can be computed based on volatility and the known risk-free rate. The algorithm also assumes that there is a single volatility in the first place, but according to q-variance, volatility is a function of z. In principle, if model error were negligible, the algorithm should compute a value for total variance; however, that only equals the actual variance at $x = \pm\sqrt{2}\sigma$.

It therefore doesn't make sense to say that the formula is model independent because the quantum model does not make these assumptions. And the result is that the algorithm is attempting to model variance by summing together numbers that may be only loosely related to the actual payout, as seen below.

The algorithm is illustrated in figure 9.1 for two data sets: an artificial lognormal time series (left column) and the data set used in the Cboe white paper (right column). Two time periods are used in the Cboe calculation; here, we show the options with thirty-two days to expiry. The three rows respectively show option prices, implied volatility, and the individual terms $\frac{2}{T}\frac{\Delta K_i}{K_i^2}e^{rT}Q(K_i)$ used in the VIX calculation. The lognormal data has a constant volatility of 0.11, as shown by the flat line in the second row.

As is customary in classical finance, a lot of attention is paid to the risk-free rate, which in the white paper is calculated to an accuracy of 0.0001 percent. Also, the time period T is divided into minutes "in order to replicate the precision that is commonly used by professional option and volatility traders." Although this gives an impression of great accuracy, in fact, the exact length of period has a negligible effect. For the data set used, the risk-free rate is $r = 0.000286$, so $e^{rT} = 1.000025 \approxeq 1$. The forward price I is determined by finding the strike price at which the absolute difference between the call and put prices is smallest, which here is $K = 1960$, and adding a term equal to e^{rT} multiplied by the difference between the call price and the put price. The result is $I = 1962.40006$, which suggests a numerical accuracy of about five parts in a billion.

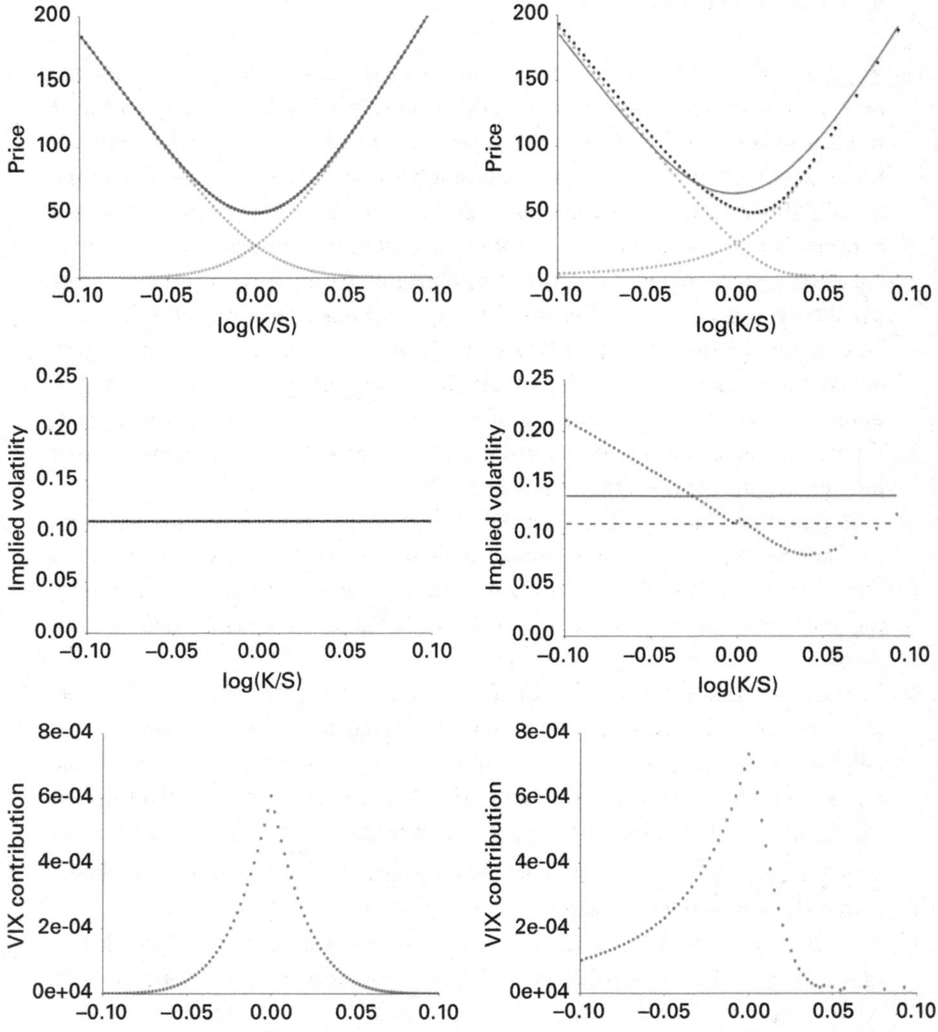

Figure 9.1
Top panels show option price data, including calls, puts, and straddles, for the lognormal (left) and Cboe (right) data sets. The solid lines show the option prices computed using the Black-Scholes formula with VIX volatility. Middle panels show implied volatilities, along with the result from the VIX calculation (solid line). The bottom panels show the contributions of option prices to the VIX calculation. The lognormal plot is symmetrical, but the Cboe case is skewed and assigns higher weights to options with small strikes.

In the top row, the solid lines show straddle option prices, which are the sum of the call and put prices, as computed using the Black-Scholes model and the VIX algorithm. Of course, the fit is perfect for the lognormal case, but for the Cboe data, the Black-Scholes prices are significantly higher than the option prices, which suggests that the formula is overestimating the applicable volatility.

The reason for this becomes clear in the bottom row of plots, which show the contributions from individual options to the VIX calculation. Whereas the lognormal case is symmetric, the Cboe case assigns a much higher weight to lower strike prices. This bias is caused by two things: the curvature of the smile and its displacement to the right. The first is related to the nonconstant volatility, whereas the second occurs in part because option prices are calculated using the risk-free rate instead of the actual growth rate. It can be checked that using an interest rate in the BSM model that equals the average annual return of around 10 percent introduces a similar horizontal shift to the implied volatility curve.[5]

The use of constant volatility and the risk-free rate—which are the core of the classical Black-Scholes/VIX approach—therefore jointly affect the volatility estimate, leading it to be too high. Although we do not know the RMS volatility that applies for the Cboe data, the vertical displacement of the solid lines in the top panels suggests that the VIX volatility is too high by around 25 percent.

It follows that, just by considering the nature of the Cboe VIX formula, one would expect the Black-Scholes/VIX option prices to be higher than the prices paid by traders because the VIX volatility is too high relative to implied volatility. This leads to a peculiar effect because if the VIX volatility is higher than the implied volatilities on which it is based, traders might lift their estimates in response, which in turn would increase the VIX, and so on, until the VIX estimate becomes detached from the relevant value.

One might therefore expect the implied volatilities to be a compromise between the higher VIX volatility, whose value is consistent with the standard formula, and the lower payout-implied volatility. In fact, something like this can be seen in markets because the implied volatility approximately splits the difference between these two volatilities, with the result that the BSM/VIX model overestimates the price of at-the-money SPX straddles by about 40 percent, while the price paid by traders reduces the error by about half.

This is shown by figure 9.2, which compares the average payout of straddle options with both the average option cost, and the cost computed using the BSM/VIX model. The BSM/VIX model consistently overprices the options, whereas the actual price paid represents a compromise between this theoretical price and the actual payout.[6]

The BSM/VIX model, by its nature, therefore systematically leads to prices that are higher than payouts. Indeed, the conclusion that VIX overestimates

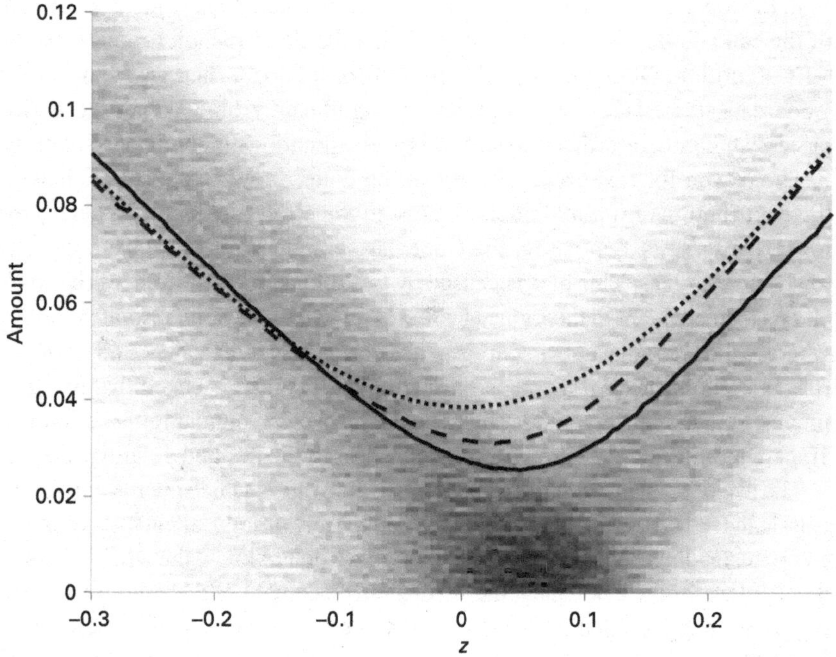

Figure 9.2
Plot of average price for one-month straddle options versus *z* for S&P 500 data over the years 2004 to 2020. The Black-Scholes/VIX model (dotted line) systematically overprices options compared to the average payouts (solid), whereas actual price paid splits the difference (dashed). The background is a heatmap of option payouts.

volatility, and therefore leads to mispricing, can be reached more easily just by noting that, on average, it is about a third higher than the rolling one-month volatility, which is what counts when pricing one-month options.[7]

Figure 9.2 also starkly illustrates the difference between prices based on model-implied volatility (dotted line), payout-implied volatility (black line), and price-implied volatility (dashed line). Classical theory treats the first two of these as being the same and attempts to model the last using the same methods.

9.3 Summary

If much of quantitative finance is about putting a price on risk, then one of the most important and widely used tools is the VIX index, which acts as an established metric of volatility and uncertainty. It is ironic then that a key step in the algorithm involves assuming that expected option payouts are exactly equal to option costs, which suggests a great amount of certainty. The so-called fear index might be a key measure in financial engineering that is routinely calculated to great precision, but it is not designed to handle the combination of q-variance and model error—and as a result, it isn't clear what it's measuring, which from an engineering perspective is a little frightening.

Together with the three anomalies reported in chapter 1, figure 9.2 effectively contradicts the key tenets of classical finance. Price changes do not follow a random walk with constant volatility, as assumed by the classical model; instead, price change and volatility are linked, as shown empirically through the property of q-variance. Markets are not perfectly efficient, as shown by the fact that option prices do not accurately reflect expected payouts. And for a system which is supposed to have no arbitrage, there appears to be plenty going on.

Of course, practitioners and theoreticians have long known that the classical random walk model is not perfect, so, for example, the price distribution is not perfectly normal, markets are not perfectly rational or efficient, and sudden crashes can occur. A common analogy, mentioned already in chapter 7, is that using the classical model is like using Newton's laws of motion to predict the trajectory of a cannonball as it flies through the air: It may not be perfectly realistic, or foresee every eventuality, but it captures the main features and can be improved by adding "frictions" such as transaction fees or randomly varying volatility. However, that is not what is going on here. The classical model is based on equilibrium and so has no real sense of dynamics. It is like trying to model the cannonball by assuming that it goes in a straight line. Again, it isn't Newtonian—it's Aristotelian.

Q-variance, which is described by a different kind of parabolic equation, therefore poses another level of challenge to classical finance. We will make this more specific in the next chapter, where we show how strategies can be devised that profit not from speculations on market movements but from the gap between classical theory and reality.

10

Beat the Options Market

> You never change things by fighting the existing reality. To change something, build a new model that makes the existing model obsolete.
> —R. Buckminster Fuller

> Past performance is not indicative of future results.
> —Standard investment disclaimer

As discussed in previous chapters, the industry standard model for option pricing has long been the BSM model. Taleb wrote in 1998 that "Most everything that has been developed in modern finance since 1973 is but a footnote on the BSM equation," and arguably, not much has changed.[1]

Of course, not everyone buys the theory. Haug & Taleb (2008) observed that "the entire argument is indeed, quite strange and rather inapplicable for someone clinically and observation-driven standing outside conventional neoclassical economics." Practitioners know that the theory has limitations, which is why they adjust the implied volatility to suit. But the BSM model is still the central reference and plays an established role as a coordination device that allows traders to communicate and do business (even if the communication is muddied somewhat by the fact that volatility is different for every strike and expiration). And in many ways, the real role of the model seems to be less about accurately pricing options than providing a kind of security blanket or foundational myth or cover story for traders.

If neoclassical economics has a theme, it is the idea that rational agents drive prices to a stable equilibrium that reflects value. Coyle (2007) wrote, for example, "The key elements of economic methodology, unchanged from the classical days, are the status of rational choice and the use of equilibrium as a modelling concept. If these are limitations, so be it: every subject has core restrictions in its methodology, which in fact represent its strengths and distinctive insights."

An abstract from a 1999 paper by Edward P. Lazear announced that "Economics is not only a social science, it is a genuine science. Like the physical sciences, economics uses a methodology that produces refutable implications and tests these implications using solid statistical techniques. In particular, economics stresses three factors that distinguish it from other social sciences. Economists use the construct of rational individuals who engage in maximizing behavior. Economic models adhere strictly to the importance of equilibrium as part of any theory. Finally, a focus on efficiency leads economists to ask questions that other social sciences ignore." It is almost as if talking about rationality and efficiency makes economics rational and efficient.

The BSM model relies, for example, on the belief that markets are efficient and so are made up of what Fama (1965) called "rational profit maximizers" whose collective actions ensure that everything is priced rationally, including assets and options. According to this theory, markets are unpredictable only because they incorporate all available information in a way no single person can do. Merton's 1973 paper was called "Theory of Rational Option Pricing" (as opposed to theory of irrational option pricing). The underlying message was that options trading is rational too, which was useful. After the Chicago Board Options Exchange opened the same year, its council could claim that "Black-Scholes was really what enabled the exchange to thrive. . . . [I]t gave a lot of legitimacy to the whole notions of hedging and efficient pricing, whereas we were faced, in the late 60s-early 70s with the issue of gambling. That issue fell away, and I think Black-Scholes made it fall away. It wasn't speculation or gambling, it was efficient pricing."[2]

Some of the shine came off the BSM model with the 1998 collapse of Long-Term Capital Management (LTCM), whose board included Scholes and Merton and whose highly leveraged bets required a $3.6 billion bailout; however, this didn't stop them both from being awarded the Nobel Prize three years later. Such catastrophic failures could always be blamed on unpredictable external factors.

According to Derman & Miller (2016), the BSM model "sounds so rational, and has such a strong grip on everyone's imagination, that even people who don't believe in its assumptions nevertheless use it to quote prices at which they are willing to trade." But speaking as a non-quant, what strikes me as strange is that for a supposedly observation-driven field, it is quite hard to find detailed empirical tests that show how the model performs, compared with historical payouts. Of course, some research along those lines is undoubtedly kept confidential for commercial reasons, but you would expect something to leak out. Samuelson, for example, claimed that the theory "is confirmed daily by millions of statistical observations," and yet when an experiment is performed that actually uses millions of observations (figure 9.2), the results do not confirm the classical model. The implied volatility used by traders also conforms more closely to the quantum model, but with a persistent bias that can be attributed to two things.

The first is the idea, derived from the dynamic hedging argument, that the value of an option does not depend on the growth of the underlying asset (apart from a risk-free growth rate) when it obviously kind of does. This is why for something like the S&P 500 index, which tends to grow, at-the-money call options (betting that price will go up) have a higher expected payout than at-the-money put options. It's like playing cards with a loaded deck.

This wouldn't be a problem if the prices were correctly adjusted, and we return to this below. However, another bias shown by figure 9.2 is that prices for at-the-money put options are generally too high. This is why, for example, the prices for at-the-money straddle options consistently exceed the expected payouts. The bias is related in part to the fact that the model and related tools such as the VIX are based on the idea that volatility is independent of strike, and this influences the prices paid in the market.

In other words, practitioners in quantitative finance may be well aware of the drawbacks and limitations of the BSM model, but its assumptions have a discernible influence on prices, which is hardly surprising given the model's pervasive role in the field. In this chapter, we will take a data-driven approach to option pricing and derive a trading strategy that exploits the yawning gap between theory and reality.

Before proceeding, there are some disclaimers. The following does not constitute investment advice. I am not a quant, or a professional trader, and would not qualify for even the lowest rung of investment adviserhood. Also, the results I will present are based on past performance, which is not a guide to future performance, especially because this is a quantum system where the observation of a strategy affects the result. In fact, if enough people read this book (unlikely), the bias would presumably vanish.

With that out of the way, this chapter will present the Quantum Fund, so named because it is the smallest hedge fund in existence. We begin with some background and context.

10.1 The Perfect Model Hypothesis

I began chapter 1 of this book discussing two doctorates: Bachelier's in finance and de Broglie's in physics. My own less momentous doctoral program (from Oxford rather than the Sorbonne) was on the topic of model error in weather forecasting. The general view at the time (late 1990s) was that forecast error was due not to model error but to the effects of chaos, where in theory, the flap of a butterfy's wing could cause a storm a few days later on the other side of the world. Since we could never measure the initial state of the atmosphere perfectly, it followed that there would be errors that would be magnified by chaos. However, by making multiple model runs starting from slightly altered initial conditions, it should still be possible as in finance to make probabilistic forecasts, a technique known as ensemble forecasting. In order to simplify the analysis, researchers had proposed a "perfect model hypothesis," which assumed that all error was due to chaos and none to the model.[3]

I had enough work experience on engineering projects to know how hard it was to eliminate all model error even when you had complete control over the system, so the idea that anyone could build a perfect model of a complex organic system like the atmosphere seemed (as quantum economics has been called) a bit of a stretch. The butterfly effect, meanwhile, was something that seemed important in highly simplified computer models, but not so much in the real world where small perturbations have a tendency of getting damped out.

My thesis claimed that if forecast errors, averaged over a number of forecasts, scaled with the square root of time, then they were probably due to model error. If they scaled exponentially, they were probably due to chaos. When during a 2000 talk at the European Centre for Medium-Range Weather Forecasting (ECMWF) I showed a plot of forecast errors growing with the square root of time, I was interrupted by the research head who said confidently that the plot must be wrong since error growth has positive curvature, not negative.

After the talk, we agreed that someone should check my results. When that was done, they were identical to the ones I had shown. However, it made absolutely no difference. The consensus remained that the errors were primarily due to chaos (though not everyone was convinced, including my thesis committee and *New Scientist* magazine, whose conclusion was "Don't blame the butterfly").[4] As I wrote in my 2007 book *The Future of Everything*, one expert even squared the same circle of saying that, as with q-variance, my results were both well known and wrong at the same time.

Unlike in engineering, it seemed there was little incentive to study model error in science. It annoyed the people who had developed the models, who were often powerful figures in the community. More generally, it seemed to undercut the credibility of the academic field. And finally, there was no financial incentive. If you thought the problem was that you needed to run a larger ensemble to address the effects of chaos, you just needed a bigger budget and more computers, which sounds good on a grant application. Fixing the model is harder.

The academic field of economics was an extreme case of the phenomenon, as I soon discovered while writing a chapter in the same book on model error in economics. In weather forecasting, theory said that forecast error could be traced back to random errors in the initial condition. In finance, the dominant efficient-market theory said that prices were randomly perturbed by news. In either case, the model itself was effectively perfect. Something like the Black-Scholes algorithm wasn't just a model—it was the nearest thing to a fundamental law of nature.

For example, look under the hood of the Cboe VIX algorithm (previous chapter), and it says $C(K) = \mathbb{E}(\max(0, K - S_T))$, so the cost of an option equals the expected payout. That is the perfect model hypothesis in action. Add some error bars on that to reflect model error, and suddenly, the calculation seems less accurate, which is one reason the VIX algorithm consistently overestimates volatility. If it was a weather model, it would be warning of a storm every day. The difference is that weather forecasters actually calibrate their models to remove systematic errors, whereas in finance, there is no need because of the perfect model.

Weather models are complicated beasts, and it is hard to correct model error with any simple fix. Processes like the formation and dissipation of clouds are best described as emergent features that defy simple analysis (maybe AI will help). Also, the weather doesn't care how we model it. Option pricing is different because as mentioned above, there are persistent biases whose roots can be traced back to the way in which quants think about risk. To profit from them, we just need to take a leaf from the BSM proof and do some hedging of our own.

10.2 Hedge Your Bets

A hedge fund can be defined as an investment fund that uses sophisticated trading strategies to deliver improved performance while managing risk. Or alternatively (nonofficial version), it can be defined as an advanced form of gambling that somehow games the system—for example, by using a probabilistic model to improve the odds. This is illustrated by the history of the first hedge fund, which was founded by the mathematician Ed Thorp.

Thorp became interested in the mathematics of gambling while working as a professor at MIT in the 1950s. His ideas were shaped by two scientific collaborators: John Kelly Jr. and Ed Shannon. Kelly had developed a formula—later known as the Kelly criterion—to determine how much to bet at any round in a game of chance. In order to use it, though, the gambler needs to have an edge. Thorp's idea was that you could apply it to a game of roulette by using physics to predict the path of the ball. All you needed was a hidden computer to do the calculations, which was where Shannon came in.

Today, Shannon is often called the father of information theory—he invented the word *bit* for the 0 or 1, yes/no basis of classical computer logic—but together with Thorp, he also developed what some consider to be the world's first wearable computer. The plan was that, with the computer hidden inside his shoe, Shannon would tap his toe to record the position of the ball and estimate its likely trajectory. The result would be communicated via an earpiece to Thorp, who would place the bets.

Testing the system in Las Vegas, they found the method did work but suffered from technical problems, such as wires breaking or earpieces falling out—not to mention the risk of getting caught at a time when the casinos were often run by organized crime. Rather than give up completely, Thorp realized that the same idea could be applied, at less personal risk, to the game of blackjack, with the difference that this time, the edge was provided by counting cards. By keeping track of the composition of cards in the remaining deck, it was possible to calculate the odds of winning a hand.

He publicized his technique in the best-selling 1962 book *Beat the Dealer*. Soon after its publication, casinos started taking measures like increasing the number of decks and shuffling more often to make life more difficult for card counters who had read his book.

By this point, though, Thorp himself had already moved on to a much larger kind of casino—the markets. Here, you couldn't predict the market directly, but it was still possible to look for arbitrage opportunities by comparing the prices of stocks and options. Together with his collaborator Sheen Kassouf from Columbia University, and well before the BSM model was published, Thorp obtained an empirical curve that described the relationship between stock price and option price. He could then look for cases where options seemed to be incorrectly priced.

If, for example, the option looked too cheap, then they could purchase the option and short the stock. That way, it didn't matter whether the stock went up or down because they profited on the price difference either way. They published their system in a 1967 book called (naturally) *Beat the Market*, claiming in the introduction that "We have used this method in the market for the past five years to earn 25% a year." Thus was born the hedge fund industry.

As a sidenote, in 1977, another mathematician named Doyne Farmer worked with a group of scientist collaborators on a nearly identical roulette scheme. As *Wired* magazine reported in 1994 (apparently unaware of the Thorp/Kassouf book), this again involved building "a set of handcrafted, programmable, tiny microcomputers into the bottoms of three ordinary leather shoes. The computers were keyboarded with toes; their function was to predict the toss of a roulette ball." Like Thorp, Farmer also ended up founding a hedge fund, called the Prediction Company, but he didn't publish his methods. As he put it, "We really have found statistically significant patterns in financial data. There are pockets of predictability. We have learned a lot, and I would love to be able to describe it all to the world, to write a technical book laying out the knowledge we have accumulated on how to extract the weak signals that exist in financial markets and trade on them—a kind of Theory of Financial Prediction. Maybe call it How to Beat the Market. But given the quantity of money involved, I'm sure our partners will never let us do that."[5]

The common factor in all these schemes, be they in roulette, cards, or the markets, is to find a persistent bias in pricing that is large enough to generate consistent profits even after accounting for trading expenses. If price changes were truly random, or markets perfectly efficient, then such opportunities would not exist. The Black-Scholes model, with its impression of rationality, may have helped the field distance itself from associations with "speculation or gambling," but really, it's an accurate description. So is it still possible to "beat the market" in a consistent manner or have all the pockets of predictability been smoothed away by "efficient markets"?

10.3 The Quantum Fund

Referring again to figure 9.2, which compares the average payout of one-month straddle options with the average costs, it is clear—as hedge-fund CTO Larry Richards and I pointed out in a 2023 paper—that purchasing at-the-money straddle options will tend to lose money over time. As we wrote, "The cost can be rationalised as a kind of insurance premium to protect against volatility, but really it is a form of mispricing caused by model error: the Black-Scholes model, which assumes strike-independent volatility, gives an overly high price, which is only partially corrected when traders adjust the implied volatility."[6]

The converse of this, of course, is that selling straddle options looks like a winning trade. The problem from a practical perspective is that when you buy a standard call or put option, your downside is limited to what you pay, but the potential upside is unlimited. When you sell the option, this is reversed. You therefore need to maintain a large reserve against loss, which reduces your potential profits as a fraction of the amount at risk. We therefore need a way to cap the maximum loss.

Since a straddle is just a put and a call, we can look at these individually. For simplicity, we will consider the case with one-month call options, though puts can also work. If we buy one call option at a lower normalized strike K_1 and sell a call at a higher strike K_2, then as shown in figure 10.1, the minimum payout is zero, so the maximum loss is limited to the amount paid for the spread.

This strategy is known as a bull spread. Usually, it would be interpreted as a bet that markets will go up in a certain range over the period of the option, but

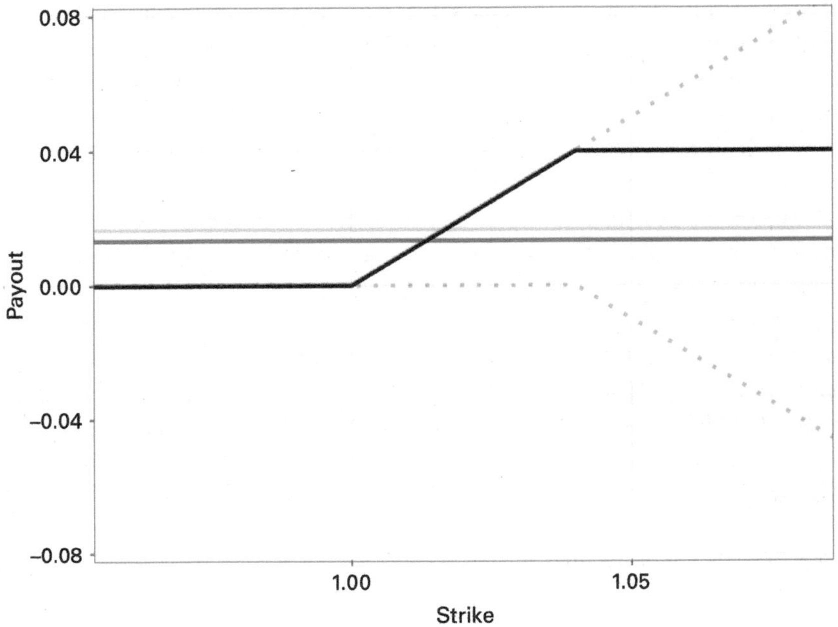

Figure 10.1
Diagram shows payouts for the call spread with normalized strikes $K_1 = 1$ and $K_2 = 1.04$. Dotted lines are for individual options, and the solid line is total. The dark gray horizontal line is the average cost, and the light gray horizontal line is the average payout, which is higher by about 22 percent.

that isn't what is going on here. We know prices don't always go up; they bounce around, especially over a timescale of a month or so. Instead, the strategy is a bet that the option cost will not properly reflect the expected payout.

The next question is how to choose the strikes. As seen in figure 9.2, the biggest difference between option payouts and costs occurs not for at-the-money options with $K = 1$, but at a slightly higher strike. The reason for this is related to the fact that the observed price distribution has a degree of positive skew. We therefore want to do a search over a range of combinations. It turns out that a reasonable strategy is to use values around $K_1 = 0$ and $K_2 = 1.04$. Again, these are normalized strikes, so in practice, we would choose the available strikes that are closest to these values.

Since $K_2 = 1.04$, the maximum payout is 4 percent or 0.04 when normalized to the initial index value. The average cost of the spread option, again normalized to the initial index value, is 0.0137, whereas the average payout is 0.0167. These values are shown by the horizontal lines in figure 10.1. Since the maximum loss, and therefore the amount at risk, is the same as the cost, the average profit is $0.0167-0.0137=0.0030$, which is about 22 percent of the maximum loss. Here, we have included transaction costs of 2 percent that are applied to the payouts.

The top panel of figure 10.2 shows density plots of the costs and payouts. The cost of the bull spread is concentrated in a fairly narrow band around the mean; however, the payout covers a larger range with two peaks around $K=0$ and $K=0.04$. The profits therefore have a bipolar nature, as shown by the bottom panel.

Buying the spread option is therefore rather like tossing a biased coin, or playing cards with a loaded deck, or betting on roulette while Claude Shannon taps a signal to your earpiece. On average, you should win. But to assess its performance more generally, we need to look at things like the risk/reward ratio.

A first step is to define an investment strategy. Suppose we start with an initial amount of \$100K, and each week, we invest 2.5 percent of the current cash holdings in new options with an expiration time of four weeks. That means that at any point, we will have 10 percent of the fund exposed to risk. In the first month, we invest \$2.5K each week for a total of \$10K, so the cash holding declines to \$90K, but then payouts begin to arrive after that.

Figure 10.3 shows how this investment would have performed over the period from mid-2012 to end-2024. The top panel shows the cumulative return, which shows a total profit of about 1,500 percent. The initial investment of \$100K grows to \$1585K. This equates to an annualized return of 25 percent, which coincidentally is the same as Thorp and Kassouf obtained for their fund.

The middle panel shows the monthly returns, whereas the bottom panel shows the drawdowns (i.e., the periods when the fund loses money). And here the news is less good. The worst drawdown occurs over the period 2015–2016 during which the fund loses nearly half its value, which is not a good look for investors.

10.4 The Pain Trade

The quantum fund described above is a bit like a person physically or virtually showing up at the stock market once per week, say every Friday, and placing exactly the same bet each time, with no variation. If one of those Solvay attendees had started doing so in 1927, and set up a fund with an initial investment of just \$1,000, and achieved a gain of around 25 percent each year, the fund would have grown over the last century to about four trillion dollars.

However, there also would have been some heart-stopping drawdowns on the way (imagine losing a trillion or so in 2015). One of the attractions of the fund from Thorp and Kassouf was that it delivered consistent returns. When Bernie Madoff was cooking the books to sell his ponzi scheme fund, he took care to

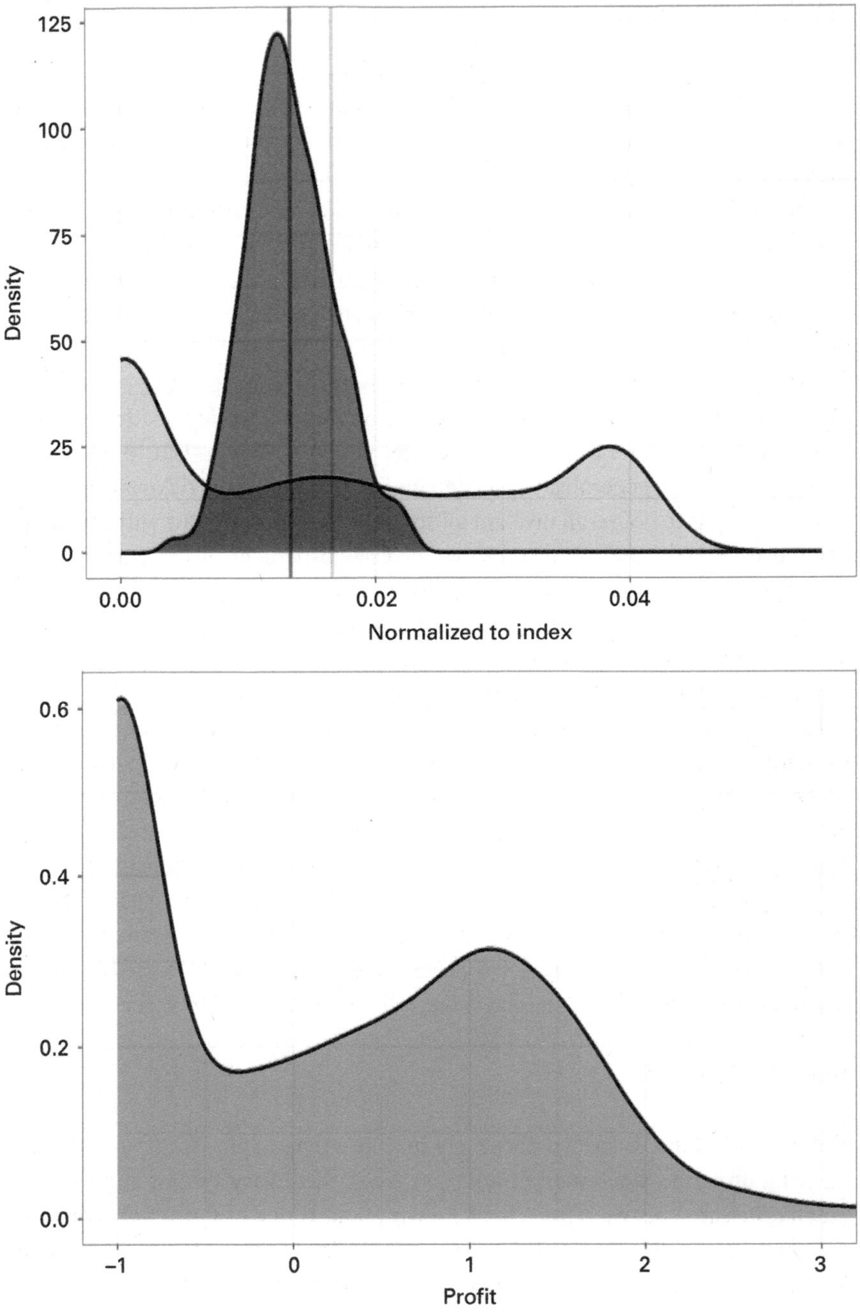

Figure 10.2
Density plot in upper panel shows costs (dark gray) and payouts (light gray), normalized to the S&P 500 index value. For normalized strikes of 1 and 1.04, the maximum payout is 0.04; however, there is some variation because the nearest strikes are used. Dark gray vertical line shows the average cost, and the light gray line shows the average payout. Data is SPX from July 2012 to December 2024. Lower panel is a density plot of profit as a fraction of maximum loss.

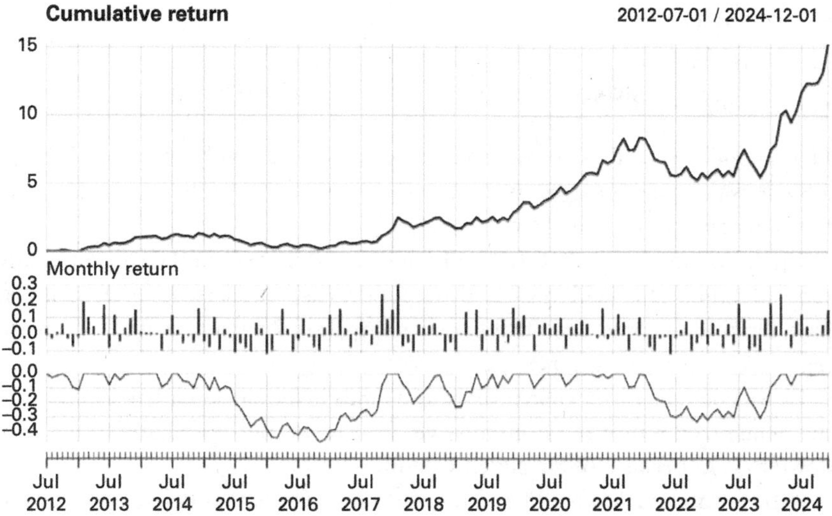

Figure 10.3
Top panel shows cumulative return for the options strategy for the period mid-2012 to end-2024. Middle panel shows the monthly returns, and bottom panel shows the drawdowns. The maximum drawdown covers the years 2015–2016 with a trough of -48 percent.

make the returns look remarkably regular and predictable (which is also what made them suspicious).

To get a better sense of the risk/reward profile, hedge fund experts therefore look at a range of metrics. Perhaps the most basic of these is the Sharpe ratio, which is defined as the difference between the returns of the investment and the risk-free return, divided by the standard deviation of the investment returns. For the quantum fund, the annualized Sharpe ratio is 0.74. A hedge fund manager would probably turn their nose up at this investment because they usually want to see a number above 1. For comparison though, over the last few decades, the S&P 500 has had a typical annual return 0.1 and volatility 0.15, which gives a Sharpe ratio of 0.67.

Other metrics generated by the software I am using[7] are something called Omega (which here is 1.90) and the Sortino ratio (0.50). Quants also have a number of terms to describe the drawdown properties, whose names sound vaguely medical. For the quantum fund, we can calculate the following:

- Calmar ratio 0.52
- Burke ratio 0.30
- Pain index 0.13
- Ulcer index 0.20

- Pain ratio 1.89
- Martin ratio 1.22
- Sterling ratio 0.43

I have no idea what these mean (some readers no doubt will), but a pain ratio of 1.89 doesn't sound good. So is there a way to make the results more stable and the experience more enjoyable?

One thing to note is that the fund only has 10 percent in the market at any time, and the rest is held in cash. If we put the cash into a savings account that pays the risk-free rate, then that boosts returns to 27 percent, with no increase in risk. The Sharpe ratio increases to 0.79.

Or we could go further and invest those funds in the stock market. This boosts the annualized return to an impressive 35 percent, but the Sharpe ratio goes down to 0.73 because of the added volatility.

A better approach would be to diversify into assets that deliver growth but are relatively uncorrelated with the S&P 500. Take your pick. (Gold? Fine art? Fine art with a gold frame?)

The best way to improve results, though, is probably to do what other hedge funds do, which is to look for trading signals. For example, I found that I could improve performance significantly and get the Sharpe ratio up around 1 by just not buying options on certain days according to a fixed rule. Also, I have only shown the results for four-week options, which is not necessarily optimal.

In order to see how the strategy performed in real trading, I tried it out over a one-year period.[8] Figure 10.4 shows the results. Here, the initial investment was only $4,000, and a single call spread worth about $800 was purchased on average every three weeks. The amount at risk each month was therefore typically about 25 percent of the initial sum instead of 10 percent. The plot includes for comparison an ensemble forecast where the price changes are randomized from historical data. The fund performance is within the expected range and also exceeds that of the S&P 500 index over the same period (dashed line); however, the results are very volatile when the initial investment amount is so small. Although this was a useful reality test and learning experience, and the returns were in line with expectations, to be used seriously, the fund would require a bigger investment and a longer horizon.

10.5 Summary

The quantum fund described here is designed to exploit the difference between option costs and expected payouts. The fact that the fund would have performed

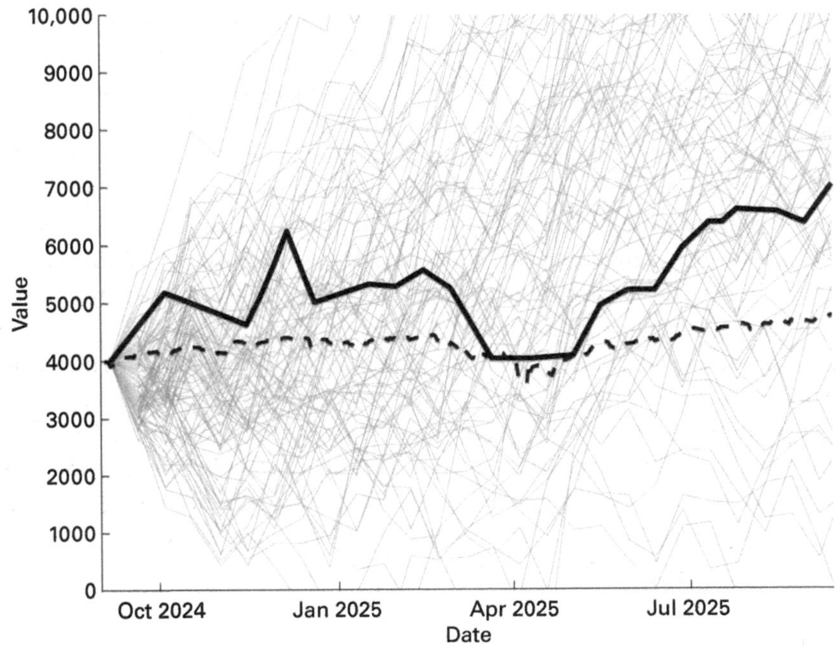

Figure 10.4
Solid line shows cumulative return for the world's smallest and noisiest hedge fund over a one-year period. Thin gray lines show historical returns with ensemble data from one hundred simulations. Price changes for the ensemble are randomized from historical data (2012–2021), trading every three weeks. Dotted line is the S&P 500 index. With a return over the period of 76 percent, the quantum fund therefore outperforms the index (19 percent) and is within the expected range. Note that the volatility is enhanced because of the small initial investment.

well in the past suggests that with a few tweaks and refinements, it could potentially form the basis of a successful trading strategy.

More important to this book, though, is that the fund (or rather the empirical backing behind it) is a concrete demonstration that the equation $C(K) = \mathbb{E}(\max(0, K - S_T))$ does not hold. The cost of an option is not the same as the expected payout. To assert otherwise is to assume that model error is negligible and can be ignored. It follows that the no-arbitrage principle does not hold either, especially given the connection between the bid–ask spread and volatility.

In physics, the crisis around the stability of the atom was resolved when the discovery of quantum energy bands explained why an electron circulating an atom would not spiral into the nucleus. The financial equivalent perhaps is the no-arbitrage idea that price can be known exactly. The main message of the quantum model is that both volatility and the bid–ask spread are reflections of uncertainty, so the bid and the ask are separated and can never collide: The "law of two prices" means they are always separated by a quantum of variance.

The veneer of determinism and rationality provided by the classical model in the 1970s was therefore an illusion. We can't compute the exact probability distribution of price change in a week's time any more than we can compute the exact probability distribution of rainfall. The Black-Scholes assumptions of zero-arbitrage and constant volatility continue to leave their mark on option prices, so, for example, the VIX consistently overestimates volatility, while traders reduce this error by about half but do not eliminate it completely. Viewed this way, the quantum fund is a way to monetize model error.

As mentioned in chapter 3, the no-arbitrage principle is ironic given that without the promise of arbitrage, much of the financial sector, including, of course, hedge funds, would have to shut up shop. However, the most ironic feature of the principle is that it can itself be arbitraged. In the next chapter, we show how the equation of cost with payout played a direct role in the 2007–2008 financial crash and more generally affects the stability of the financial system.

11

The Money Bomb

There cannot, in short, be intrinsically a more insignificant thing, in the economy of society, than money.
—John Stuart Mill, *Principles of Political Economy*, 1848

The question is not what you look at, but what you see.
—Henry Thoreau, Journal of 5 August 1851

Although quantum mechanics was invented to address anomalies such as the ultraviolet crisis, it soon found practical applications. Many technological inventions, such as microchips or lasers, rely on properties of matter that are related to quantum processes. But one of the first—which also had a huge impact on society—was the atomic bomb. In this penultimate chapter, we ask what the quantum approach to finance can tell us about things like financial stability.

11.1 Chain Reaction

Quantum processes in matter are usually limited to small scales, simply because Planck's constant $\hbar$ is associated with a miniscule amount of energy. A quantum harmonic oscillator at higher energy levels converges to a classical oscillator. A tennis ball stuck in an "infinite well" such as the one defined by a fence around a tennis court is not limited to a set number of bounces or show other nonclassical behaviors. However, quantum properties can scale up by design in engineered systems, such as a bomb.

The path from understanding the structure of atoms to making them blow up was remarkably fast. In 1938, the German scientists Otto Hahn and Fritz Strassman showed that bombarding uranium with a beam of neutrons could cause the unstable atoms to split in half. This would convert some of their mass into energy via Einstein's $E = mc^2$ and also release new neutrons that could in turn collide with neighboring atoms. In 1939, a team led by Leó Szilárd at Columbia University demonstrated the nuclear chain reaction and found that if the quantity of material present was above a certain critical mass, which for uranium-235 turned out to be just a few kilograms, the reaction would be self-sustaining. The energy could be harnessed for a nuclear fission reactor—or a nuclear weapon.

During the Manhattan Project, which followed after America entered the war, one of the biggest challenges faced by scientists was, in fact, not just how to generate a nuclear chain reaction but how to slow it down enough to make a functioning device. The main advance was made by Enrico Fermi, who argued that graphite was the ideal substance to soak up neutrons and therefore moderate the reaction rate. To test it, he set up a top secret experiment known as Chicago Pile-1 in a rackets court under the University of Chicago's football stadium.

The apparatus consisted of a large pile of uranium blocks weighing almost 500 tons, interspersed with graphite blocks to slow the reaction rate. Graphite control rods functioned as a further brake. The pile was activated on December 2, 1942, by removing the control rods, while detectors monitored activity. As Fermi's wife Laura later wrote, "The counters stepped up; the pen started its upward rise. It showed no tendency to level off. A chain reaction was taking place in the pile. In the back of everyone's mind was one unavoidable question, 'When do we become scared?'"[1]

The question perhaps was answered four and a half minutes later, when Fermi ordered that the control rods be reinserted to shut down the experiment. A little longer, and Chicago might have been the site of the world's first nuclear meltdown.

The development of the bomb was therefore a kind of fast-moving chain reaction in its own right, but one where ideas were propagated instead of energy, and neurons inside physicists' heads played the role of neutrons packed inside the nucleus. The new theory of quantum mechanics guided the process by explaining the structure of the atom and making sense of phenomena such as quantum tunneling, where particles can seemingly pass through barriers that classical physics would deem impossible (think the infinite well problem from chapter 2, but where the forces aren't actually infinite).

After the war, many physicists career-switched into finance, where some of the same techniques carried over. For example, random walk theory, the mainstay of classical quantitative finance, was familiar to physicists who had used it to compute the motion of neutrons in fissile material, and therefore the critical mass needed for a nuclear device.

But when it came to building explosive devices, quants took the opposite route. First, they built a bomb. And now, they are still trying to figure out how it works.

11.2 The Stock Market

Money is a fissile substance. We often think of money either in terms of something solid and inert, like old coins or a gold bar, or as merely a number on a statement. Economists, meanwhile, have tended to ignore it as a thing in itself, on the basis as Samuelson wrote in his classic textbook *Economics* that trade "largely boils down to barter" so money is just a medium of exchange.[2] But as with quantum matter money has two sides.[3] A money object such as a coin, a check, or a bank transfer is not really a thing in a classical physical sense; instead, it is a kind of information transfer, which acts as a measurement device by putting a hard number on the fuzzy concept of value. The word quantum is from the Latin for "how much," and the role of money is to say how much something is worth in terms of some unit of currency.

Money also acts as an entanglement device, in the sense that it entangles a debtor and creditor. (Here, the word *entanglement* is used in the financial sense, although the debt relationship can also be modeled mathematically using quantum entanglement.[4]) An early form of money was the Medieval tally stick, which was first used as a way to collect tax debts. A wooden stick would be marked with notches that indicated the value of the debt, and then split down the middle. One part was handed to the debtor, and the other part was held by the creditor, with the wood grain acting as a form of counterfeit prevention. The creditor's part was known as the stock, which is the source of that word in finance. Because it represented the right to collect a debt, it had a well-defined value and could be used as a money object in transactions. Today, when we analyze price changes in the stock market, we are analyzing the worth of instruments that represent ownership of firms, though the tallies are now electronic instead of made of wood.

The dualistic, entangling properties of money make it suitable material for a chain reaction. Suppose that instead of a sovereign issuing a tax on a Medieval landowner, a bank grants a mortgage to a customer so that they can buy a house. The tally in this case is a mortgage contract. The money paid to the customer, which is passed on to the seller, is not taken from a vault somewhere but is new money created by the bank. In countries such as the US or UK, some 95 percent of money is created in this way.[5]

We therefore have the seeds for a potential chain reaction. Much of the new money created by the bank will end up back in the real estate market (for example, the seller may want to buy a new, larger home). This will boost the price of property, which means that the value of the mortgage contract—which allows a claim on the property in the case of default—is secured. The bank can therefore issue more mortgages for larger amounts, with the new money again acting to boost house prices.

To achieve full criticality, though, it would help to have some way to speed up the process. Mortgages are ultimately a source of credit risk for the bank, so it would be much better if they could find a way to remove these from their balance sheets. Quants therefore came up with the idea to bundle loans up and sell them as packaged investments, using complex derivatives such as collateralized debt obligations (CDOs) and credit default swaps (CDSs). The former were used to combine loans such as mortgages into products with calibrated levels of risk that could be sold on to investors, whereas CDSs offered insurance against default.

These instruments had been around for a while but gained popularity in the early 2000s. According to economists, or regulators, their use just made the system more stable. As the International Monetary Fund purred approvingly in January 2006, "The dispersion of credit risk by banks to a broader and more diverse group of investors, rather than warehousing such risks on their balance sheets, has helped to make the banking and overall financial system more resilient." Ben Bernanke echoed them a few months later, saying that "because of the dispersion of financial risks to those more willing and able to bear them, the economy and financial system are more resilient."[6]

Just as quantum physicists had performed the alchemy of turning matter into energy, quants had seemingly transformed mortgages into a new source of money while at the same time reducing risk. Or as anthropologist David Graeber put it, "Financiers had managed to convince the public—and not just the public, but social theorists, too (I well remember this)—that with instruments such as collateralized debt obligations and high-speed trading algorithms so complex they could be understood only by astrophysicists, they had, like modern alchemists, learned ways to whisk value out of nothing by means that others dared not even try to understand."[7]

Underpinning this elaborate structure of financial derivatives, though, was the idea that mathematical models could be used to understand and put a price on risk. For example, CDOs were priced using models known as Gaussian copulas, which attempt to evaluate the probability of default by assuming, as the name suggests, that price changes follow a normal distribution and also that correlations between different assets could be assessed.

Some people did try to warn them. As early as 2000, Paul Wilmott wrote that the models used to evaluate derivatives were flawed: "It is clear that a major rethink is desperately required if the world is to avoid a mathematician-led market meltdown ... The underlying assumptions in the models, such as the importance of the normal distribution, the elimination of risk, measurable correlations, etc., are incorrect." In Berkshire Hathaway's 2002 Annual Report, Warren Buffet wrote that "derivatives are financial weapons of mass destruction, carrying dangers that, while now latent, are potentially lethal."[8] But such warnings fell on deaf ears. Quants were too busy making money, and regulators had long ago been captured by the story that markets were rational and self-correcting.[9]

11.3 When Do We Become Scared?

In chapter 1, I described three anomalies in finance that the quantum approach helped address. However, a much larger anomaly, if that is the word, was the 2007–2008 financial crisis, which was similarly unpredicted by conventional models and was again met by almost blanket denial among economists.

In a 2008 testimony to Congress, Alan Greenspan said, "A Nobel Prize was awarded for the discovery of the pricing model that underpins much of the advance in derivatives markets. This modern risk management paradigm held sway for decades. The whole intellectual edifice, however, collapsed in the summer of last year because the data inputted into the risk management models generally covered only the past two decades, a period of euphoria. Had instead the models been fitted more appropriately to historic periods of stress, capital requirements would have been much higher and the financial world would be in far better shape today, in my judgment." In other words, the problem was not with the Nobel-certified models, only their calibration.

The majority of mainstream economists agreed; in fact, some even took the crisis as confirmation of their beliefs. Robert Lucas wrote in 2009 that the unpredictability of markets "is nothing new. It has been known for more than 40 years and is one of the main implications of Eugene Fama's 'efficient-market hypothesis.' "[10] Fama himself told a 2010 interviewer that "I think it did quite well in this episode."[11] Paul Krugman summed it up a decade later when he announced that "Neither the financial crisis nor the Great Recession that followed required a rethinking of basic ideas."[12]

Obviously, there had been some lapses, such as the fact that the models did not include banks, or money, or derivatives, which, after all, were at the heart of the crisis. Vítor Constâncio of the European Central Bank observed, for example, in a 2017 speech, so a bit late, "In the prevalent macro models, the financial sector was absent, considered to have a remote effect on the real economic activity." In particular, the models "ignored the fact that banks create money by extending credit ex nihilo" (out of nothing).

In other words, the quants knew how to build a bomb, but they had no way of modeling how it worked or monitoring it for signs of danger. It was like someone trying to assemble a nuclear core without geiger counters, graphite rods, or an instruction manual.

In fact, economists and financial regulators did have an instruction manual, but it was the wrong kind. Conventional models, in finance and in economics more broadly, were based on a picture of equilibrium, where unspecified forces of supply and demand drive prices to their optimal level. And this feature was exactly the source of the alchemy that blew up the financial system.

Recall that the magic of the $\mu = r$ dynamic hedging argument behind the Black-Scholes model implied that risk can be hedged away by buying and selling securities (or as Merton said, one could "eliminate all of the risk."[13]). A conclusion was that, in theory at least, the Black-Scholes price of an option exactly equaled its expected payout. Model error was zero.

Scaling this argument up, it followed that risk could be reduced by encouraging the development of derivatives. And if risk can be hedged away, at least on paper, because you have a perfect model—what Samuelson had called "the perfect formula to evaluate and to price options"—then there is no limit to the amount that you can invest. In 2010, Wilmott estimated the nominal value of derivatives to be over a quadrillion dollars, which was larger than the actual economy that was supposed to support it.[14] It's as if everyone in an area has a massive mortgage not only on their own house but also that of their neighbors.

If there is one main lesson of the quantum approach though, it is that risk can never be reduced to zero. There is no perfect model. And the market for derivatives only exists in the first place because there is always an irreducible level of uncertainty—a quantum of variance—that under the right conditions can explode.

11.4 Virtual Estate

Although complex derivatives act as accelerants for money creation and ensuing financial crises, there are, of course, other ways of achieving the same ends. An example is the old-fashioned real estate bubble, of the sort recently demonstrated in Canada.

The Canadian economy did quite well during the 2007–2008 crisis, in part because banks did not resort to the same complex derivatives as did their counterparts in the US. However, the greatest risk is not so much derivatives themselves but the mental models used by economists to evaluate risk.

The housing market is similar to the stock market in the sense that buyers and sellers come together to trade assets. The difference is that in the housing market, people live in the assets, which complicates matters. For one thing, it slows transactions down, with real estate at the opposite end of the spectrum from stock markets in terms of holding periods and turnover time.

As an example of how markets may remain out of balance for extended periods, figure 11.1 shows prices and monthly transaction volumes for two-story homes in Toronto, Canada, for the period 2010 to 2025. House prices showed explosive growth over most of this period, which is usually attributed to demand from a growing population. This fits with the classical view that price rises are typically driven by excess demand for a finite number of units. However, as shown by the lower panel, the volume of transactions in the period 2023–2025 was much lower than in the earlier period 2010–2016. Instead of representing a happy equilibrium between supply and demand, the market was in a severe state of imbalance.

Mainstream economists saw no problem with this because on the surface, it seemed the economy was doing fine. The central bank cut interest rates to the bone since according to their metrics, inflation showed no signs of life at the time. But as I argued at the time (early 2022), Canada had created its own version of a financial fusion device, which did not produce a sudden mighty explosion but instead simply lifted house prices to a level where ordinary Canadians could no longer afford them.[15] Canada as a country had somehow contrived a way to price itself out of a place to live.

This had little to do with population growth. A bigger factor was the fact that bond yields had been on a downward trend for some four decades. This meant that when mortgages came up for renewal, which in Canada was typically after five years, the payment was often lower, and house prices had often raised to compensate, resulting in tax-free capital gains. The net worth of homeowners therefore ramped up, but when interest rates effectively hit zero during the COVID pandemic, then bounced (compare figure 5.9), the result was a deep imbalance between what houses were worth on paper and what new buyers could actually afford.

Just as in the stock market a large order leads to a price change, we can ask what price change would hypothetically correct this imbalance. If we estimate the imbalance to be about $\iota = 0.5$, then the log price change required to correct the price impact is $-\sqrt{2\iota}\sigma = -\sigma$, which requires an estimate of the price uncertainty σ. In terms of turnover, the timescales for housing markets are again more leisurely than for a typical stock market, so significant changes in actual and perceived value take place over years rather than days (compared to the stock market, price impact therefore occurs in slow motion).

House prices also have a strong cyclical component. The annual volatility of log price change for the S&P/Case-Shiller U.S. National Home Price Index

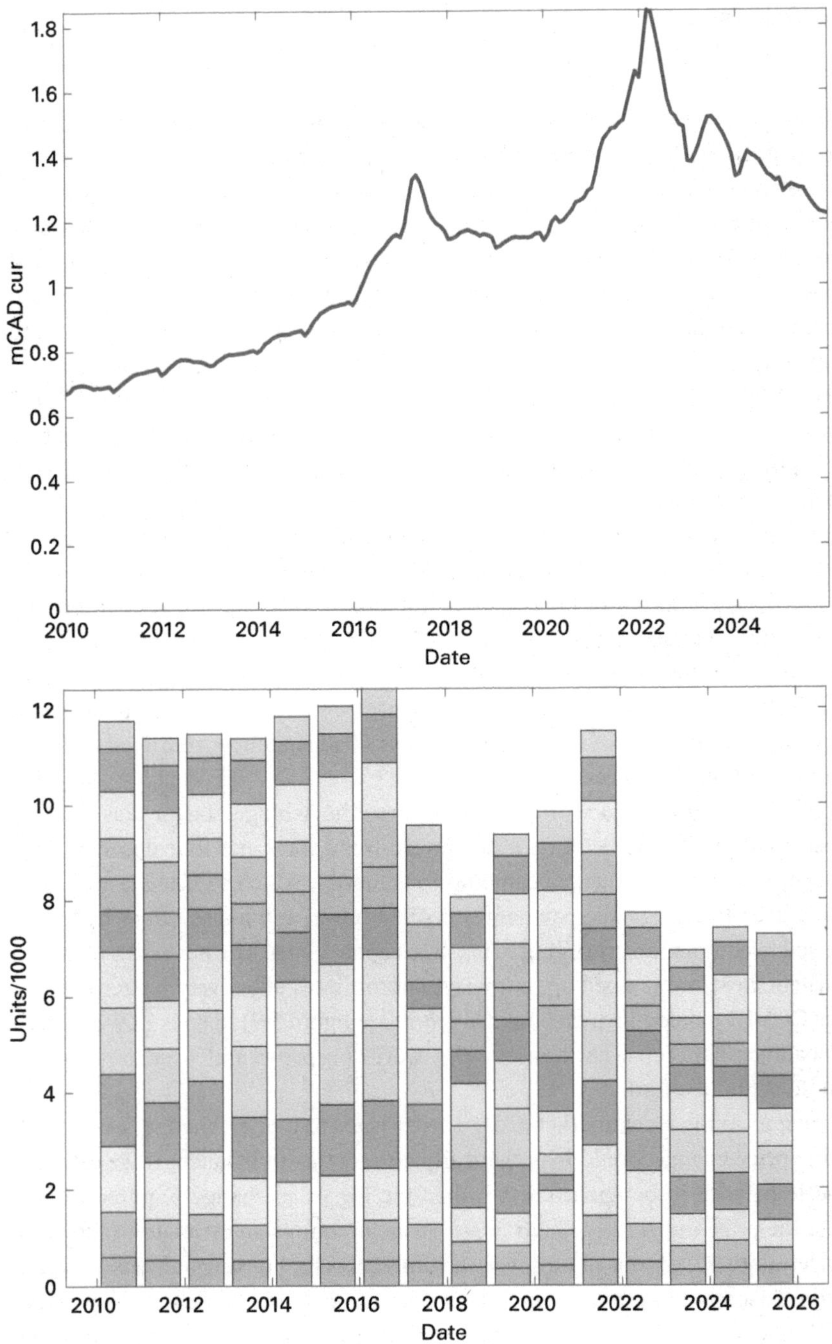

Figure 11.1
Top panel shows real house prices for two-story homes in Toronto, Canada, from 2010 to 2025 (MLS index in millions, normalized to 2025 dollars). Bottom panel shows house sales per month, in thousands of units. Grayscale indicates month from January (bottom) to December (top).

(1987–2023) is about 0.06, so if the data scaled in the usual way with time, then we would expect the five-year volatility to be $0.06\sqrt{5} = 0.13$. But instead, it is measured to be 0.26. This suggests that in order to assess the underlying price uncertainty, we need to take a longer-term perspective. If we assume that the price impact—and a corresponding shift in perceived valuations—takes place over a period of five years, and set $\sigma = 0.26$ to reflect the price uncertainty, then this translates to a fall in price (as opposed to log price) of around 30 percent in total. Of course, there are many other factors at work, especially the effect of interest rates on affordability, and an imbalance that grew up over four decades of declining bond yields will not disappear quickly. However, this result suggests that house prices need to moderate substantially (experience a negative impact) in order to restore the number of transactions and bring the market back into balance. It also shows that approaches that assume equilibrium work no better for assets such as houses than they do for stocks.

Given that real house prices have so far fallen by slightly over 30 percent, it seems at the time of writing that the market should start to move back to a more balanced state; however, markets do tend to overcorrect, which is what leads to oscillations. Price changes can lag the underlying dynamics, so a state of balance may equate to the peak or trough of a cycle, which would imply we are only partway through the process.[16]

Also, a difference between the housing market and the stock market is that the money creation process in the former directly affects the general availability of credit, so there is a powerful feedback loop between it and the national economy. We often associate houses with "real" value (as in "real estate") and assets such as stocks with "virtual" value, but a price is just a number, and the fact that the housing market is built on massive loans makes it inherently fragile. Real estate distortions, of course, do not compare with the existential danger of nuclear devices, but they can siphon investment from more productive uses, threaten housing security, damage the prospects of a generation, and, as with any large economic factor, can even have national security implications by financially weakening the country.[17]

11.5 Summary

Since its invention, classical finance and mainstream economics in general have emphasized rationality and equilibrium. Phenomena such as financial crises can't be made to fit into this picture (although economists try). The quantum approach, in contrast, views the financial system as inherently both dynamic and uncertain—features that also make it susceptible to extreme events.

Quantum finance might not predict the exact timing of a market crisis, but applying its principles can help to avoid one in the first place—for example, by improving the risk metrics used by regulators. For the housing market, the quantum approach draws attention to the underlying dynamics, which often have less to do with supply and demand for actual houses than with money creation through loans. In the final chapter, we summarize some of the book's main findings and ask what the quantum approach tells us about not just markets but the field of economics.

12

Blinded by Science

In T.S. Kuhn's theory of "normal science" research, the puzzle-solving ordinary practice depends on uncritical faith in the dogma of the overarching "paradigm". . . . This present case shows how the disease of blind faith can now infect the science-based intellectual systems as easily as the religious ones, and how the consequent debauchery of reason has outcomes here that are even more disastrous.

—Jerome Ravetz, Faith and Reason in the Mathematics of the Credit Crunch, 2008

Given that the models can never be perfect in this "soft" science, why is there so much focus on detail at the expense of the big picture? Some are easily blinded by science, unable to see the wood for the trees.

—Paul Wilmott, *Frequently Asked Questions in Quantitative Finance*, 2010

In some ways, this book has been the easiest and most fun to write of the dozen-plus books that I have authored or coauthored over the years. The material was based on my research in quantum finance over the past several years, and the work itself has been enjoyable. After working in areas like computational biology, where the modeler has to contrive equations that somehow approximate the incredible complexity of organic systems, it was nice to return to simple models. And of the many mathematical models that I have worked with throughout my career, the quantum oscillator has been the rare example of a model that actually tells you new things that you didn't already know. For example, I had no idea that stock markets would exhibit q-variance until the model suggested I look, or that the q-distribution would emerge almost unblemished from the average of a jumble of stock market data (figure 12.1 recaps these results). It was also a surprise to see the deep structure revealed by the quantum model in an implied volatility surface.

In a 1924 eulogy for Alfred Marshall, Keynes wrote that "Professor Planck, of Berlin, the famous originator of the Quantum Theory, once remarked to me that in early life he had thought of studying economics, but had found

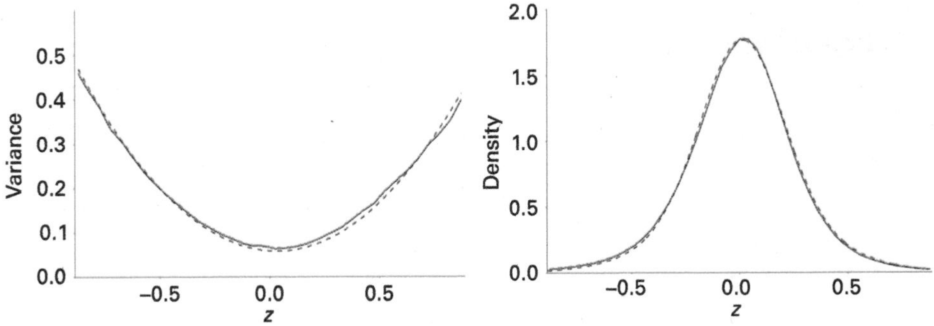

Figure 12.1
Q-variance and the normalized q-distribution for 350 stocks from the S&P 500 from figures 5.10 and 6.5. In both cases, with a small horizontal offset, the simple quantum model (dashed lines) provides an excellent fit to the average of the data (solid lines); however, the results appear to be inaccessible to—and therefore falsify—the classical random walk approach.

it too difficult! Professor Planck could easily master the whole corpus of mathematical economics in a few days. He did not mean that! But the amalgam of logic and intuition and the wide knowledge of facts, most of which are not precise, which is required for economic interpretation in its highest form is, quite truly, overwhelmingly difficult for those whose gift mainly consists in the power to imagine and pursue to their furthest points the implications and prior conditions of comparatively simple facts which are known with a high degree of precision."[1] Apparently, as alluded to earlier, the other attendees at the 1927 Solvay conference, along with their intellectual heirs, felt the same way. However, although economics is certainly not physics, it seems that some simple facts at least can be predicted and tested to a reasonably high degree of precision (also, is it still physics envy when the results look cleaner than most physics experiments?).

However, what might be called the "outreach" component of this unfunded and generally uncalled for "research program" has been at times somewhat exasperating. My feeling is that quantitative finance, and economics more broadly, is a field that actively resists reform or new ideas or exploring different paths. Economics as a discipline has long been obsessed with equilibrium, but it turns out that extends to its own theories. This makes it challenging to develop a new theory that is based on a different mathematical framework—even if that framework has existed for over a century. One of the main conclusions of this book is in a way less about stocks or options than it is about the practice of economics.

12.1 A New Paradigm

Since the time of Bachelier, classical quantitative finance has been based on the idea that price follows a random walk, so price changes conform closely to a normal distribution. His model of option pricing was an extension of the neoclassical model into the future: One couldn't predict prices, but one could predict their probability. Some seventy years later, efficient market theory argued that the reason price changes were random was because they were reactions to a random flow of news that was instantly absorbed by the market super-intelligence. The lesson of the story was that no one could beat the market, but at least you could predict its statistics.

The Black-Scholes model took this argument to the next level by appearing to mathematically demonstrate that risk can be removed by a process of dynamic hedging. Its adoption coincided with and contributed to an explosive growth in options and complex derivatives, helping to create a new industry in financial centers around the world. Economists over the years were happy to set aside the occasional malfunction such as the 1987 Black Monday crash, the 1998 LTCM blow-up, and the 2007–2008 financial crisis. Any nagging doubts could be addressed by inventing elaborate excuses or by noting that no model is perfect, the Black-Scholes model has the advantage of simplicity, it is very useful as a mental tool, traders adjust the price anyway, its incompleteness actually liberates traders' creativity, and so on.[2]

However, the reason for the success of the Black-Scholes model was not really the equation itself, since a similar equation had been developed by others to much less fanfare, or even option pricing per se. Instead, it was in the dynamic hedging story, which said that the subjective estimate of a stock's growth rate μ could be replaced by the objective risk-free rate r, and risk could be made to vanish, as in a kind of magic trick. That story is why we now have a quadrillion dollars worth of derivatives hanging over the world economy, built and maintained by financial engineers. Risk didn't vanish—it just got bigger.

The quantum finance approach is completely different. A recap follows:

- Quantum finance is motivated by the need to develop a probabilistic model of transactions that accounts for dynamics.
- The quantum oscillator model is derived by quantizing a linear entropic force and so can be considered a first-order dynamical model that correctly captures effects such as the square root law of price impact.
- The main prediction of the model, obtained by considering the variance of a displaced quantum oscillator, is the property of q-variance, which has been experimentally verified using market data.

- A corollary is that price change follows the associated q-distribution, which is a time-invariant, Poisson-weighted sum of Gaussians.
- Volatility clusters in time, and these clusters do not average out with increasing horizon, so realized variance fails to converge to a single value even over long periods.
- The quantum model suggests that the implied volatility smile can be viewed as largely an attempt by traders to account for the fact that volatility is related to price change through q-variance (theory did not include this, so traders had to put it in).
- However, q-variance and the q-distribution are incompatible with the classical random walk model, which forms the backbone of classical quantitative finance.
- Risk can never be eliminated even in theory, as claimed in the classical model, but is always subject to a fundamental level of uncertainty.

In this quantum model, price changes are treated as a dynamic probabilistic process. Volatility is not constant but along with price change is affected by imbalance. Hedging arguments don't work if they ignore the bid—ask spread, which represents an irreducible level of uncertainty. Whereas the normal distribution serves as a reasonable zero-order approximation to price behavior, the classical approach fails to describe volatility (actual or implied), which is key to the pricing of options. The risk-free rate, which plays such an important role in classical finance, is less useful: $\mu \neq r$. And the culprit is not just exogeneous shocks, or unpredictable surprises, but the basic properties of markets, where even something as staid as bond yields shows q-variance. The entire random walk model breaks down.

According to Myron Scholes (2009), "To say something has failed, you have to have something to replace it, and so far we don't have a new paradigm to replace efficient markets."[3] That isn't quite true—you can tell a model has failed (been falsified) without having a new paradigm, the same as I can tell my car has broken down without getting a new one. What is true is that in economics, people will continue to pretend the old model still works. But why are economists still following that paradigm in the first place? Why haven't they explored different roads?

12.2 Model Error

Back in 2010, I wrote a book called *Economyths: Ten Ways Economics Gets It Wrong*, which was in part my reaction to the financial crisis. A theme in the book was that economists are modern versions of Pythagoreans, who are obsessed with the idea that everything can be reduced to number; or as Paul Romer put it more recently, "that math could tell you the deep secrets of the universe."[4] The book ended with an exhortation for economics students to overturn neoclassical orthodoxy and "do something new." The section was reproduced by *Adbusters* magazine during Occupy Wall Street, an event that the magazine had initiated.

The original Pythagoreans were inspired by the discovery that musical harmony is based on mathematical ratios—for example, the ratios of string lengths when playing notes on a lute (as John Burnet wrote in *Early Greek Philosophy*, "It is not too much to say that Greek philosophy was henceforward to be dominated by the notion of the perfectly tuned string."[5]). They valued principles such as symmetry and simplicity and also saw patterns in numbers, believing, for example, that odd numbers were superior to even numbers because they could not be divided in two and so were in a sense indivisible.

Quantum finance was my own, somewhat belated, attempt to do something new. In one sense, ironically, the q-distribution may be the most Pythagorean contribution to economics ever, given that it involves a sum of perfectly symmetric, odd-numbered wave functions.[6] However, the model is based on the idea that markets are dynamic and subject to imbalance, so the apparently stable q-distribution represents a kind of dynamic balance between opposing forces. A better description is supplied by Pythagoras's contemporary (and critic) Heraclitus, who wrote, "What is at variance comes to terms with itself—a harmony of opposite tensions, as in the bow or the lyre."[7]

Also ironic is that a main technical contribution of the research is a new algorithm for valuing options, which is not exactly the revolution we had in mind back in 2010. However, the acknowledgment of model error might limit their misuse, and as already mentioned, it is the story that counts. In the quantum model, it is impossible to magic away risk because an irreducible quantum of variance is written in the bid–ask spread. There is no point in pretending to calculate implied volatility to the sixth decimal place if prices are only known to a few percent. And derivatives don't just diversify risk—they can also amplify it. (Also to be fair, the field of quantum economics is much broader and uses quantum models to address topics such as decision theory and game theory, which might be more useful.[8])

Perhaps a more interesting question, though one for sociologists or anthropologists more than economists, is what the subject tells us about the field of economics.

The methods presented in this book, which I started developing back in 2016, were for a long time—until mid-2025—extremely hard to publish in non-heterodox economics or finance journals (with the critical exception of *Wilmott*). Part of the problem was that anything with the word *quantum* seemed to elicit a jaded feeling of distrust and anatagonism. (I mentioned some of the reviews I received in chapter 1; however, this was just the tip of the iceberg. I should thank these critics for their disparaging comments since they often turned out to be quite motivating. After a while, I came to view hostile reviews as part of the process.) Until quite recently, quantum ideas have seen very little use outside of physics. The reason has nothing to do with their efficacy or lack thereof; instead, as I have argued elsewhere, and touched on in chapter 1, it is because there is what amounts to a scientific taboo around their use by non-physicists.[9] The quantum road has long been closed to general traffic.

However, although physicists may be deeply uncomfortable with the perceived misuse of quantum mathematics, it's not up to them to decide how models can be used in the social sciences. A bigger obstacle, as became evident in the aftermath of the financial crisis, is that economists themselves don't seem to exhibit much of the scientific spirit when it comes to engaging with new ideas. This explains the continued emphasis on concepts like equilibrium and rationality—which are then repackaged as "strengths and distinctive insights."[10]—and why proponents of new approaches often face surprisingly fierce resistance.

This is true, of course, in other fields, including the life sciences. As Jay Bhattacharya, in his (sometimes controversial) role as director of the US National Institutes of Health, told the New York Times in 2025, "You have, in field after field after field, a kind of set of dogmatic ideas held by the people who are at the top of the field. And if you don't share those ideas, you have no chance of advancing within those fields."[11] Testing and replication of empirical results is important because it "turns over the determination of what's true to nature rather than authority." (As mentioned already, the empirical phenomena of q-variance and the q-distribution are easily checked.) However, economics and finance take this to the next level, where theories replicate endlessly whether they agree with data or not. Biology has progressed enormously since the 1970s—quantitative finance not so much.

Part of the problem comes down to the typical groupthink—as Romer noted, there is "a disregard for and disinterest in ideas, opinions, and work of experts who are not part of the group"[12]—accompanied and fortified by what Claudia Sahm, who was formerly a section chief at the Federal Reserve, described in 2020 as the "toxic culture" of their profession, where gatekeepers "punch down and attack those with opinions different than theirs."[13] The physicist César A. Hidalgo, whose work in complexity economics at places including the MIT Media Lab has drawn wide note, similarly described "an academic world of exclusion, fear, and deception" in which "toxicity consumes the minds of younger students."[14] Economist, author, and YouTuber Cahal Moran did a whole video called "The Toxic Culture of the Economics Profession."[15]

I am not an academic, so haven't actually experienced this directly; however, a related problem, which affects even independent researchers, concerns the concept of conflict of interest. According to the film maker Charles Ferguson, who directed the Oscar-winning documentary *Inside Job* in 2010, the economics academy "has become so compromised by conflicts of interest that it now functions almost as a support group for financial services and other industries."[16] But they also function as a support group for themselves and their university departments, which makes criticizing old ideas or arguing for new ones a fraught exercise. Nowhere is this seen more clearly than with the review process (I am going to write about this because the culture of anonymity and silence about the process makes it open for abuse).

Academic journals use a (usually anonymous) review process to evaluate submissions. Reviewers, who are sourced by editors from experts working in the same field, are supposed to declare whether they have a conflict of interest (this needn't disqualify them since it can be hard to find experts with no potential conflicts, but it is important to be up-front). In economics, although I have been fortunate to work with some very good editors and reviewers, more broadly, the norms seem different. An example was a paper of mine from 2024 (so two years after I had first published on q-variance), which was an early attempt to falsify key ideas including the no-arbitrage principle. The reviewers did not discuss this but just said they "do not see the point of the paper" and "there is no scientific novelty, the discussion is extremely incomplete and partial, and no results support the approach" (which would apply also to this book since it makes all the same points).

When one of the reviewers later outed himself (in response to something I wrote), it turned out that his most-cited paper was exactly on building models that apply the no-arbitrage principle (this is not giving too much away, as there are scores of such papers). He seemed completely unaware that there might be a conflict. Instead, he said that he had rejected my paper because it was "very pseudo-philosophical. . . . There is nothing quantum about Economics or Finance. Prices of shares or options are real valued, not in superposition."

Such assertions are typical of the sort that I have had directed at me over the last decade, but they have little meaning.[17] Of course, prices are real valued. No one is saying that the money in your wallet is in multiple states. The idea is that you can model probability using a complex-valued wave function. The rejected paper was about empirical results, not "pseudo-philosophical" speculation.[18] (Maybe it comes down to framing. Saying that stock prices behave just like subatomic particles: sounds spiritual. Saying subatomic particles behave just like stock prices: not so spiritual.)

But really, such comments are the sound of someone colliding with a paradigm shift. This points to a deeper reason why reviewers often failed to engage seriously with quantum approaches, which comes down to worldview, or what one paper on "the ethics of scholarly peer review" called an epistemological conflict of interest (Souder, 2011). This cites Shimp (2004), who "identifies through a Kuhnian analysis a similar epistemological conflict of interest. Scientists from different paradigms view data differently, and therefore Shimp recommends that when peer reviewers represent radically different perspectives from those of the author under review, they must openly acknowledge such differences as conflicts of interest. More broadly, Shimp calls for the peer-review communities to develop and foster a 'tolerance for competing paradigms.'"

As an article in *Nature* argued, "Journals should take action against toxic peer reviews" especially because of the effect they can have on early-stage scientists. One idea is that journals should maintain a checklist for editors. "This could include things like confirming that the reviewer has maintained integrity and impartiality, has no conflicts of interest, and has been courteous and constructive."[19] Or at least keep an open mind.

12.3 The Collapse of Time

However, maybe skeptics are right to worry about the ontological question of whether something like the stock market is "really quantum." After all, we are not using quantum physics just as a metaphor (as mentioned in chapter 3 this would be pointless since most people in finance are going to know more about stock prices than they do about electrons). And if a physicist analyzes data that only makes sense in a quantum model, would they not conclude that the underlying phenomenon must be quantum? (I had an experience like this with superconducting magnets, where the odd behavior of a measurement apparatus turned out to be caused by quantum fluctuations.[20])

A skeptical physicist-turned-quant told me once that quantum mechanics has "many totally unintuitive predictions that make it special," so the onus was on me to justify its use in finance. But the real test is not to surprise people (the assertion $\mu = r$ is surprising[21])—it is to make accurate predictions; and perhaps quantum (in the mathematical sense) phenomena present differently, and more intuitively, in social systems than they do in physical ones, while also resisting prediction using classical means. Also, the quantum model used here is based on the core properties of a quantum harmonic oscillator: The linear restoring force gives the square root law of price impact, the energy increase caused by displacement gives q-variance, and the energy harmonics give the q-distribution. The only parameter in all cases is a ground-state standard deviation. If anyone could come up with a one-parameter classical model with the same properties, then in effect, they would also have a classical version of the quantum oscillator, which would probably surprise physicists.

If there is one aspect of the quantum approach that seems deeply unintuitive, though, it is in the treatment of time. The whole point of mechanistic science—and indeed much of Western philosophy over the last couple of thousand years—is that to understand a system, you break it down into parts, figure out the forces which act on them, and solve. Time itself is treated as a substance that can be sliced and diced into separate units rather than viewed as a whole.[22] Brownian motion, for example, is modeled as a random walk over discrete time steps. Stochastic calculus takes this to the limit of steps that are infinitely short.

When I first started working with quantum models, I did the same thing, breaking a time period T down into steps Δt to build up a time series in the traditional manner. At some point, though, I switched to working with the time period T as a whole, which was when things became much easier (if harder to explain).

For example, it was remarked in chapter 5 that the quantum approach does not model the exact price trajectory during the period. For both q-variance and the q-distribution, the wave function is only collapsed at the end, and variance is computed not from individual points or transactions but by measuring the energy over the complete period. This is fine for things like option pricing since we can adjust the period to whatever we want, and as mentioned in chapter 6 we can also use ensemble techniques (equation 6.19) to simulate the distribution, however it does raise a kind of ontological problem. For anyone trained in classical finance, or the tenets of Western science, a model of price is an algorithm that tells you how price evolves over time in a continuous fashion, not one that just tells you the distribution after a set period has elapsed. And it seems intuitively reasonable that we should be able to produce such a time series—after all, the market does. And yet as seen in chapter 6, classical continuous-time models are not consistent with q-variance or its associated q-distribution. Certainly no predictive[23] model has been developed, and the clock ran out on that test.

Also, while it is true that markets constantly collapse price through transactions, that only applies to past and current prices. If we change the context to think about how market forces play out over a future period, then there is no collapse, but the expected price change distribution should be the same.

And this points to an interesting question: What would it mean if the stock market produces behavior that can only be satisfactorally modeled using a quantum approach, and so is in a sense inaccessible to conventional methods? As with emergent phenomena, it would imply that we can model the effect without knowing exactly how it is created in classical step-by-step terms—which is not unreasonable given that the stock market obviously qualifies as a complex system. It also suggests that the subatomic world is not as foreign as we thought. Žižek (2012) wrote that "in the quantum universe, the human spirit encounters itself outside itself," and perhaps that is true of traders as well.

12.4 The Quantum Joke

However, the main reason quantum finance has not caught on is not so much about ontology, or uneasiness about quantum models, or "toxic peer reviews." Instead, it is that in many respects, economics has evolved in such a way that it is less what we think of as a real "hard" science, where even established theories are at risk of falsification, than a kind of performance. It is about telling a story. And from the point of view of the financial sector, which supports much of the work, the story that markets are rational and efficient and stable and optimize utility is hard to beat. And the idea that you can mathematically eliminate risk is the Holy Grail, to use Samuelson's phrase.

Markets are quantum, not just in the sense that money is dualistic, prices are uncertain, price changes can be modeled using a wave function, or that when you look at it the right way, volatility is seen to be smiling, as if it's in on a rather funny joke. At a deeper level, they are quantum because their nature is shaped by, and has itself shaped, a kind of mental substrate of theories and attitudes and beliefs and stories. Financial transactions are a way of attaching a precise number to the fuzzy concept of value. But the reverse is also true. By attaching prices to value, we shape our values. The observation affects not just the system but also the observer.

The best evidence for that—the biggest anomaly—is to look at the value system of mainstream economics and marvel at its incredible stability. In what other field would generations of researchers attempt to model a complex dynamic probabilistic system such as the interaction between buyers and sellers by drawing two lines that intersect at a fixed and stable point? (I, for one, have never encountered this in another field.) And then draw conclusions that impact society by airily referring to the "law of supply and demand"? Or non-jokingly assert that markets instantaneously absorb all available information—and that a devastating crisis proves their point? Or build entire theories around the assertion that the expected growth rate equals the risk-free rate, which, if true, would make much of the financial sector—including the part which helps fund such research—disappear into the void?

Economics always selects theories that are consistent with the idea that value can be expressed exactly using numbers (with controlled allowance for "frictions" such as behavioral effects[24]). The efficient market hypothesis, the law of one price, and the Black-Scholes model are all ways of saying the same thing. According to these theories, the future may be unknown, but the uncertainty is a tame kind because the probability distribution can be computed. Again, the idea ultimately goes back to the Pythagorean notion that "number is all." This is why the implied volatility smile—a clue hidden in plain sight—is commonly explained away as being the product of trader irrationality, when instead, it is largely due to the effort to correct the imperfect model. And it is why economists can ignore empirical evidence, like the fact that supposedly parallel lines in a plot of price impact actually intersect, or options have a minimum cost so their price violates the no-arbitrage principle, or derivative prices do not match average payouts, or the financial system blows up on their watch. Empirical observations can never falsify your theory if you just refuse to look.

As mentioned in chapter 1, finance is overdue a wake-up call. Stock market behavior is driven not so much by "news" or the efficient processing of information by the market hive-mind, but—here's some news—by a quantum of variance that is related to information and can be measured in the spread of expectations between a buyer and a seller. Even if economists do not "believe" the quantum model, they should start believing the empirical evidence that has long been in front of them and act accordingly. Teaching something like the Black-Scholes model, while not mentioning that volatility varies by a factor of two depending on strike, would be misleading, and coding such models into the heart of the economy through financial engineering could constitute negligence. Embracing real uncertainty—that irreducible quantum—and truly letting go of the dream of efficiency, rationality, and the perfect model may be hard, but it's long past time. (And to be honest, all that talk about efficiency and rationality was starting to sound a little crazy.)

Also, finance may be mostly about the story, but the story is changing, in part because of the growing interest in quantum technology. Just as neoclassical economics came of age with the advent of classical computing, so new approaches to finance are being sparked by ideas from quantum computing. After all, if the language of finance is quantum, then quantum computers are the appropriate translators. As of the time of writing in mid-2025, the mood music around quantum economics and finance certainly seems to be shifting, at least from where I sit.[25] (In particular, for reasons that are not well understood but I would like to think have at least something to do with the scientific process creaking into life, quantum results are becoming easier to publish.[26])

However, it may turn out that the jump to a new paradigm depends more on the human quality of embarrassment—or rather the moment when it becomes less risky to ditch the old ways than to support them. Speaking about the difficulty of upsetting the status quo in areas from tobacco policy to (more recently) concussions in ice hockey, the late Canadian former politician (and ex-NHL goalie) Ken Dryden noted that the impetus for change is not really up to scientists or communicators. Instead, it only occurs when decision-makers start to worry about how things will be perceived by "our kids and grandkids . . . 10, 20, 30 years from now."[27]

In economics, a good test might be the property of q-variance. Anyone can check that variance over a period depends in a quadratic fashion on price change. The corresponding quantum model of price dynamics is consistent with both implied and actual volatility but is incompatible with a random walk. This means that the proofs for key theories such as Black-Scholes do not apply. How long will these tired ideas continue to be propagated in universities? Will AI speed things up? Economic theories probably won't give you a concussion (even if it sometimes feels like it), but defenders of the status quo might want to adjust their metaphorical seatbelts.

My hope for this book, then, is that by providing a quantum alternative to the classical model, it will help open more eyes to the fact that the financial system is not a stable, self-equilibrating, clockwork machine that ticks along in a sequence of rational steps, but is something far more complex and interesting. Economics has been stuck on its boring road for a long time, as if marooned by the faulty instructions of an outdated GPS map. Other routes are available, and the views of the scenery are better.

But the main question raised and only partially answered by this book is not what quantum approaches tell us about markets. It is what they tell us about what we tell ourselves about markets. And that, of course, is the most quantum thing of all.

Notes

Introduction

1. See Courtault et al., 2000.
2. De Broglie, 1929.
3. Kumar, 2008.
4. Clark, 1999.

Chapter 1

1. Kyle & Obizhaeva, 2018.
2. Lillo, 2023.
3. Bucci et al., 2019.
4. Orrell, 2022a.
5. Let's Do Quantum Economics! Certificate of Quantitative Finance Institute, July 13, 2022.
6. One physicist-turned-quant who scanned the paper spoke for many when he volunteered that "I unfortunately cannot follow your argument nor reproduce your train of thought." Even so, I felt that the price impact paper should have been corrected because the plot concealed the fact that the data was clearly inconsistent with the stated hypothesis.
7. Unless otherwise specified, the data source is Yahoo Finance. The ticker symbol for the S&P 500 index is ^GSPC.
8. Let's Do Quantum Economics! Certificate of Quantitative Finance Institute, July 13, 2022; Imaginary Oscillations: Quantum Uncertainty and the Black-Scholes Formula; Certificate of Quantitative Finance Institute, June 14, 2023; An Introduction to Quantum Economics; The Fields Institute for Research in Mathematical Sciences, March 23, 2023.
9. Orrell & Richards, 2023; Orrell, 2023, 2024c.
10. For a journal that shall not be mentioned.
11. Mackenzie, 2006.
12. Derman & Miller, 2016, p. 311.
13. Gross & Waltners, 1995.
14. Simons, 1997.
15. Orrell, 2023. See also Certificate of Quantitative Finance Institute, June 5, 2024; A Quantum Finance Approach to Option Pricing.
16. Orrell, 2024a.
17. Wilmott & Orrell, 2025.
18. Volatility and Risk with Dr. Paul Wilmott. Quant Insights: Volatility and Risk in Quant Finance Conference 2025, June 5, 2025.
19. See the competition website at https://github.com/q-variance/challenge.

20. Akerlof, 2020.

21. Aaronson, 2013.

22. The field of quantum economics was founded by a physicist; see Qadir, 1973.

23. One anonymous critic pointed out that "In markets there's no literal wavefunction anyway," so I had to describe my model in terms of "the analogy . . . of a quantum harmonic oscillator," the "analogy to a coherent state," and volatility modes that "themselves are analogous to [oscillator] energy levels."

24. See discussion in Tudball, 2024.

Chapter 2

1. Keynes, 1936.
2. See www.oxfordreference.com.
3. Jevons, 1957 (first published 1871).
4. Walras, 1889.
5. Fama, 1965.
6. Jensen, 1978.
7. Cochrane, 2011.
8. Robinson, 1968.
9. Orrell, 2025a.
10. Orrell, 2024d.
11. Sokolov, 2010; Roos, 2014.
12. Orrell & Houshmand, 2022.
13. Kondratenko (2015) proposed similar force terms, without a corresponding expression for mass, on the basis that these terms cancel at equilibrium.
14. Frisch, 1933, 1936.

Chapter 3

1. Galbraith, 1994.
2. The physics in this chapter and the next is standard and is explained in fuller detail in texts such as Rae (2007) and Zwiebach (2022).
3. Belloni & Robinett, 2014.
4. Schrödinger, 1935
5. Danchin, 2002.

Chapter 5

1. Jevons, 1878.
2. Juglar, 1862; Kitchin, 1923; Kuznets, 1930; Kondratiev, 1925.
3. Frisch, 1933, 1936.
4. Fama, 1965.
5. Tóth et al., 2011.
6. Orrell, 2022c, 2025a.
7. Wilmott & Orrell, 2025.

Chapter 6

1. Mandelbrot & Hudson, 2004; Wilmott, 2010: 219.
2. These chapters draw on material from Orrell, 2025, 2025a.
3. Merton, 1976.

4. Navas, 2003.
5. Orrell, 2025a.
6. Orrell, 2025a.
7. For the S&P 500 stocks studied, the value of σ used for q-variance is typically about 15 percent larger than $\Sigma/\sqrt{2}$, whereas the value used for the q-distribution is smaller by a similar amount.
8. The term is usually applied to moments of the price process rather than of variance. Andersen & Piterbarg, 2007.
9. See the competition website at https://github.com/q-variance/challenge.
10. For a discussion, see (Orrell, 2026).
11. Mandelbrot, 1963.

Chapter 7

1. Boness, 1964.
2. Bodie, 1999.
3. Scholes similarly claimed that "We were able to build a portfolio that was essentially riskless"; Clark, 1999.
4. Clark, 1999.
5. Quoted in Haug & Taleb, 2008.
6. Derman & Miller, 2016.
7. Merton, 1976.
8. Wilmott, 2013.
9. Orrell, 2024b.
10. Indeed, the BSM model can be understood in terms of a magic trick; see Orrell, 2023.
11. For a transcript, see https://www.feynmanlectures.caltech.edu/I_01.html.
12. A Stylized History of Quantitative Finance. Talk by Emanuel Derman at Quant Insights: Volatility and Risk in Quant Finance Conference 2025, June 5, 2025.
13. Clark, 1999.

Chapter 8

1. Since $\log(0.5) = -0.69$ and the weekly volatility is 0.028.
2. Tett & Gangahar, 2007.
3. Zhu, 2015.
4. Lee, 2004; Raval & Jacquier, 2023.
5. Gatheral, 2006.
6. As obtained from figure 1 of Gatheral & Jacquier, 2014.
7. For comparison, Enrico Fermi quoted John von Neumann as saying, "With four parameters I can fit an elephant, and with five I can make him wiggle his trunk"; Dyson, 2004.
8. Derman & Miller, 2016.
9. Orrell, 2024c.
10. See (Orrell, 2021a) for a discussion.
11. As just one example, Modern Portfolio Theory shows how to select a portfolio of assets that maximizes the expected return for a given level of risk, but assumes that returns are lognormal; Markowitz, 1952.
12. Romer, 2016.
13. See https://wilmott.com/financial-modelers-manifesto/.

Chapter 9

1. Cboe, 2019.
2. See Hull (1993) along with his Technical Note No. 22, available at http://www-2.rotman.utoronto.ca/~hull/technicalnotes/TechnicalNote22.pdf.
3. Itô, 1951.
4. Carr & Madan, 2001.
5. Orrell & Richards, 2023.
6. Orrell & Richards, 2023.
7. See figure 1 in Ahmad & Wilmott, 2005.

Chapter 10

1. Taleb, 1998.
2. Quoted in Mackenzie, 2006, p. 158.
3. Orrell, 2007.
4. Matthews, 2001.
5. Kelly, 1994.
6. Orrell & Richards, 2023.
7. The "PerformanceAnalytics" package in R.
8. Results were followed by Paul Wilmott.

Chapter 11

1. Fermi, 1954.
2. Samuelson, 1973.
3. Orrell, 2016, 2018a, 2018b, 2020b.
4. See Orrell, 2020b.
5. McLeay et al., 2014.
6. Bernanke, 2006.
7. Graeber, 2018.
8. See www.berkshirehathaway.com/2002ar/2002ar.pdf.
9. Tett, 2009.
10. Lucas, 2009.
11. Cassidy, 2010.
12. Krugman, 2018.
13. Clark, 1999.
14. Wilmott & Orrell, 2017.
15. My book *Money, Magic, and How to Dismantle a Financial Bomb* was published at the start of 2022, which coincided with the peak of the bubble.
16. Faced with some of the weakest sales in a quarter century, the CEO of the Toronto Regional Real Estate Board explained that "Canadian residents, both homeowners and renters alike, are increasingly having to deal with the nightmare of violent home invasions and carjackings." Nothing to do with ridiculous prices then. See GTA REALTORS Release June Stats, https://trreb.ca/wp-content/files/market-stats/market-watch/mw2506.pdf.
17. If only because a "secure Canada requires affordable places to call home"; Maddeaux, 2025. In Europe, meanwhile, the "housing crisis is as big a threat to the EU as Russia," according to the mayor of Barcelona; Hernández-Morales, 2025.

Chapter 12

1. Keynes, 1924.
2. Svetlova, 2018; Triana, 2009.
3. Anonymous, 2009.
4. Mayeda, 2016.
5. Burnet, 1920.
6. Or a power chord, if you prefer. For example, the notes C1 (frequency 32.703), G2 (97.999), and E3 (164.81) make a major C chord and have frequency ratios of 1, 3, and 5. When I mentioned this as a humorous aside in a paper, one of the reviewers, who had rejected the quantum argument, rejected this as well: "It is true that a major chord is composed of the tonic (1), major third (3) and dominant (5), but this has nothing to do with frequencies, only with the position of the notes in the diatonic scale—and actually there are 2 tones between 1 and 3 and 1.5 tone between 3 and 5, therefore the frequency ratios are absolutely not 1, 3 and 5." Again, it seemed telling that the reviewer trusted their hazy knowledge of music theory instead of just looking at something like a guitar.
7. Heraclitus, Fragment 51.
8. See Holtfort & Horsch, 2024, and references therein.
9. Orrell, 2022b.
10. Coyle, 2007.
11. Schulman, 2025.
12. Romer, 2016.
13. Sahm, 2020.
14. Hidalgo, C. A. (2021, February 24). https://twitter.com/cesifoti/status/1364699994012459009.
15. As part of his YouTube channel *Unlearning Economics*. See https://www.youtube.com/watch?v=AeMcVo3WFOY.
16. Ferguson, 2010. See also Carrick-Hagenbarth & Epstein, 2012.
17. For a sample of typical comments, see "Ten Reasons to (Not) be Quantum": https://futureofeverything.wordpress.com/2021/11/11/reasons-to-not-be-quantum/.
18. The reviews were for a paper called "Blinded by Science: The Empirical Case for Quantum Models in Finance," which was later published in unmodified form by Real-World Economics Review; Orrell, 2024e.
19. Beaumont, 2019; Conroy, 2019.
20. Quantum Judder for Financial Engineers. Quant Insights Conference 2025. November 4, 2025.
21. As Bouchaud (2023) notes, "There are two surprises. . . . The first surprise is that, in the world of Black–Scholes, the insurance premium does not depend on the value of the expected average return of the stock market over the next year. . . . The second, perhaps even more disturbing surprise is that the insurer can follow a strategy known as 'hedging,' which allows it to take no risk at all." In an appendix of a textbook on option pricing, Dadachanji (2015) included the following joke dialogue:
Junior quant: "Should I be surprised that μ drops out?"
Senior quant: "Not if you want to keep your job."
22. See McGilchrist, 2009, p. 137 for a discussion of how this relates to psychiatry and brain lateralization.
23. As opposed to one that postdicts the known result.
24. As I have argued elsewhere, although behavioral economics has certainly made valuable contributions, it has won a degree of acceptance in mainstream economics in part because it does not pose too much of a challenge to core assumptions; Orrell, 2021b.
25. For my part, the July 2025 issue of *Wilmott* featured a cover story written with Paul Wilmott on q-variance, a separate technical article, and the last in a series of extracts from my *Quantum*

Economics and Finance book. Related papers were also accepted for publication in the *Journal of Derivatives* and *Philosophical Transactions of the Royal Society A*. Most importantly, the proposal for this book was accepted by MIT Press.

26. And we even have a proper journal called "Quantum Economics and Finance."

27. What Will Future Generations Look Back On in Horror? The Agenda, TVO Today, June 26, 2025.

Bibliography

Aaronson, S. (2013). *Quantum computing since Democritus*. Cambridge University Press.

Ahmad, R., & Wilmott, P. (2005). Which free lunch would you like today, sir?: Delta hedging, volatility arbitrage and optimal portfolios. *Wilmott, 2005*(November), 64–79.

Ahn, K., Choi, M. Y., Dai, B., Sohn, S., & Yang, B. (2017). Modeling stock return distributions with a quantum harmonic oscillator. *EPL, 120*(3), 38003.

Akerlof, G. A. (2020). Sins of omission and the practice of economics. *Journal of Economic Literature, 58*(2), 405–418.

Andersen and Piterbarg. (2007). Moment explosions in stochastic volatility models. *Finance and Stochastics, 11*(1), 29–50.

Anonymous (2009, July 16). Efficiency and beyond. *The Economist.*

Bachelier, L. (1900). Théorie de la spéculation. *Annales Scientifiques de l'École Normale Supérieure, 3*(17), 21–86.

Baaquie, B. E. (2021). Merton's equation and the quantum oscillator: Pricing risky corporate coupon bonds. *Physica A: Statistical Mechanics and Its Applications, 541*, 123367.

Ball, P. (2023, February 28). Can we use quantum computers to make music? *Physics World.*

Beaumont, L. (2019). Peer reviewers need a code of conduct too. *Nature, 572*(7769), 439–440.

Belloni, M., Robinett, R. W. (2014). The infinite well and Dirac delta function potentials as pedagogical, mathematical and physical models in quantum mechanics. *Physics Reports, 540*(2), 25–122.

Bernanke, B. (2006). *Basel II: Its promise and its challenges.* http://www.federalreserve.gov/newsevents/speech/bernanke20060518a.htm

Black, F., & Scholes, M. (1973). The pricing of options and corporate liabilities. *Journal of Political Economy, 81*(3), 637–654.

Bodie, Z. (1999). *Investment management and technology: Past, present, and future*. https://ssrn.com/abstract=178629

Boness, A. J. (1964). Elements of a theory of stock-option value. *Journal of Political Economy, 72*(2), 163–175.

Bouchaud, J. P. (2023). From statistical physics to social sciences: The pitfalls of multi-disciplinarity. *Journal of Physics: Complexity, 4*(4), 041001.

Bucci, F., Mastromatteo, I., Benzaquen, M., & Bouchaud, J. P. (2019). Impact is not just volatility. *Quantitative Finance, 19*(11), 1763–1766.

Burnet, J. (1920). *Early Greek philosophy* (3rd ed.). A. & C. Black Ltd.

Carr, P., & Wu, L. (2006). A tale of two indices. *Journal of Derivatives, 13*(3), 13–29. https://doi.org/10.2139/ssrn.871729

Carr, P., & Madan, D. (2001). Towards a theory of volatility trading. Option pricing, interest rates and risk management. *Handbooks in Mathematical Finance, 22*(7), 458–476.

Carrick-Hagenbarth, J., & Epstein, G. A. (2012). Dangerous interconnectedness: Economists' conflicts of interest, ideology and financial crisis. *Cambridge Journal of Economics, 36*(1), 43–63.

Cassidy, J. (2010, January 13). Interview with Eugene Fama. *The New Yorker*.

Cboe (2019). Cboe volatility index. https://www.sfu.ca/ poitras/419_VIX.pdf

Clark, M. (director) (1999). *The Midas Formula* (motion picture). https://www.pbs.org/wgbh/nova/transcripts/2704stockmarket.html

Cochrane, J. (2011). How did Paul Krugman get it so wrong? *IEA Economic Affairs*, (June), 36–40.

Conroy, G. (2019). *Q&A Linda Beaumont: Journals should take action against toxic peer reviews*. https://www.nature.com/nature-index/news/linda-beaumont-research-journals-should-take-action-against-toxic-peer-reviews

Courtault, J. M, Kabanov, Y., Bru, B., Crépel, P., Lebon, I., & Le Marchand, A. (2000). Louis Bachelier on the centenary of Théorie de la spéculation. *Mathematical Finance, 10*(3), 339–353.

Coyle, D. (2007). *The soulful science: What economists really do and why it matters*. Princeton University Press.

Dadachanji, Z. (2015). *FX barrier options: A comprehensive guide for industry quants*. Palgrave Macmillan.

Danchin, A. (2002). *The Delphic boat*. Harvard University Press.

De Broglie, L. (1929). The wave nature of the electron, Nobel Lecture, December 12, 1929. https://www.nobelprize.org/uploads/2016/04/broglie-lecture.pdf

Derman, E., & Miller, M. B. (2016). *The volatility smile*. John Wiley & Sons.

Dyson, F. (2004). A meeting with Enrico Fermi. *Nature, 427*(6972).

Fama, E. F. (1965). Random walks in stock market prices. *Financial Analysts Journal*, 21(5), 55–59.

Ferguson, C. (2010, October 30). Larry Summers and the subversion of economics. *The Chronicle of Higher Education*.

Fermi, L. (1954). Success. In M. Gardner (Ed.) (1984). *The sacred beetle and other great essays in science*. Oxford University Press.

Feynman, R. (1964). *The Feynman lectures on physics*. Addison-Wesley.

Feynman, R. (1985). *QED: The strange theory of light and matter*. Princeton University Press.

Fisher, I. (1910). *Introduction to economic science*. Macmillan Company.

Frisch, R. (1933). Propagation problems and impulse problems in dynamic economics. In *Economic essays in honor of Gustav Cassel* (pp. 171–205). George Allen & Unwin.

Frisch, R. (1936). A note on the term 'econometrics'. *Econometrica, 4*(1), 95.

Gao, T., & Chen, Y. (2017). A quantum anharmonic oscillator model for the stock market. *Physica A, 468*, 307–314.

Galbraith, J. (1994, Winter). Keynes, Einstein, and scientific revolution. *The American Prospect*.

Gatheral, J. (2006). *The volatility surface: A practitioner's guide*. Wiley.

Gatheral, J., & Jacquier, A. (2014). Arbitrage-free SVI volatility surfaces. *Quantitative Finance, 14*(1), 59–71.

Gatarek, D. (2023). The principle of two models: The cases of Black-Scholes formula for interest rates and of Gaussian copula for credit. *Wilmott, 2023*(125), 78–82.

Graeber, D. (2018). *Bullshit jobs: A theory*. Simon & Schuster.

Gross, L., & Waltners, N. (1995). S&P 500 options: Put volatility smile and risk aversion. Salomon Brothers, mimeo.

Haug, E. G., & Taleb, N. N. (2008). *Why we have never used the Black-Scholes-Merton option pricing formula*. Social Science Research Network Working Paper Series.

Heisenberg, W. (1971). *Physics and beyond: Encounters and conversations* (A. J. Pomerans, Trans.). World Perspectives (Vol. 42). Harper & Row.

Hernández-Morales, A. (2025, February 27). Housing crisis is as big a threat to the EU as Russia' according to the mayor of Barcelona. *Politico.*

Holtfort, T., & Horsch, A. (2024). Quantum economics: A systematic literature review. *SocioEconomic Challenges, 8*(1), 62–77.

Hull, J. (1993). *Options, futures, and other derivative securities* (7th ed.). Prentice Hall.

International Monetary Fund. (2006). Global financial stability report: Market developments and issues, April. International Monetary Fund.

Itô, K. (1951). On a formula concerning stochastic differentials. *Nagoya Mathematical Journal, 3*, 55–65.

Jensen, M. (1978). Some anomalous evidence regarding market efficiency. *Journal of Financial Economics, 6*, 95–102.

Jevons, W. S. (1878). Commercial crises and sun-spots. *Nature, 19*, 33–37.

Jevons, W. S. (1957). *The theory of political economy* (5th ed.). Kelley and Millman.

Juglar, C. (1862). *Des crises commerciales et de leur retour périodique en France, an angleterre et aux États-Unis. Guillaumin.*

Kelly, K. (1994, July 1). Cracking Wall Street. *Wired.*

Keynes, J. M. (1924). Alfred Marshall, 1842–1924. *The Economic Journal, 34*(135), 311–372.

Keynes, J. M. (1936). *Theory of employment, interest and money.* Harcourt, Brace.

Kitchin, J. (1923). Cycles and trends in economic factors. *The Review of Economics and Statistics, 5*(1), 10–16.

Kondratenko, A. V. (2015). *Probabilistic economic theory.* Nauka.

Kondratiev, N. D. (1925). The major economic cycles. *Voprosy Konjunktury, 1*(1), 28–79.

Kuznets, S. (1930). *Secular movements in production and prices. Their nature and their bearing upon cyclical fluctuations.* Houghton Mifflin.

Krugman, P. (2018). Good enough for government work? Macroeconomics since the crisis. *Oxford Review of Economic Policy, 34*(1–2), 156–168.

Kumar, M. (2008). *Quantum: Einstein, Bohr and the great debate about the nature of reality.* Icon Books.

Kyle, A. S., & Obizhaeva, A. A. (2020). *The market impact puzzle* (Working Paper No. w0270). New Economic School (NES).

Lazear, E. P. (2000). Economic imperialism. *The Quarterly Journal of Economics, 115*(1), 99–146.

Lee, R. W. (2004). The moment formula for implied volatility at extreme strikes. *Mathematical Finance, 14*, 469–480.

Lillo, F. (2023). Order flow and price formation. In A. Capponi & C. A. Lahalle (Eds.), *Machine learning and data sciences for financial markets: A guide to contemporary practices.* Cambridge University Press.

Lucas, R. (2009, August 6). In defence of the dismal science. *The Economist*, 66–67.

Mackenzie, D. (2006). *An engine, not a camera: How financial models shape markets.* MIT Press.

Maddeaux, S. (2025, March 20). Young people who can't afford homes feel betrayed by their country. Why should they stand up against Trump when Canada has let them down? *Toronto Star.*

Mandelbrot, B. (1963). The variation of certain speculative prices. *The Journal of Business, 36*(4), 394–419.

Mandelbrot, B. B., & Hudson, R. L. (2004). *The (Mis)behaviour of markets: A fractal view of risk, ruin and reward.* Profile.

Markowitz, H. M. (1952). Portfolio selection. *The Journal of Finance, 7*(1), 77–91.

Matthews, R. (2001, August 4). Don't blame the butterfly. *New Scientist.*

Mayeda, A. (2016, November 18). *The rebel economist who blew up macroeconomics*. Bloomberg.com

McGilchrist, I. (2009). *The master and his emissary*. Yale University Press.

McLeay, M., Radia, A., & Thomas, R. (2014). Money creation in the modern economy. *Quarterly Bulletin 2014 Q1* (Bank of England).

Meng, X., Zhang J-W., Xu, J., & Guo, H. (2015). Quantum spatial-periodic harmonic model for daily price-limited stock markets. *Physica A: Statistical Mechanics and Its Applications, 438*(15), 154–160.

Meng, X., Zhang J-W., & Guo, H. (2016). Quantum brownian motion model for the stock market. *Physica A: Statistical Mechanics and Its Applications, 452*, 281–288.

Merton, R. C. (1976). Option pricing when underlying stock returns are discontinuous. *Journal of Financial Economics, 3*(1–2), 125–144.

Merton, R. C. (1990). *Continuous-time finance*. Basil Blackwell.

Navas, J. F. (2003). Calculation of volatility in a jump-diffusion model. *Journal of Derivatives, 11*(2), 66–72.

Nelson, S. A. (1904). *The A B C of options and arbitrage*. The Wall Street Library.

Orrell, D. (2007). *The future of everything: The science of prediction*. Basic Books.

Orrell, D. (2016). A quantum theory of money and value. *Economic Thought, 5*(2), 19–36.

Orrell, D. (2018a). Quantum economics. *Economic Thought, 7*(2), 63–81.

Orrell, D. (2018b). *Quantum economics: The new science of money*. Icon Books.

Orrell, D. (2020a). A quantum model of supply and demand. *Physica A, 539*, 122928.

Orrell, D. (2020b). The value of value: A quantum approach to economics, security and international relations. *Security Dialogue, 51*(5), 482–498.

Orrell, D. (2021a). A quantum walk model of financial options. *Wilmott, 2021*(112), 62–69.

Orrell, D. (2021b). *Behavioural economics: Psychology, neuroscience, and the human side of economics*. Icon Books.

Orrell, D. (2022a). Market impact through a quantum lens. *Wilmott, 2022*(122), 50–52.

Orrell, D. (2022b). *Money, magic, and how to dismantle a financial bomb: Quantum economics for the real world*. Icon Books.

Orrell, D. (2022c). *Quantum economics and finance: An applied mathematics introduction* (3rd ed.). Panda Ohana.

Orrell, D. (2023). The Black-Scholes magic trick, explained! *Wilmott, 2023*(126), 90–93.

Orrell, D. (2024a). Is non-quantum finance too much of a stretch? *Wilmott, 2024*(129), 26–28.

Orrell, D. (2024b). Quantum uncertainty and the Black-Scholes formula. *Quantum Economics and Finance, 1*(1), 82–91.

Orrell, D. (2024c). A quantum model of implied volatility. *Wilmott, 2024*(131), 70–73.

Orrell, D. (2024d). Quantum economics and physics. *Quantum Economics and Finance, 1*(2), 95–102.

Orrell, D. (2024e). Blinded by science: The empirical case for quantum models in finance. *Real-World Economics Review, 107*, 68–79.

Orrell, D. (2025). A quantum jump model of option pricing. *Journal of Derivatives, 33*(2) (in press).

Orrell, D. (2025a). Quantum impact and the supply-demand curve. *Philosophical Transactions of the Royal Society A, 383*(2309), 20240562.

Orrell, D. (2026). Q-Variance: A quadratic constraint on variance. SSRN discussion paper. Available at: https://papers.ssrn.com/sol3/papers.cfm?abstract_id=6140027

Orrell, D., & Houshmand, M. (2022). Quantum propensity in economics. *Frontiers in Artificial Intelligence, 4*:772294.

Orrell, D., & Richards, L. (2023). Keep on smiling: Market imbalance, option pricing, and the volatility smile. *Wilmott, 2023*(124), 58–64.

Popper, K. R. (1959). *The logic of scientific discovery*. Basic Books.

Qadir, A. (1978). Quantum economics. *Pakistan Economic and Social Review, 16*(3/4), 117–126.

Rae, A. I. M. (2007). *Quantum mechanics* (5th ed.). Taylor & Francis.

Raval, V., & Jacquier, A. (2023). The log-moment formula for implied volatility. *Mathematical Finance, 33*(4), 1146–1165.

Ravetz, J. (2008). Faith and reason in the mathematics of the credit crunch. *Oxford Magazine*, eighth week, 14–16.

Robinson, J. M. (1968). *An introduction to early Greek philosophy: The chief fragments and ancient testimony, with connecting commentary*. Houghton Mifflin.

Romer, P. (2016). The trouble with macroeconomics. https://paulromer.net/trouble-with-macro economics-update/WP-Trouble.pdf

Ross, S. A. (1987). Finance. In J. Eatwell, M. Milgate, & P. Newman (Eds.), *The new palgrave: A dictionary of economics* (vol. 2). Macmillan.

Roos, N. (2014). Entropic forces in Brownian motion. *American Journal of Physics, 82*(12), 1161–1166.

Rubinstein, M. (1994). Implied binomial trees. *Journal of Finance, 49*(3), 771–818.

Sahm, C. (2020, July 29). *Economics is a disgrace*. http://macromomblog.com/2020/07/29 /economics-is-a-disgrace/

Salam, A. (1990). *Unification of fundamental forces*. Cambridge University Press.

Samuelson, P. A. (1973). *Economics* (9th ed.). McGraw-Hill.

Schulman, A. (2025, September 22). Jay Bhattacharya wants to fix science. Is he in over his head? *New York Times*.

Szent-Gyorgyi, A. (1972). Dionysians and Apollonians. *Science, 176*, 966.

Schrödinger, E. (1935). Die gegenwärtige situation in der quantenmechanik. *Naturwissenschaften, 23*, 823–828.

Shimp, C. P. (2004). Scientific peer review: A case study from local and global analyses. *Journal of the Experimental Analysis of Behavior, 82*(1), 103–116.

Simons, K. (1997). Model error. *New England Economic Review, 1*, 17–28.

Smith, A. (1776). *An inquiry into the nature and causes of wealth of nations*. W. Strahan & T. Cadell.

Sokolov, I. M. (2010). Statistical mechanics of entropic forces: Disassembling a toy. *European Journal of Physics, 31*(6), 1353–1367.

Souder, L. (2011). The ethics of scholarly peer review: A review of the literature. *Learned Publishing, 24*, 55–72.

Svetlova, E. (2018). *Financial models and society: Villains or scapegoats?* Edward Elgar.

Taleb, N. (1998). How the ought became the is. In *Futures and OTC world* (pp. 35–36). Black-Scholes-Merton.

Tett, G., & Gangahar, A. (2007, August 14). Limitations of computer models. *Financial Times*.

Tett, G. (2009, August 27). Could 'Tobin tax' reshape financial sector DNA? *Financial Times*.

Thorp, E. O. (1962). *Beat the dealer: A winning strategy for the game of twenty-one*. Random House.

Thorp, E. O., & Kassouf, S. T. (1967). *Beat the market: A scientific stock market system*. Random House.

Tóth, B., Lemperiere, Y., Deremble, C., De-lataillade, J., Kockelkoren, J., & Bouchaud, J.-P. (2011). Anomalous price impact and the critical nature of liquidity in financial markets. *Physical Review X, 1*(2), 21006.

Triana, P. (2009). *Lecturing birds on flying: Can mathematical theories destroy the financial markets?* John Wiley & Sons.

Tudball, D. (2024). Psi ops. *Wilmott, 2024*(131), 42–48.

Walras, L. (1889). Éléments d'économie politique pure ou théorie de la richesse sociale (2ème éd.). Lausanne, F. Rouge, Guillaumin, Duncker & Humblot.

Wilmott, P. (2000). The use, misuse and abuse of mathematics in finance. *Philosophical Transactions of the Royal Society of London A, 358*(1765), 63–73.

Wilmott, P. (2010). *Frequently asked questions in quantitative finance.* Wiley.

Wilmott, P. (2013). *Paul Wilmott on quantitative finance (2nd ed.).* Wiley.

Wilmott, P., & Orrell, D. (2017). *The money formula: Dodgy finance, pseudo science, and how mathematics took over the markets.* Wiley.

Wilmott, P., & Orrell, D. (2025). Q-Variance: or, a duet concerning the two chief world systems. *Wilmott, 2025*(138), 34–38.

Wyart, M., Bouchaud, J. P, Kockelkoren, J., Potters, M., & Vettorazzo, M. (2008). Relation between bid–ask spread, Impact and volatility in order-driven markets. *Quantitative Finance, 8*(1), 41–57.

Ye, C., Huang, J. (2008). Non-classical oscillator model for persistent fluctuations in stock markets. *Physica A: Statistical Mechanics and Its Applications, 387*, 1255–1263.

Zhu, L. (2015). Options with extreme strikes. *Risks, 3*(3), 234–249.

Žižek, S. (2012). *Less than nothing: Hegel and the shadow of dialectical materialism.* Verso.

Zwiebach, B. (2022). *Mastering quantum mechanics: Essentials, theory, and applications.* MIT Press.

Index

Publisher contact:
The MIT Press
Massachusetts Institute of Technology
77 Massachusetts Avenue, Cambridge, MA 02139
mitpress.mit.edu

EU Authorised Representative:
Easy Access System Europe, Mustamäe tee 50,
10621 Tallinn, Estonia
gpsr.requests@easproject.com

Printed by Integrated Books International,
United States of America